Philipp Jostarndt

Financial Distress, Corporate Restructuring and Firm Survival

Beiträge zur betriebswirtschaftlichen Forschung

Herausgegeben von

Prof. Dr. Dr. h.c. Sönke Albers, Kiel
Prof. Dr. Bernhard Pellens, Bochum
Prof. Dr. Dieter Sadowski, Trier
Prof. Dr. Martin Weber, Mannheim

Band 116

Die „braune Reihe", wie die „Beiträge zur betriebswirtschaftlichen Forschung" häufig kurz genannt werden, ist eine der bekanntesten und angesehensten Buchreihen ihres Fachs. Seit 1954 erscheinen hier besonders qualifizierte, oft richtungsweisende Forschungsarbeiten (vor allem Dissertationen und Habilitationsschriften) der jeweils „neuen Generation" der Betriebswirtschaftslehre.

Philipp Jostarndt

Financial Distress, Corporate Restructuring and Firm Survival

An Empirical Analysis of German Panel Data

With a foreword by Prof. Dr. Bernd Rudolph

Deutscher Universitäts-Verlag

Bibliografische Information Der Deutschen Nationalbibliothek
Die Deutsche Nationalbibliothek verzeichnet diese Publikation in der Deutschen Nationalbibliografie; detaillierte bibliografische Daten sind im Internet über <http://dnb.d-nb.de> abrufbar.

Dissertation Universität München, 2006

1. Auflage Februar 2007

Lektorat: Brigitte Siegel / Sabine Schöller

Der Deutsche Universitäts-Verlag ist ein Unternehmen von Springer Science+Business Media.
www.duv.de

Umschlaggestaltung: Regine Zimmer, Dipl.-Designerin, Frankfurt/Main
Gedruckt auf säurefreiem und chlorfrei gebleichtem Papier
Printed in Germany

ISBN 978-3-8350-0590-7

Foreword

Research on corporate distress and bankruptcy and the accompanying efforts of firms to restructure their operations and balance sheets have become an increasingly important field in financial economics and business administration. Especially in Germany where the recent period of economic downturn and large-scale bankruptcy filings coincided with extensive reforms of the bankruptcy legislation the topic has enjoyed controversial debates among economists, legal scholars and public policy makers.

Yet so far insights from empirical research that can provide valuable guidance in these debates have remained sparse and inconclusive. One reason for the lack of evidence is that common financial theory on corporate restructuring is not fully compatible with the German institutional background and thus often allows only ambiguous predictions. Moreover, empirical investigations of German restructurings have so far been almost impossible due to the lack of exhaustive data. This holds in particular for private reorganizations, which present the predominant form of restructuring distressed firms in Germany. Many economically highly interesting aspects pertain to this final stage in the corporate lifecycle. For example, the question whether the firm's management, shareholders or creditors should trigger a formal bankruptcy proceeding or, alternatively, pursue a going-concern in an out-of-court workout has a myriad of economic implications.

In his dissertation Philipp Jostarndt tries to shed first light on this highly relevant topic. Applying advanced econometric methods to large-scale data sets, which were assembled specifically for the purpose of this thesis, he investigates corporate responses to financial distress. His analyses embrace the impact of distress on corporate governance, firms' choices between private workouts and formal insolvency procedures as well as the role of claimholder conflicts in distressed equity offerings. In his concluding chapter, Jostarndt conducts a survival analysis to decipher the determinants of survival, acquisition and failure as alternative paths of exit from financial distress. In his studies, the author considers both the measures taken on the firm level as well as market valuations thereof. The obtained results thus not only help explaining how beleaguered firms make capital structure decisions but also allow an inference on how these decisions relate to the extreme return patterns that are typically observed in the trading of distressed securities. Finally, the author makes a valuable contribution by relating his results to existing evidence on distress and bankruptcy of U.S. firms. Above all, this concerns the seminal studies by Gilson (1990), Gilson, John and Lang (1990) and Asquith, Gertner and Scharfstein (1994) all of which deal with the aftermath of the collapse of the high-yield bond market and the savings and loans crisis in the U.S. at the end of the 1980s. Insights gained from this comparison are extremely helpful in assessing the relative efficacy of alternative institutional and legislative bodies in their role as screening mechanism for economically viable and non-viable firms.

This book is the product of more than three years of intensive research which earned the author not only a doctoral degree at the Ludwig-Maximilian-University of Munich but also several best paper awards, among others at the 2006 Zürich Meeting of European Finance Association and the 2006 Porto Meeting of the Portuguese Finance Network. Philipp Jostarndt's studies on financial distress and restructuring in Germany deal with an important and methodologically very demanding topic. They present a remarkable contribution to the field – I am sure his results will attract the attention of practitioners and researchers alike.

Prof. Dr. Bernd Rudolph

Preface

It is a myth that doing a doctorate is a solitary pursuit that can only be accomplished under pain-staking personal privations. And though I claim this dissertation to be an individual work, I must acknowledge that I could have never reached the heights or explored the depths without the help, support, guidance and efforts of many. To all of them I owe thanks.

I would like to express my deep gratitude to Bernd Rudolph, my doctoral advisor, for his trust and encouragement during the past years. He has been granting me a remarkable degree of freedom in defining my theme and pursuing my research and yet has been a constant and reliable source of advise and guidance. I further wish to thank him for giving me the opportunity to stay at the University of Oxford towards the end of my dissertation project. This courtesy is unparalleled and has been invaluable.

I am also very grateful for having Dietmar Harhoff as my thesis referee and scientific advisor. Already early into my graduate studies, he inspired me with his passion for empirical research and his almost intimidating knowledge of methodology. Ever since, his support and counsel in all of my endeavors have been outstanding.

During my MBR studies, Hubert Job and Hans-Ulrich Küpper were my course advisors. I very much appreciate their help and encouragement.

I wish to thank Colin Mayer and Oren Sussman for inviting me to Oxford for a research stay at the Finance and Economics Group of the Saïd Business School. My work benefitted very much from their extensive knowledge of corporate distress and bankruptcy and the German financial system. Living and studying at Oxford has been an intriguing experience. Research and financial support from the German Academic Exchange Service (DAAD) during this stay is gratefully acknowledged.

Thanks also to all my past and present peers at the Institute of Capital Market Research and Finance in Munich for maintaining an atmosphere of high spirit and mutual support. Our joint ventures in research and teaching were both an exciting challenge and great fun.

I was fortunate to spend the past years accompanied by four fellow doctoral students to whom I owe special thanks. Raimo Reese, Felix Treptow, Hannes Wagner and Stefan Wagner. Their intellect, curiosity and bohemian wit not only constantly nurtured this thesis but also greatly impacted my views of almost every aspect of life. I also thank them for sharing with me all the distractions from academia a city like Munich can offer. I further wish to thank my friends Rainer Bloch, Marc Petry for their time and tolerance. I take pride in my friendship to all of them.

Finally, my deepest gratitude goes to my family. I owe my parents and my sister for the great examples they are in life and academia, and my brothers for sharing their sense of humor and keeping me young-spirited. The unconditional faith and support by all of them has been contributing to my well-being in ways immeasurable. Thank you!

Philipp Jostarndt

Table of Contents

List of Tables

List of Figures

Chapter 1

Introduction

1.1 Motivation

Corporate financial distress has changed dramatically over the past decade. From the onset of the general economic recession at the turn of the century to the present, there has been a tremendous increase in default rates and bankruptcy activity in the corporate sector throughout Europe. Firms that only a few years before had been labelled the rising stars of a new epoch and had raised massive amounts of funds on very generous terms, now suffered from inherently unprofitable business models and excessive burdens of debt. This twist of fate for the industry along with the increasing number of company scandals in recent years have raised concerns about the corporate sector's financial stability.

As a result, financial scholars have become increasingly interested in analyzing the ramifications of financial distress. Motives for an in-depth investigation of this topic are manifold. First, financial distress typically engenders a reallocation of corporate resources. When defaults and bankruptcies are widespread in the economy, misallocations arising from inefficiencies in corporate reorganization potentially inhibit economic growth. Accordingly, financial distress has garnered considerable attention in recent public debates in which policy makers and legal scholars ever more turn to economists for advise on the optimal design of frameworks guiding the reorganization of distressed firms. Second, the states of distress and convalescence typically exert a strong attraction to professional investors. As one of them puts it, "Resolving financial distress is an arduous, time-consuming process. [...] But the rewards are there, because this environment really represents the ultimate definition of an inefficient market; and inefficient markets produce extraordinary rates of return. And that's what this business is all about."[1] However, in

[1] Sam Zell, Chairman, Equity and Financial Management Company, quoted in the Journal of Applied Corporate Finance Roundtable Discussion on "Bankruptcies, Workouts, and Turnarounds, April 1991.

order to successfully exploit the intricate risk-return characteristics of distressed securities a sound comprehension of the underlying economics is required. Finally, financial distress amplifies conflicts of interest between various stakeholders. Managers face a greater job-risk, shareholders fear the loss of their equity's option value, and creditors fight over the firm's waning resources. Also, the firm as a whole will find it harder to maintain long-term relationships with its suppliers and customers. Studying distressed restructurings, therefore, is a promising approach to testing and potentially challenging established capital structure theory.

Evidence on European firms in distress is sparse. In particular, the recent era of economic turmoil has not yet undergone exhaustive scrutiny. Previous empirical studies are almost exclusively restricted to the Anglo-Saxon domain and mainly cover the aftermath of the collapse of the high-yield bond market and the savings and loans crisis in the U.S. at the end of the 1980s.[2] The transferability of these insights is limited, however, because the economic implications of financial distress strongly differ, depending on the microstructure of the national financial and legal system [e.g. Franks, Nyborg, and Torous (1996)]. Germany is a particularly interesting case because in this country financial distress has traditionally been confronted in a singular manner. Mainly due to the strong bank-orientation in corporate financing, an insider-oriented corporate governance, and an overly creditor-friendly bankruptcy legislation, distressed firms were either privately resuscitated by their main creditor banks or, if deemed non-viable, liquidated under court supervision. Unlike in the U.S., large bankruptcies were a rarity and most restructuring activity occurred without public disclosure [e.g. Kaiser (1996)].

In recent years, however, corporate restructuring in Germany has undergone considerable changes. Not only did Germany exhibit an all-time record in the total number of bankruptcies. It also experienced some of the biggest corporate failures in the nation's history, among them highly disputed cases such as Philipp Holzmann, Babcock Borsig, and Kirch Media.[3] These developments were accompanied by several significant reforms in the institutional setting under which corporate reorganization in Germany takes place.[4] First and foremost, a new bankruptcy legislation was introduced in 1994 and came into effect in 1999. The new code repairs several inefficiencies inherent in the old procedure that often caused liquidations of economically viable debtors. For example, the code introduces an automatic stay of three months on secured claims and considers a bankruptcy plan reorganization an equitable alternative to formal liquidation. Moreover, it provides a distressed debtor the opportunity to file a voluntary (pre-packaged) bankruptcy peti-

[2] Senbet and Seward (1995) provide a survey of that era.

[3] According to the Federal Statistical Office (StBA) corporate bankruptcies in Germany increased from 15.148 in 1993 to 39.320 in 2003, among the highest numbers and the biggest rise throughout Europe.

[4] A survey of recent reforms is provided by Nowak (2001) and Rudolph (2003).

tion prior to actual insolvency. In this more debtor-friendly setting in- and out-of-court restructurings of distressed firms bear more economic resemblance and occur in a more timely and orderly manner.

Another major change in the institutional setting in Germany occurred with the adoption of the Corporate Sector Supervision and Transparency Act (KonTraG) in 1998. The KonTraG set a milestone in improving monitoring effectiveness of German supervisory boards. As part of the law, legal liability of senior executives in case of dishonest or fraudulent behavior was tightened and deviations from one share–one vote principle were prohibited. Also, the KonTraG strengthened the powers of the shareholders' general assembly and established the groundwork for a more detailed and cash flow oriented accounting reform. Investor protection and corporate transparency were further promoted by the introduction of "ad-hoc disclosure" requirements in 1995. Since then, corporations listed on a German stock exchange have been required to disclose immediately any "inside" information that is likely to affect the value of the firm's outstanding securities. Other than before fundamental corporate policy decisions were now timely and accurately conveyed to the market.

With improved investor protection and corporate transparency in place, German corporate finance, and especially the financing of distressed firms, has recently developed a considerably stronger arm's length orientation. Firms' ownership structures, which were traditionally held very closely, are gradually disentangling and provide new investment opportunities for specialized institutional investors. For example, so called "vulture investors" that deliberately invest in distressed targets and actively engage in the firm's restructuring present a comparatively novel trend on the German capital market, which has recently enjoyed considerable coverage in the financial press [e.g. Becker (2003)]. Relationship-based banking is also on retreat. Traditionally, German commercial banks used to hang on to their credit agreements over the loan's entire life-cycle. More recently, however, banks increasingly dispose of non-performing loans and leave the restructuring to the market.[5] While a liquid market for distressed debt is still in the making, the public trading of claims has greatly reduced the opacity in private debt restructurings.

Combined, these developments in Germany over the past decade have created the opportunity to conduct empirical work on corporate financial distress that had very long been out of reach. Other than before, there now exists a sufficient number of German firms that have undergone formal and informal reorganization and whose restructuring path is actually traceable. In my thesis, I seek to exploit this opportunity. I empirically analyze how firms encounter and respond to financial distress. My analysis is based on a

[5] See "Barbarians at the gates of Europe" in: *The Economist*, 18 February 2006.

sample of 267 German corporations that experienced repeated interest coverage shortfalls and steep share price declines between 1996 and 2004. My research design follows prior work by Gilson (1990) and Asquith, Gertner, and Scharfstein (1994) in that I (1) create a stratified sample of firms that meet a pre-determined distress-criterion at some time during the sampling period and (2) track each firm's development over the distress interval. Thus, my data set is dynamic following the cycle of distress from its onset to its resolution. I collect data on financial accounts, ownership and board composition, and restructuring activity.

My focus is on how firms restructure to avoid formal bankruptcy proceedings, i.e. I mainly study private reorganizations. I analyze changes in ownership and control, management turnover, distressed equity infusions as well as in- and out-of-court debt restructurings. Moreover, I conduct a survival analysis to decipher the determinants of survival, acquisition, and bankruptcy as distinct outcomes of financial distress. My analyzes embrace both the firm perspective as well as the market valuations of the undertaken restructurings and, where applicable, relate the findings to the microstructure of Germany's revised bankruptcy legislation. To the best of my knowledge, no study of similar scope has been undertaken before. Thus, I provide genuine insights into the anatomy of distress in German corporations that have not been provided by previous research.

One distinguishing feature of my analysis is that it focuses on a non-interventionist regulatory setting in which most reorganizations take place privately, prior to actual bankruptcy. This makes my data set particularly interesting because observed restructuring efforts are not distorted by legal or regulatory influence but remain a matter of choice. In contrast, much of the previous evidence on distress analyzes U.S. firms who tend to enter formal proceedings under Chapter 11 prematurely and on their own free will and thus perform a great deal of restructuring under court supervision [e.g. Franks and Torous (1989)]. Moreover, my approach is methodologically different to most previous studies in that my sample is not, as often the case, conditioned on a particular firm-type, restructuring event, or outcome of distress but relies on more objective and pre-determined criteria in form of interest coverage ratios.[6] Accordingly, I create a cross-section of financially distressed firms that ensures sufficient heterogeneity with respect to specific firm or industry characteristics. This approach presents exogenous stratified sampling that allows consistent estimation and inference uncontaminated by problems of sample selection [e.g. Manski and McFadden (1983)].

6 For example, Asquith, Gertner, and Scharfstein (1994) and Andrade and Kaplan (1998) condition upon high-yield bond issuers and leveraged buy-outs, James (1996) conditions upon defaults of publicly traded debt, and Franks and Torous (1989) condition upon Chapter 11 bankruptcy filings.

1.2 Course of examination

My dissertation thesis is divided into 6 chapters. Chapter 2 presents the data and sample selection. Chapter 3 scrutinizes distress related issues of corporate control. Chapter 4 and Chapter 5 contain an in-depth investigation of two related financial restructuring measures, debt restructurings and equity infusions, that are common responses to distress by the firms in my sample. Finally, in the concluding chapter, I study the determinants of firm exit and survival in financial distress. In the following, I briefly review each of the chapters and highlight the main findings.

In Chapter 2 I explain the sample selection process and provide a detailed description of my data sample. Following definitions of financial distress provided by theory I apply a cash flow based criterion for my initial sample stratification: A firm is classified as financially distressed, if in any two consecutive years the firm reports insufficient interest coverage ratios. Departing from this definition I apply a simple methodology established by Asquith, Gertner, and Scharfstein (1994) to assess the relative importance of excessive leverage, firm-specific operating performance, and industry-wide operating performance in causing the initial coverage shortfall for the firms in the sample. It shows that firm-specific operating performance rather than leverage or industry shocks is the major source of financial distress for the vast majority of the firms. From this finding I conclude that corporate (i.e. firm-level) restructuring is a mandatory response to distress and thus presents a promising subject for empirical research.

The first part of this thesis' main body, Chapter 3, investigates the effect of financial distress on corporate ownership and control. While financial theory traditionally proposes that the states of distress and default provoke substantial changes in the ownership of firms' residual claims and the allocation of rights to manage corporate resources, empirical evidence on how precisely these changes evolve has remained sparse. In my analysis, I find a significant decrease in ownership concentration over the distress cycle. Private investors, typically the bulwark in corporate ownership structures in Germany, gradually relinquish their dominating role and cease to be an effective source of managerial control. By contrast, ownership representation by banks and outside investors almost doubles although both groups of investors only acquire comparatively small stakes. Shareholdings by managers and directors also increase substantially. I further perform panel data regressions to investigate the relation between (changes in) corporate ownership and management turnover. It shows that disciplinary turnover of key executives is mostly initiated by outside investors and banks and often occurs subsequent to debt restructurings, block investments, and takeovers. Managerial ownership and blockholdings by private investors do not significantly affect turnover. Collectively, the evidence suggests that financial distress provokes a shift from internal to external mechanisms of corporate control.

Chapter 4 investigates debt restructurings for a sub-sample of 116 firms of which about half successfully restructure their debt in a workout while the other half fail and file an insolvency petition under the new bankruptcy code. I provide detailed summary statistics on both sub-samples that describe the most commonly observed features of private workouts and shed a first light on how firms choose between alternative bankruptcy triggers. Evidence from multivariate analysis suggests that firms more likely to succeed in their restructuring attempt are higher leveraged, owe more debt to banks, and exhibit higher going concern values. Bankruptcy, on the other hand, is more likely for firms with deficient lender coordination and high fractions of collateralized debt. Evidence from stock returns over the entire restructuring interval reveals that the market uses similar information to predict successful workout attempts and that shareholders fare significantly better if bankruptcy is ultimately avoided. The results are consistent with the predictions that high leverage may serve as catalyst for efficient reorganization [e.g. Jensen (1989)] and that conflicts among creditors may impede an otherwise successful restructuring [e.g. Bolton and Scharfstein (1996)].

In Chapter 5 I analyze firms' decision to recapitalize by raising fresh equity. Distressed equity issues are a particularly German phenomenon, which mainly results from institutional impediments to raising senior funds in a state of crisis. More than one third of the firms in my sample complete such an issue. Theoretic arguments by Myers (1977) and Gertner and Scharfstein (1991) hold that a debt-overhang problem arising from financial distress should make the contribution of new funds prohibitively costly to shareholders. Only if the gains from rescuing the firm through the infusion exceed the wealth transfers to creditors, shareholders will find it in their self-interest to complete the issue. Alternatively, corporate managers may use distressed equity issues as an entrenchment device to sidestep hostile takeover attempts. I first analyze the recapitalization from a firm-perspective using a Heckman two-stage selection model. I find that the debt-overhang problem dominates the terms of the equity issue. The amount raised is negatively related to the firms' indebtedness and positively related to future growth opportunities. Also, firms are more inclined to raise equity if creditors accommodate them with debt concessions. A subsequent analysis of stock price reactions confirms this finding from a market perspective. However, the market also puts considerable weight on the managerial entrenchment hypothesis. Cross-sectional regression results suggest that announcement returns are substantially lower for firms issuing equity while being subject to takeover speculation and substantially higher for firms replacing top-management in the course of the issue. Market reactions are also significantly more favorable if the issued shares are subscribed by existing blockholders or strategic investors.

Finally, in Chapter 6, I investigate the determinants of survival, acquisition, and failure as distinct outcomes of distress. This concluding analysis seeks to compliment my previous work as it goes beyond explaining how distress affects corporate governance and restructuring to demonstrating what actually fosters ultimate survival or failure. Alternative outcomes of distress differ substantially in their impact on shareholder wealth. While bankruptcy filings provoke announcement returns of below -40% around a 20 day event window, corresponding returns for takeover agreements between a bidder and a distressed target are significantly positive ranging between 12% and 17%. This suggests that there exist distinct economic features that help identifying the potential candidates of either form of "exit" beforehand. Using simple multinomial logit and Cox proportional hazard rate models, I find considerable differences across alternative exits in the factors determining the type of exit as well as the time elapsed until a particular exit occurs. Acquired firms exit earlier than their bankrupt counterparts and, and the onset of distress, are characterized by low leverage, high ownership concentration, and high industry liquidity. By contrast, bankruptcies are largely driven by high leverage, low liquidity, low ownership concentration, and low industry growth opportunities. Bankruptcies are also accelerated in cases where managers hold significant blocks of voting stock. Finally, firms seem to be able to retard their exit by issuing fresh equity and divesting considerable amounts of assets. While overall results are consistent with a large set of capital structure theory, the applied competing risk design in my study provides an alternative approach to identifying and explaining some of the critical drivers of a firm's financial distress costs.

My dissertation contributes to the literature in several ways. It is the first exhaustive study on corporate financial distress in Germany. At present, there exists almost no evidence on how German firms are affected by distress, why they choose certain restructuring measures over others, and how private reorganizations are influenced by the rules of formal bankruptcy. Because Germany is often considered as the as prime representative for the Central-European bank-based financial system, the insights gained in my study are among the first to supplement and potentially challenge the established view on distress that has so far focused on the Anglo-Saxon market-based domain. Considering the EU's recent pursuit of a unified corporate insolvency law such comparative insights are of high practical relevance [e.g. Sussman (2005)]. Moreover, my investigation is the first of its kind that embraces the prelude and aftermath of the stock market hype and technology bubble at the turn of the century. Thus, it allows to study if and how ramifications of distress differ between so-called old and new economy firms. If results vary across enterprize-types, this would have valuable implications for regulators and policy makers interested in how distress and bankruptcy affect the resource allocation in the economy.

One principle objection to my study design could be made: It is not clear *ex ante* whether the particularities of the recent epoch as well as the relatively short time span of ten years affect the generality my results. Where applicable, I use several time and market segment dummy variables to address this concern and test the sensitivity of the results across different time-windows and industry types. The evidence suggest that the allegedly distorting influences are statistically as well as economically small. However, since my thesis analyzes a novel data set and provides the first empirical investigation covering this recent epoch it is yet to be determined whether some of the obtained evidence is specific to my sample. To reconsider or complement the insights of this study will be the task of future research in this area.

Bibliography for Chapter 1

ANDRADE, G., AND S. N. KAPLAN (1998): "How Costly is Financial (Not Economic) Distress? Evidence from Highly Leveraged Transactions That Became Distressed," *The Journal of Finance*, 53, 1443–1493.

ASQUITH, P., R. GERTNER, AND D. SCHARFSTEIN (1994): "Anatomy of Financial Distress: An Examination of Junk-Bond Issuers," *The Quarterly Journal of Economics*, 109, 625–658.

BECKER, W. (2003): "Geier oder Notärzte? US-Investoren wittern in deutschen Turnaround-Kandidaten hohe Renditen," *Börsen-Zeitung*, (158 [08.19.03]), 13.

BOLTON, P., AND D. S. SCHARFSTEIN (1996): "Optimal Debt Structure and the Number of Creditors," *The Journal of Political Economy*, 104, 1–25.

FRANKS, J. R., K. NYBORG, AND W. TOROUS (1996): "A Comparison of US, UK, and German Insolvency Codes," *Financial Management*, 25, 19–30.

FRANKS, J. R., AND W. N. TOROUS (1989): "An Empirical Investigation of U.S. Firms in Reorganization," *The Journal of Finance*, 44, 747–769.

GERTNER, R., AND D. SCHARFSTEIN (1991): "A Theory of Workouts and the Effects of Reorganization Law," *The Journal of Finance*, 46, 1189–1222.

GILSON, S. C. (1990): "Bankruptcy, Boards, Banks, and Blockholders," *Journal of Financial Economics*, 27, 355–387.

JAMES, C. (1996): "Bank Debt Restructurings and the Composition of Exchange Offers in Financial Distress," *The Journal of Finance*, 51, 711–727.

JENSEN, M. C. (1989): "Active Investors, LBO's and Privatization of Bankruptcy," *Journal of Applied Corporate Finance*, 2, 35–44.

KAISER, K. M. (1996): "European Bankruptcy Laws: Implications for Coporations Facing Financial Distress," *Financial Management*, 25, 67–85.

MANSKI, C., AND D. MCFADDEN (1983): "Alternative Estimators and Sample Designs for Discrete Choice Analysis," in *Structural Analysis of Discrete Data with Econometric Applications*, ed. by C. Manski, and D. McFadden, pp. 2–50. MIT Press, Boston, MA.

MYERS, S. C. (1977): "Determinants of Corporate Borrowing," *Journal of Financial Economics*, 5, 147–175.

NOWAK, E. (2001): "Recent Developments in German Capital Markets and Corporate Governance," *Journal of Applied Corporate Finance*, 14, 35–48.

RUDOLPH, B. (2003): "Unternehmensfinanzierung und Corporate Governance - Entwicklungen und weiterer Anpassungsbedarf," *Betriebs-Berater*, 58, 2053–2060.

SENBET, L. W., AND J. K. SEWARD (1995): "Financial Distress, Bankruptcy and Reorganization," in *Finance*, ed. by R. A. Jarrow, V. Maksimovic, and W. T. Ziemba, pp. 921–957, Amsterdam, N.H. Elsevier.

SUSSMAN, O. (2005): "The Economics of the EU's Corporate-Insolvency Law and the Quest for Harmonisation by Market Forces," University of Oxford Working Paper 2005-FE-16.

Chapter 2

Data selection and sample descriptives

2.1 Sampling procedure

The objective of this study is to analyze how firms encounter and respond to financial distress. My sampling procedure follows a two-step approach in which I (1) create a stratified sample of firms that fulfill a specified distress-criterion and (2) track each firm's development over the distress interval. Thus, my data set is dynamic following the cycle of distress from its onset to its resolution. I collect data on financial accounts, ownership and board composition, and restructuring activity. My sampling period covers the years 1996-2004 and begins by identifying all publicly traded German corporations with stock price and basic financial statement data available on the German tapes of DATASTREAM and WORLDSCOPE, respectively.[1] The choice of the sample period results from data availability constraints: Mandatory ad-hoc publication of corporate news (such as restructuring-measures) are systematically obtainable from 1996 forward and 2003 was the last year for which financial statements were available when the sample was collected.

The pivotal step in my sampling procedure is to identify the right definition of financial distress. Corporate finance theory defines financial distress as a situation where a firm's cash flow is insufficient to meet the compulsory payments on its outstanding debt.[2] In this case a firm will ultimately be forced to breach its debt contracts, which in turn causes a gradual transfer of control rights to the firm's creditors and thus triggers distress related restructuring. I therefore base my empirical definition of financial distress on interest coverage ratios.[3] In this manner,

[1] Collection of financial statements ended 2003. However, I tracked corporate restructuring activities until the end of 2004.

[2] See Wruck (1990), pp. 421-422.

[3] This definition follows a widespread convention in literature. Among others, Asquith, Gertner, and Scharfstein (1994), and Hoshi, Kashyap, and Scharfstein (1990) use this sampling approach. Moreover, the Basel Committee (2004) uses interest coverage ratios for estimating a firm's default risk.

a firm is classified as financially distressed, if in any two consecutive years—beginning 1996—the firm's earnings before interest and taxes (Ebit) is less than its reported interest expense. The first year in which the firm meets the insufficient coverage criterion, is denoted as year 0. Importantly, this definition understates the severity of distress since it does not include contractual redemption payments or other obligations and covenants arising from non-interest bearing debt and liabilities.[4]

I am aware that this sampling approach is based on a rather unsophisticated distress criterion and fails to cover firms with only minor or short-term decreases in interest coverage.[5] However, several advantageous properties of this criterion prevail. First, initial sampling on repeated coverage shortfalls helps to create a sample of firms that suffer from a sustained bout of financial difficulty. The incidence of default, bankruptcy, and financial restructuring can be assumed to be fairly common for these firms. This is important because creating a sample of seriously distressed firms in Germany is less straight forward than for an equivalent sample of U.S. firms.[6] Most German firms have no public debt outstanding and thus defaults are usually not directly observable. Moreover, other than in the U.S., bankruptcies occur comparatively rarely in Germany and mostly present the end of a failed restructuring path rather than its beginning. Thus, initial sampling conditioned on discrete events such as public defaults or bankruptcy filings is likely to result in a selection bias towards large bond issuers or firms that were not deemed economically viable in the first place.

Another advantage of coverage shortfalls as sampling criterion is that it presents an unambiguous indicator of financial trouble for all firm-types and does not impose any further restrictions on firm or capital structure characteristics for a firm to be included in the sample. My approach therefore ensures a sufficiently heterogenous sample composition, which permits a more comprehensive inference of the obtained results.[7]

Finally, my approach does not share the shortcomings associated with constructing a sample on basis of market data such as poor stock performance.[8] As argued by Asquith, Gertner, and Scharfstein (1994), such a measure could, by design, include some information on how well the

[4] The use of Ebit is based on the assumption that investments equal in magnitude to depreciation are needed to keep the firm a going concern. See Rajan and Zingales (1995), p. 1429. However, the used criterion is highly correlated with alternative measures of distress such as Ebitda to interest expenses or Altman's Z-score. A robustness check for the year 2002 in which both alternatives measures where available, yielded very similar distress samples.

[5] In focusing on repeated coverage shortfalls, I rely on Asquith, Gertner, and Scharfstein (1994) who argue that firms with only minor shortfalls do not take discernible actions in response to distress. A more sophisticated, yet not necessarily more reliable proxy for a firm's default risk is presented by Altman's Z-score, which also measures the relation between operating performance and interest expenses.

[6] For example, James (1996) conditions upon defaults of publicly traded debt, and Franks and Torous (1989) and Denis and Rodgers (2006) condition upon Chapter 11 bankruptcy filings.

[7] In contrast, Asquith, Gertner, and Scharfstein (1994) and Andrade and Kaplan (1998) restrict their sample to highly leveraged transactions and thus can only make inference about this particular firm-type.

[8] This approach is followed by Gilson, John, and Lang (1990), and Ofek (1993).

market perceives the firm's chances to resolve financial distress and thus result in a sampling bias towards firms with relatively unfavorable resolution chances. By contrast, sampling on a backward-looking criterion such as coverage ratios produces an exogenous stratified sample in the sense of Manski and McFadden (1983) that allows consistent estimation and inference uncontaminated by problems of sample selection.

After excluding observations from the open market trading segment of the German Stock Exchange (*Freiverkehr*) as well as firms from the Financial Services industries, the sampling procedure provides a stratified sample of 267 financially distressed firms. Since when the sample was initially created, financial statement data was only available until 2003, the last year of entry is 2002. Not surprisingly, a large number of entries are centered around the years 1999-2001, which coincides with the burst of the technology bubble and onset of the general economic downturn shortly afterwards. In the final sample firms appear for a mean and median of 3.56 and 4.0 years, respectively. Only three firms appear the maximum number of nine years. A more detailed description of the time-series distribution of the final sample is given in Chapter 3.[9]

To inspect the validity of my distress criterion I conduct several robustness checks. In particular, I want to confirm that sampling on interest coverage shortfalls creates a cross-section that (1) contains firms that are seriously financially constraint and (2) does not leave a significant portion of the underlying population of distressed firms systematically unconsidered. I do so by using three legal guideposts that unambiguously identify firms at the cusp of bankruptcy by triggering mandatory revelations of firms' drastic financial conditions. The applied guideposts are mandatory bankruptcy filings pursuant to to § 92 II and III of the German Companies Act (AktG), mandatory notices of the loss of at least 50% of the firm's book equity capital pursuant to § 92 I AktG (*Verlustanzeige*), and mandatory notices of equity capital write-offs to accommodate asset depreciations or accrued losses pursuant to § 229 AktG (*Vereinfachte Kapitalherabsetzung*).[10] All three indicators are subject to mandatory ad-hoc disclosure and are thus easy to verify. I consequently search the database of the German Society of Ad-hoc Disclosure (*DGAP*) for all German public corporations during the sampling interval and compare figures for firms in and out of my sample.

The results of the comparison are summarized in Table 2.1. In total 43% of the firms in the distress sample make at least one of the three mandatory filings during their distress interval. Almost 30% file a bankruptcy petition. These are very high figures given that firms have strong incentives to forego any of such filings since they frequently cause steep share price declines

---

[9] A detailed list of firms included in the final sample can be obtained from the author upon request.

[10] In particular with respect to the the § 92 I AktG guidepost the Ebit criterion proved to be more reliable than, say, the Ebitda criterion since a considerable number of firms in my sample fell into distress after significant write-offs of earlier investments, which immediately resulted in imminent indebtedness.

Table 2.1: Robustness of distress criterion

List of legal guideposts that trigger mandatory notices of bankruptcy, imminent overindebtedness, and capital write-offs according to §§ 92 and 229 of the German Companies Act (AktG). Figures are based on a sample of 267 financially distressed corporations in Germany between 1996 and 2004. All figures are obtained from the database of the Deutsche Gesellschaft für Ad-hoc Publizität (DGAP).

	Distress sample		DGAP Database	
	(1)	(2)	(3)	(4)
Legal guideposts of distress	Number of firms	Fraction of total	Number of firms	Fraction of (1) in (3)
Mandatory insolvency filing pursuant to § 92 II and III AktG	76	0.28	89	0.85
Mandatory notice of capital loss pursuant to § 92 I AktG	55	0.21	60	0.91
Mandatory notice of capital write-off pursuant to § 229 AktG	29	0.11	37	0.79
Total	115	0.43	186	0.85

and deliberately initiate lengthy and cost-intensive administrative proceedings.[11] Thus, to most firms in the sample a mandatory filing denotes last resort on a failed restructuring path. In fact, a considerable number of the most heavily distressed firms in the sample restructure their liabilities without ever making any mandatory filing.[12] From columns 3 and 4 of Table 2.1 it can also be inferred that my final sample presents a highly representative cross-section of the underlying population of distressed firms in Germany. In total, the distress sample includes 85% of all bankruptcies of German public corporations, 91% of all § 92 I AktG filings, and 79% of all § 229 AktG filings during that interval. I interpret these figures as a strong confirmation of my sampling procedure.

2.2 Data sources and sample structure

The final distress sample contains basic firm data, stock market data, balance sheet and financial statement data, data on corporate ownership structure, data on firm's management and supervisory board structure, event data on corporate restructuring activity, and event data on firm exit. For stock market and balance sheet data figures are also available on an industry-adjusted level, i.e. I gather data on industry affiliation and industry performance. Subsequently, I briefly describe the sources for each data type. Because the used data types vary across studies, supplementary overviews of data types and variable definitions are also included in the individual chapters.

11 In the case of §§ 92 I and 229 this essentially a subsequent convening of an exceptional general shareholder assembly is required.

12 These cases include the public bond restructurings of Augusta Technologie AG in 2004 and EM.TV AG in 2003 as well as private restructurings of Walter Bau AG in 2002 and 2003 and Primacom in 2001.

Balance sheet and financial statement data are obtained from three different sources. The primary source is Thomson Financial's WORLDSCOPE database.[13] Company accounts data on WORLDSCOPE for Continental European firms are available from 1980 onwards. Since in several cases time series data on financial statements are incomplete or missing or not yet available electronically, I use supplementary data from the print edition of the HOPPENSTEDT Financial Information Stock Guide. For a subset of firms further information about capital and liability structure as well collateralization is directly obtained from the appendices of the company's annual reports. For some of these more sophisticated data types no exhaustive coverage by commercial databases is available.

Stock price data are obtained from Thomson Financial's DATASTREAM database. DATASTREAM coverage of German firms is available from 1973 onwards. It contains stock price information of all stocks traded on the Frankfurt Stock Exchange as well as any other exchange, though the latter may not date back as long. Stock prices as well as several market indices (e.g. CDAX and DAFOX) are collected on a daily basis. All quotes are corrected for dividend payments, stock splits, and other nominal factors that are likely to have an influence on stock prices. From DATASTREAM also the number of common shares outstanding is obtained. It is mainly used to determine the total market value of a firm's common stock.

Ownership data are obtained from the print edition of the HOPPENSTEDT Financial Information Stock Guide (*Hoppenstedt Aktienführer*). It contains data on firm characteristics such as domicile and trade register accounts, dates of foundation, incorporation, and initial public offering, group structure, basic financial statement data as well data on corporate ownership distribution for all corporations listed on a German stock exchange.[14] Ownership data are collected on an annual basis and contain information on direct holdings of common stock (*Stammaktien*). The information is used to calculate measures of ownership concentration and to account for the distribution of shares among different types of owners separated into management and non-management blockholders as well as different forms of private and corporate investors.[15]

Board data are also obtained from HOPPENSTEDT on an annual basis. The source contains information on the composition of the supervisory board (*Aufsichtsrat*) and the management board (*Vorstand*). Personal information on the board members entails residence and departmental responsibility (*Ressort*). Information on management and director ownership are

[13] For further information on these sources, see `http://www.thomson.com/financial/financial.jsp`.

[14] For further information on this source, see `http://www.hoppenstedt-aktienfuehrer.de/`. Köke (2002) also provides an exhaustive description of the various Hoppenstedt database products.

[15] A detailed description of the different ownership definitions and the calculation of the ownership variables is provided in Chapter 3 of this thesis.

obtained from matching board and ownership data. Furthermore, HOPPENSTEDT lists information on remuneration for both boards, though not allocated to the individual board members.

Restructuring data are obtained through a news research of the firm's press releases as well as all publicly available media sources. The research covers all documents on the following databases: LEXIS-NEXIS, DOWJONES&REUTERS (FACTIVA) and the electronic archive of the BÖRSENZEITUNG (the gazette of all German stock exchanges).[16] Collectively, these sources embrace all major German newspapers, business periodicals, electronic news-wires, adhoc information disclosures, trade register filings as well as the most relevant international sources. For each firm in the sample all available documents over the entire distress cycle are scrutinized. Observed restructurings are categorized in operational measures (e.g. divestitures, management turnover, layoffs) and financial measures (debt restructurings, equity issues, blocktrades). Information on distress resolution and firm exit, i.e. bankruptcy filings or acquisitions are also obtained from these sources.

The resulting structure of the distress sample is illustrated in Figure 2.1. The total sample comprises 267 firms with a maximum time-series of 1024 firm-years. Notably, sample sizes are not constant across chapters. This is due to different lengths of available time-series for different types of variables. Prior research by Köke (2002) suggests that incomplete time-series and missing data are a common side-effect of empirical studies relying on German firm data. The critical data type in my study that causes samples sizes to vary across chapters is corporate ownership and the degree of sophistication with which it is measured. For example, in Chapter 5, the sample size is 1024 because I only use data on ownership concentration and a management ownership dummy. In Chapter 3, by contrast, I distinguish ownership types in more detail, which causes the sample to be slightly reduced to 914 observations. Finally, in Chapter 6, I do not rely on sophisticated ownership data but I deliberately exclude observations from year -1 in distress time, which results in the sample size to shrink further to 878 observation. Furthermore, note that the structure of the panel is unbalanced, i.e. the number of observations is not the same for all firms. This is a result of the sampling approach: The time spent in distress differs across firms. Whether or not this fact causes methodological concerns due to panel attrition is inspected in Chapter 3.

[16] For further information on these sources, see `http://www.genios.de`, `http://www.lexisnexis.com`, and `http://www.factiva.com`.

Figure 2.1: Sample structure

Scope and structure of data set. Stock price and balance sheet data are obtained from DATASTREAM and WORLDSCOPE, respectively. Basic firm data, ownership data, and board data are obtained from HOPPENSTEDT. Restructuring data is obtained from GENIOS, DOWJONES&REUTERS, and LEXIS-NEXIS. Competition and industry segment data is obtained from WORLDSCOPE.

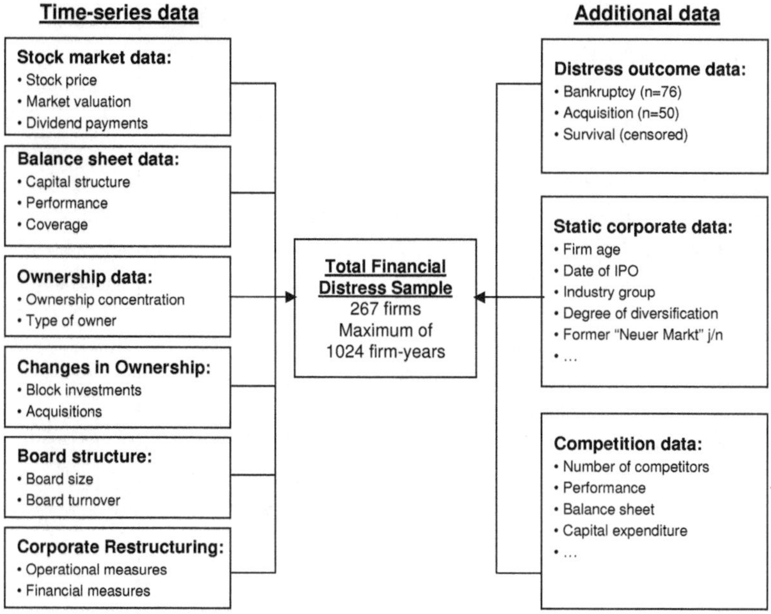

2.3 Sample representativeness

My distress sample is a subset of the universe of German listed firms covered by the German tapes of DATASTREAM and WORLDSCOPE, respectively. In every year during the 1996-2002 period a certain fraction of firms in this universe enter the distress sample, whereas the fraction varies between roughly 1.1% in 1997 and 7.2% in 2000. At the end of 2004, when the sample was initially collected, this universe contains a total of 1074 firms.[17] I am interested in whether

[17] Of course this population is not constant over time. Firms enter due to initial listing and exit due to bankruptcy or merger. In my sampling I control for this flotation by cross-checking the WORLDSCOPE sample with filings of firm entries and exits in the annual edition of the HOPPENSTEDT Akienführer. However, for a comparison of the industry distribution this static perspective should suffice.

the resulting industry distribution of firms in the distress sample broadly corresponds with the overall distribution of industries in the universe.

The industry distributions of the distress sample and the underlying WORLDSCOPE universe are comprised in Table 2.2. Industry classifications are based on the one-digit FTSE Global Classification Industry Code obtainable in WORLDSCOPE.[18] In both samples, General Industrials, Cyclical Services, and Information Technology present the most prevalent industry types. Also noteworthy, Utilities and Non-Cyclical Services only have a dismal relevance in both samples. Yet, two differences are evident: First, there are no Financials in the distress sample. This is a deliberate result of the sampling approach, as I stick to the convention of analyzing non-financial Corporates only.[19] The second and more important difference is that Information Technology firms are over-represented in the distress sample. In the WORLDSCOPE reference universe of 2004 the fraction of IT firms amount 17% whereas the overall fraction in the distress sample is 35%. Clearly, this is not surprising given that the sampling period embraces the burst of the technology bubble at the *Neuer Markt*, the former growth segment of the German Stock Exchange. In fact, almost all IT firms in the IT sample were formerly listed on the Neuer Markt. However, it is not clear *ex ante* whether and how this tilt towards technology firms in the distress sample adversely affects the generality of the results. In the subsequent analyses I address this concern by explicitly controlling for the effect of a listing at the *Neuer Markt.* After controlling for observations in the Financials and Information Technology sector the industry distribution in both samples are roughly the same. A combined Kolmogorov-Smirnov test for the equality of distribution functions cannot reject the hypothesis that industry distributions are equal for both samples (corresponding p-value is 0.808).

2.4 Sources of financial distress

Firms enter the distress sample in case repeated interest coverage shortfalls. The year of the initial coverage shortfall is denoted as year 0 in distress time. Three distinct factors can cause a firm's inability to cover its debt obligations: (1) Excessive leverage, (2) an industry downturn, and (3) poor firm-specific operating performance. In the following I apply a simple methodology established by Asquith, Gertner, and Scharfstein (1994) and Andrade and Kaplan (1998) to assess the relative importance of these factors in triggering financial distress for the firms in my sample.[20]

---

[18] For a detailed description of the FTSE sectorial breakdown, see `http://www.ftse.com`.

[19] Financials are subject to different disclosure rules and much stricter regulation, which forbids comparison with regular Corporates.

[20] The methodology was developed by Asquith, Gertner, and Scharfstein (1994). In their article Andrade and Kaplan (1998) adapt the framework by adding short-term interest changes as fourth possible source of distress, however they find that this factor has little explanatory power. In the following, I strictly follow the approach of Asquith, Gertner, and Scharfstein (1994), pp. 632-634.

Table 2.2: Sample industry distribution

Industry distribution of distress sample and underlying universe of publicly traded firms on the German Tape of WORLDSCOPE and DATASTREAM as of the end of 2002. Figures are based on a sample of 267 financially distressed corporations in Germany between 1996 and 2004. Industry classifications pertain to the one-digit FTSE Global Classification Industry Code. Note that the sampling procedure precludes Financial firms (one-digit FTSE Code 80) from the distress sample.

	Distress sample		WORLDSCOPE Universe	
FTSE Clobal Classification Industry Code	Number of firms	Fraction of total	Number of firms	Fraction of total
[10] Basic Industries	17	0.06	102	0.09
[20] General Industrials	42	0.16	155	0.14
[30] Cyclical Consumer Goods	26	0.10	115	0.11
[40] Non-cyclical Consumer Goods	26	0.10	127	0.12
[50] Cyclical Services	52	0.19	181	0.17
[60] Non-cyclical Services	9	0.03	23	0.02
[70] Utilities	2	0.01	24	0.02
[80] Financials	0	0.00	161	0.15
[90] Information Technology	93	0.35	186	0.17
Total	267	1.00	1074	1.00

Basic firm characteristics at year 0 are displayed in Table 2.3.[21] Industry medians are based on the two-digit FTSE Global Classification Industry Codes.[22] Figures in Panel A indicate that firms are only moderately higher indebted than the median firm in their industry. This contrasts with the samples in Asquith, Gertner, and Scharfstein (1994) and Andrade and Kaplan (1998) who find their firms to be substantially higher leveraged than their industry peers. However, because both studies exclusively analyze junk-bond issuers and highly leveraged transactions, this contrast appears very plausible. Panel A of Table 2.3 also shows that firms are poor operating performers. The *return on assets* variable, which is defined by the ratio of a firm's earnings before interest depreciation and amortization (Ebitda) to total assets, is negative on an absolute scale as well as relative to the firms' industry median. The profitability shortfall relative to the industry median is substantial: On average, firms in the distress sample trail the representative firm in their industry in return on assets by 17%. However, during the year of the initial coverage shortfall, overall industry operating performance is also substantially worse than in the previous year. The mean decline in return on assets by the median firm in the industry is 2.5% between years -1 and 0.[23] Therefore, firms in the distress sample are not only performing poorly relative to the their industry peers, but their industry peers are also performing poorly.

[21] A more detailed description of the firm characteristics and the features of the designated sub-samples is contained in the subsequent chapters.

[22] Two-digit Codes (Industrial Sectors) rather than three digit Codes (Industry Sub-sectors) are chosen as benchmark to ensure a sufficient number of peer firms within the same category. By that means, the median number of firms within the same industry is 62. Only for 7 firms, the number of industry peers is below 10.

[23] The corresponding figure in the Asquith, Gertner, and Scharfstein (1994) is -2.8%.

Similar to Asquith, Gertner, and Scharfstein (1994), I make the following calculations to uncover the relative weight of leverage, firm-specific operating performance, and industry operating performance in causing financial distress.

1. Leverage factor (λ): The amount that firm cash flow, defined as Ebitda less interest expenses, would improve in year 0 if the firm had the same ratio of interest expense to total assets as the median firm in the industry. Thus, if the firm is more highly leveraged than its representative peer, the adjustment will increase cash flow by the amount $\lambda = \delta_{ita} * TA$, where δ_{ita} is the positive difference of the interest expense to assets ratio and TA is the amount of the firm's total assets.

2. Firm-specific operating performance factor (θ): The amount that cash flow would improve in year 0 if the firm performed equally well as the median firm in the industry. If the firm's operating performance, measured by the Ebitda to total assets ratio (*return on assets*), is worse than that of its representative peer, the adjustment will increase cash flow by the amount $\theta = -\delta_{roa} * TA$, where δ_{roa} is the negative difference in the *return on assets* ratio.

3. Industry operating performance factor (ϕ): The amount that cash flow would improve in year 0 if the firm had the same operating performance as the median firm in its industry and the industry performed as well as in the previous (pre-distress) year -1. If industry performance fell between years, the adjustment will increase cash flow by the amount $\phi = \delta_{iop} * TA$, where δ_{iop} is the difference in the industry median of the Ebitda to total assets ratio between year -1 and year 0.

Note, that the sum of all these cash flow changes $\Delta CF = \lambda + \theta + \phi$ would, by definition, augment my sample firms' cash flows to those of the median firm in an average pre-distress industry. Thus, to calculate the marginal contribution of each factor to the total cash flow change I build simple quotients. In that manner, the portion of distress caused by excessive leverage is $\lambda / \Delta CF$, the portion of distress caused by a firm-specific operating performance decline is $\theta / \Delta CF$, and the portion of distress caused by the sole instance of an industry downturn is $\phi / \Delta CF$.

The results of this procedure are presented in Panel B of Table 2.3. Evidently, firm-specific operating performance declines are the dominant factor in causing financial distress to the firms in my sample. On average, more than 75% of the cash flow shortfall is attributable to this source. For 216 firms firm-specific performance it is the primary source of distress, i.e. its effect on cash flow exceeds that of leverage and industry performance. Corresponding figures for the factors of leverage and industry performance are 7.2% and 14, and 15.1% and 37, respectively. Overall, the results are very similar to those reported by Asquith, Gertner, and Scharfstein (1994).[24]

One implication of the above analysis is that firms rarely become financially distressed for solely financial reasons. This is consistent with arguments by Wruck (1990) and others

[24] The impact of the leverage factor their study is somewhat higher (21.4%), which mainly results from their sample's restriction on high-yield bond issuers.

Table 2.3: Sources of coverage shortfall in year 0

Decomposition of the coverage shortfall at year 0 into three potential sources of financial distress. Figures are based on a sample of 267 financially distressed corporations in Germany between 1996 and 2004. Industry medians pertain to the universe of firms with the same two-digit FTSE Global Classification industry code. Portions of distress attributable to a specific factor in Panel B are calculated as the ratio of the cash shortfall due to source to the sum of cash shortfall du to all sources. Cash shortfall due to factor leverage is calculated as the amount that cash flow (Ebitda less interest expense) would improve in year 0 if the firm had the same ratio of interest expenses to assets as the median firm in its industry. Cash shortfall due to factor firm operating performance is calculated as the amount that cash flow would improve in year 0 if the firm performed as well as the median firm in its industry. Cash shortfall due to factor industry operating performance is calculated as the amount that cash flow would improve if the firm had the same performance relative to its industry, but the industry performed as well as in the previous (pre-distress) year -1.

Panel A: Sources of coverage shortfall in year 0

Variable	Mean	Median	St.Dev	Min.	Max.
A. Interest expense/assets					
Sample firms	0.017	0.012	0.019	0.000	0.172
Industry median	0.012	0.011	0.007	0.003	0.055
Deviation from industry median	0.005	0.001	0.017	-0.033	0.160
B. Return on assets					
Sample firms	-0.099	-0.037	0.221	-1.386	0.258
Industry median	0.072	0.087	0.056	-0.319	0.193
Deviation from industry median	-0.171	-0.112	0.223	-1.522	0.250
C. Industry median change in Return on assets from year -1 to year 0	-0.025	-0.024	0.036	-0.251	0.169

Panel B: Normalized sources of coverage shortfall in year 0

Factor	Mean	Median	St.Dev	Primary cause
Leverage ($\lambda/\Delta CF$)	0.072	0.011	0.302	14
Firm operating performance ($\theta/\Delta CF$)	0.777	0.890	0.668	216
Industry operating performance ($\phi/\Delta CF$)	0.151	0.100	0.599	37

that financial distress often coincides with economic distress, i.e. poor operating performance. Another implication is that most of the firms' poor financial and operational condition is in fact caused by firm-specific rather than industry-wide factors. In consequence, the resolution of financial distress and the return to at least industry-average profitability, to most firms, seems unfeasible without adequate corporate (i.e. firm-level) restructuring. In fact, firms in my sample engage heavily in restructuring their operations and balance sheets.

Table 2.4 provides a synopsis of selected restructuring activities (and their definitions) that are identified by researching the news databases for all firms in the sample. Panel A contains common operational responses to distress, the most prevalent being asset divestitures and replacements of key executives. Panel B contains common financial restructurings. Firms heavily engage in debt restructurings and equity infusions. Other measures, such as equity write-offs and shareholder loans are less frequently observed. In total, more than 80% of all firms engage

Table 2.4: Synopsis of corporate restructuring activities

Panels A and B contain summary statistics on restructuring activities undertaken by a sample of 267 financially distressed corporations in Germany between 1996 and 2004. Panel C lists different outcomes of financial distress for the sampled firms. Restructuring activities and outcomes are identified from LEXIS-NEXIS, DOWJONES&REUTERS, and the BÖRSENZEITUNG. Definitions of restructurings measures are similar to Ofek (1993). *Layoffs* are announcements of employee layoffs unrelated to corporate downsizing. *Asset divestitures* are sales of subsidiary business units, abroad business divisions, or parts of the production facilities. *Asset shutdowns* are discontinuing of operations. *Management turnover* presents regular and irregular replacement of CEO's and CFO's. *Director turnover* presents regular and irregular replacement of the chairman of the supervisory board. *Equity issues* are capital raises through cash infusion (*Barkapitaleinlage*), *equity write-offs* are reductions of book equity pursuant to § 229 of the German Companies Act (AktG), *shareholder loans* present credit agreements between the firm and one of its shareholders (*Aktionärsdarlehen*), private and public *debt restructurings* present reductions or deferrals of contractual payments, provisions of fresh money, or swaps of debt securities against securities with residual of mezzanine claim.

Panel A: Operational Restructurings	Number of occurrences	Number of firms	Mean of total sample
Employee layoffs	105	78	0.29
Asset divestiture	181	112	0.41
Asset shutdowns	55	37	0.14
Management turnover	254	167	0.61
Director turnover	246	168	0.62
Total operational actions	841	239	0.88
Panel B: Financial Restructurings			
Equity issue	123	97	0.36
Equity write-down	29	29	0.11
Shareholder loan	21	21	0.08
Debt restructuring	123	98	0.37
Public-debt restructuring	4	4	0.01
Total financial actions	298	174	0.64
Panel C: Outcomes of financial distress	Number of firms		Mean of total sample
Bankruptcy	76		0.28
Acquisition	54		0.20
Survival	146		0.54

in some kind operational restructuring and more than 60% of all firms engage in some kind of financial restructuring.

Finally, Panel C of Table 2.4 partitions the sample by the outcome of financial distress. Roughly half of the firms do not survive distress as independent entities. 28% ultimately file for bankruptcy while 20% are acquired by other firms.[25] An the end of the sampling period, at 2004, 50% of the firms are denoted as survivors. However, for a majority of these firms the state of distress is still pending, i.e. the outcome variable is left-censored. In the subsequent chapters

[25] Five firms file for bankruptcy after being acquired. For transparency, these double counts are not eliminated here. Chapter 6 distinguishes more clearly between the different outcomes of distress.

I will explore in more detail how firms chose between alternative restructurings and whether restructuring is related to the final outcome of distress. However, because not all restructuring measures are equally important and some of them, such as employee layoffs and asset divestitures are highly correlated, I will restrict my attention in the subsequent analyses to the most prevalent responses to distress. In Chapter 3 I explore changes in ownership and management turnover. In Chapters 4 and 5 I study debt restructurings and equity issues, respectively. Finally, in Chapter 6, I analyze the determinants of survival, acquisition, and bankruptcy as alternative outcomes of distress.

Bibliography for Chapter 2

ANDRADE, G., AND S. N. KAPLAN (1998): "How Costly is Financial (Not Economic) Distress? Evidence from Highly Leveraged Transactions That Became Distressed," *The Journal of Finance*, 53, 1443–1493.

ASQUITH, P., R. GERTNER, AND D. SCHARFSTEIN (1994): "Anatomy of Financial Distress: An Examination of Junk-Bond Issuers," *The Quarterly Journal of Economics*, 109, 625–658.

DENIS, D. K., AND K. J. RODGERS (2006): "Chapter 11: Duration, Outcome, and Post-Reorganization Performance," *Journal of Financial and Quantitative Analysis (forthcoming)*, 41.

FRANKS, J. R., AND W. N. TOROUS (1989): "An Empirical Investigation of U.S. Firms in Reorganization," *The Journal of Finance*, 44, 747–769.

GILSON, S. C., K. JOHN, AND L. H. LANG (1990): "Troubled Debt Restructurings, An Empirical Study of Private Reorganization of Firms in Default," *Journal of Financial Economics*, 27, 315–353.

HOSHI, T., A. KASHYAP, AND D. S. SCHARFSTEIN (1990): "The Role of Banks in Reducing the Costs of Financial Distress in Japan," *Journal of Financial Economics*, 27, 67–88.

JAMES, C. (1996): "Bank Debt Restructurings and the Composition of Exchange Offers in Financial Distress," *The Journal of Finance*, 51, 711–727.

KÖKE, J. (2002): *Corporate Governance in Germany: An Empirical Investigation*. Physica, Heidelberg.

MANSKI, C., AND D. MCFADDEN (1983): "Alternative Estimators and Sample Designs for Discrete Choice Analysis," in *Structural Analysis of Discrete Data with Econometric Applications*, ed. by C. Manski, and D. McFadden, pp. 2–50. MIT Press, Boston, MA.

OFEK, E. (1993): "Capital Structure and Firm Response to Poor Performance," *Journal of Financial Economics*, 34, 3–30.

RAJAN, R., AND L. ZINGALES (1995): "What Do We Know About Capital Structure? Some Evidence from International Data," *The Journal of Finance*, 50, 1421–1460.

WRUCK, K. H. (1990): "Financial Distress, Reorganization, and Organizational Efficiency," *Journal of Financial Economics*, 27, 419–444.

Chapter 3

Financial distress, corporate control, and management turnover: A German panel analysis*

3.1 Introduction

According to corporate financial theory, the states of financial distress, default, and bankruptcy present a fundamental stage in the life-cycle of corporations that provokes substantial changes in the ownership of firms' residual claims and the allocation of rights to manage corporate resources [e.g. Jensen (1988), Wruck (1990)]. However, empirical results on how precisely these changes evolve have remained sparse and inconclusive.[1] For example, neoclassical models on financial distress typically suggest that default engenders a wholesale transfer of control to the firm's lenders who can costlessly restructure their claims to maximize firm value [e.g. Haugen and Senbet (1978)]. Yet, the actual role of creditors in the restructuring of financially distressed firms has not been exhaustively scrutinized. Similarly, while financial theory traditionally proposes that managers personally suffer when their firms default or go bankrupt [e.g. Ross (1977)], there exists little evidence on what forces actually discipline managers in financially distressed firms.

---

* I would like to thank Dietmar Harhoff, Christoph Kaserer, Colin Mayer, Bernd Rudolph, Oren Sussman, and Felix Treptow for helpful discussions. Markus Ampenberger provided excellent research assistance. Earlier drafts of this chapter are also conference papers at the Association of University Professors of Management Conference (VHB Pfingstagung), Dresden 2006, the Annual Conference on Corporate Strategy (ACCS), Berlin 2006, and the International Conference on Business and Finance (ICBF), Punjagutta, Hyderabad 2005. I would like to thank four anonymous referees for their thoughtful comments.

1 Most notable previous studies on corporate financial distress include Franks and Torous (1989) on reorganization of bankrupt firms under Chapter 11, Gilson (1989) on private costs of distress, Gilson (1990) on ownership and board composition of firms in default or bankruptcy, Gilson, John, and Lang (1990) on debt restructuring, and Gilson and Vetsuypens (1993) on CEO compensation. Wruck (1990) and Senbet and Seward (1995) provide surveys of the theoretic as well as empirical strands of literature.

Finally, we currently know little about the intricate causes and consequences of control transfers in firms at the cusp of bankruptcy.

In this study I seek to address these and related issues. In applying panel data methodology I analyze the impact of sustained financial distress on corporate ownership and management turnover as well as the interaction between these two. A focus is set on the relative weight and effectiveness of internal and external monitoring mechanisms as well as monitoring by bank-lenders. Thereby, I account for the theoretic postulate that the relative effectiveness of alternative ownership and governance structures is mirrored by their ability to replace poorly performing managers [e.g. Fama and Jensen (1983), Franks and Mayer (2001)]. One crucial aspect of my study is the explicit consideration of the particularities of German ownership structures, which were traditionally dominated by large family investors and proxy-vote representation by powerful house-banks, but have undergone substantial change in recent years [Gorton and Schmid (2000), Köke (2002)]. My study thus aims at providing genuine insights into the anatomy of distress in German corporations and seeks to complement as well as challenge previous evidence that is almost exclusively restricted to the Anglo-Saxon domain.

My analysis is based on a sample of 267 German corporations that experienced back-to-back interest coverage shortfalls and steep share price declines between 1996 and 2004. This period coincides with the youngest economic crisis and the subsequent convalescence thereof and thus offers the analysis of a sample that was previously not obtainable. My research design follows prior work by Gilson (1990) and Asquith et al. (1990) in that I (1) create a stratified sample of firms that meet a pre-determined distress-criterion at some time during the sampling interval and (2) track each firm's development over the distress cycle. Firms exit the sample upon bankruptcy or financial recovery. Data coverage is censored at the year 2004.

My analysis follows a three-step approach. First, I examine the impact of financial distress on corporate ownership. I find that ownership structures undergo substantial changes. Median ownership concentration, measured by a Herfindahl index, significantly declines from 26% in year -1 to 16% in year +4 relative to the onset of financial distress. The decline in ownership concentration is mostly attributable to a systematic retreat of individual and family investors, traditionally the bulwark in corporate ownership structures in Germany. Conversely, ownership representation by banks and financial investors almost doubles over the same interval, although both groups of investors only acquire comparatively small stakes. Ownership by corporate managers, i.e. executives and directors, also significantly increases over the distress interval.

Second, I analyze how turnover of key-executives is affected by persisting distress. I find that average turnover rates in my sample are almost twice as high as conventional levels of turnover in Germany. Only 14% of chief executives and 22% of chief directors who hold respective seats at the onset of financial difficulties are still in office at year +4 in distress time. Third, I perform panel data regressions to investigate the relation between (changes in) corporate ownership and management turnover. After controlling for performance, I find that turnover is significantly affected by ownership composition and changes therein. For one, increasing insider ownership cannot insulate management from disciplinary turnover. Also, turnover is not affected by overall ownership concentration or the size of holdings by private investors. Instead, turnover is mostly triggered by firm outsiders, especially banks and financial investors who acquire distressed claims through block investments and takeovers. Banks also replace managers upon defaults and in debt restructurings. Thus, managerial tenure under financial distress is more affected by actual shifts in ownership and control rather than by absolute levels of ownership. The results are robust to alternative ownership specifications and definitions of management turnover and are not inflicted by panel attrition problems.

Collectively, my results offer strong support for the hypothesis that financial distress provokes a shift from internal to external mechanisms of corporate control. One ancillary contribution of my study is the revealing that German corporations seem to heavily engage in restructuring prior to actual bankruptcy. While roughly one-third of my sampled firms ultimately go bankrupt, formal proceedings appear to be protracted as long as possible. This sharply contrasts to previous evidence on distressed U.S. firms who tend to enter formal proceedings under Chapter 11 prematurely and on their own free will and thus perform a great deal of restructuring under court supervision [Franks and Torous (1989)].[2] This national peculiarity makes German data particularly interesting for studying the impact of financial distress because observed restructuring measures are not distorted by legal or regulatory influence but remain a matter of choice.

This study is structured as follows. Section 2 surveys the relevant theoretic literature as well as related empirical studies and derives testable propositions. Section 3 describes the data structure and discusses key measurement issues. The empirical results, their interpretation and robustness checks are contained in section 4. Section 5 concludes with a summary of the study's main findings and a brief outlook. Complimentary empirical results and detailed variable definitions are contained in the Appendix.

3.2 Theory and propositions

3.2.1 Theory on distress, ownership, and management turnover

Financial distress may affect corporate control in various ways. Yet there exists no single theoretic framework modelling this relationship. Therefore, my derivation of testable hypotheses must rely on an array of in part conflicting theoretic contributions, related empirical studies as well as anecdotal evidence. In this respect the following analysis will deliberately retain some explorative traits.

[2] Most likely this reflects the more debtor-friendly bankruptcy legislation in the U.S. Franks, Nyborg, and Torous (1996) provide a review of that issue.

3.2.1.1 Financial distress and the separation of ownership and control

The fundamental principle underlying the separation of ownership and control in modern corporations is that managers who act as agents on behalf of the firm's claimholders and have no or only a limited financial interest in the firm can be made accountable for poor performance. Accountability of managers and thus the required return on investment to financial claimholders in ensured by mechanisms of corporate governance [Shleifer and Vishny (1997)]. Perhaps the most apparent indication for the effectiveness of these mechanisms is the outright replacement of unsuccessful executives.[3] While managers' actual contribution to firm value is not directly observable, (adjusted) measures for firm performance are usually applied as proxies. The so-postulated inverse relation between stock price or operating performance and management turnover has been confirmed in several previous empirical studies.[4]

Aside from low profits and poor stock returns, several types of corporate finance and investment decisions seem to be particularly influenced by the personal costs that managers incur when their firms face financial nemesis such as default and bankruptcy. For example, to avoid the negative personal consequences of distress managers might choose less risky (and rewarding) investment projects [Smith and Stulz (1985)] or employ below optimum levels of leverage in the firm's capital structure [Ross (1977)]. While corporate and financial performance are strongly interrelated, empirical evidence by Gilson (1989) suggests that financial distress independently engenders higher rates of management turnover. For a sample of poorly performing firms Gilson finds that turnover in firms that are also financially distressed exceeds turnover in non-distressed entities almost by a factor of three. Similarly, Franks et al. (2001) argue that financial distress is the only focused and significant force in disciplining poor management.

Perhaps surprisingly, the question of who stands behind the disciplining of managers in distressed firms has so far remained almost entirely disregarded. This is an interesting void to fill. Under financial distress, conflicts of interest are pronounced as various classes of claimants dispute about the distribution of the firm's waning resources. In such a setting, the allocation of rights to appoint or replace key executives directly reflects the effects of distress on the balance of power within the corporation.

In the following I restrict my attention to three non-mutually exclusive sources of corporate control. I distinguish internal monitoring by blockholders and the board of directors, external monitoring by the market for corporate control, and monitoring by creditors.

---

3 Gilson (1989) shows that non-routine turnovers have a sustainably bad influence on the personal wealth of individuals as well as their value on the market for managers.

4 References include Warner, Watts, and Wruck (1988), Weisbach (1988), and Gibbons and Murphy (1990) for the U.S., Franks, Mayer, and Renneboog (2001) for the U.K. as well as Te Wildt (1996) and Jostarndt et al. (2005) for Germany.

3.2.1.2 Ownership structure and internal monitoring

In Germany, the governance of corporations is organized in a two-tier system. The first tier is the supervisory board (i.e. the board of directors), which appoints the management-executive board, nominates a chief executive, determines managerial compensation schemes, and approves the annual accounts as well as the firm's long term strategy. Unlike in the anglo-saxon domain, the two tiers in Germany are strictly separated in that no member of the management board simultaneously holds a seat in the supervisory board.[5] The supervisory board consists of employee and owner representatives and is appointed by the general shareholder assembly. Thus, blockholders of voting stock typically exert a strong influence on the board composition and, along with it, on management. Whether or not this influence is appreciable is ambiguous from a theoretic point of view. In principle, concentrated ownership bears the advantage that large shareholders have the power and the incentive to effectively monitor management and thus overcome the free-riding problem associated with dispersed ownership [Shleifer and Vishny (1986)]. On the other hand, powerful blockholders, especially majority owners, may also use their influence to reap private benefits at the expense of minority owners [Bebchuk (1999), Barclay and Holderness (1989)]. Concerning the disciplining of poor management, prior empirical studies generally provide evidence in favor of concentrated ownership. For example, Denis, Denis, and Sarin (1997) find a positive relation between ownership concentration and performance related management turnover.[6]

A second dimension of internal monitoring pertains to the type of blockholder. In Germany the most powerful owners in listed corporations are private investors (families and individuals) and non-financial corporates [e.g. Gorton and Schmid (2000), Köke (2001)]. Economic theory suggests that monitoring by private blockholders may be more effective because they present ownership at the ultimate level and thus have better incentives to obey their fiduciary duties. Corporate shareholders, by contrast, are fraught with additional agency conflicts and may therefore be weak monitors [Von Thadden (1990)]. In Germany, this discrepancy is pronounced due to the traditionally intensive ties between private shareholders and the firms they own [e.g. Ehrhardt and Nowak (2003)]. For this reason, private investors in Germany are typically assigned the attribute of active "inside" blockholders [Gray (1998)].[7] Anecdotal evidence consistent with the argument of more effective monitoring by private investors is provided by Wenger and Kaserer (1998). They find that management errors in German corporations are more likely to be corrected if the supervisory board is dominated by private rather than by corporate blockholders. The effect of financial distress on blockholder monitoring is somewhat

5 A more detailed comparison of both governance systems is provided by Edwards and Fischer (1994) and Rudolph (2003).

6 Similarly Jostarndt, Rudolph, and Thierauf (2005). By contrast, Franks and Mayer (2001) find no relation between ownership concentration and turnover.

7 Ownership representation by private investors in Germany is particularly strong for younger firms formerly listed on 'Neuer Markt' in which the founding entrepreneurs and/or family descendants take active roles on the firm's supervisory board.

ambiguous. On the one hand, distress and corporate crises increase the need for effective monitoring. Provided that inside blockholders are better informed and represent better monitors, economic theory may assert that distress engenders a consolidation of voting stock in the hands of few private blockholders [Gilson (1990)]. If, on the other hand, private investors are less diversified and more wealth constrained than, say, institutional investors, they may be more hesitant to increase their ownership stakes in distressed targets.

A final dimension of internal monitoring considered in this study concerns the incentive-based compensation for managers and directors in the form of stock ownership. According to Jensen and Meckling (1976) and Baker, Jensen, and Murphy (1988), the incentive-related virtues of compensating managers and directors with firm's stock are greatest when the firm is distressed. However, the expected impact of stock-based compensation of both groups on management turnover should be directly opposed. I should expect direct holdings by management-executives to reduce irregular turnover. In part, this stems from the fact that managers have better entrenchment possibilities if they hold voting stock in the firm and thus are more insulated from disciplinary board decisions [Denis, Denis, and Sarin (1997)]. In part, however, this is also due to the disciplining effect of granting poor management undervalued stock (other than options), which may serve as substitute to outright replacement. Increasing ownership by directors, in turn, should provoke higher rates of performance related turnover if ownership participation of directors induces them to monitor management more effectively.

Throughout this text I will refer to this interaction of ownership concentration, holdings by private investors, and holdings by corporate managers and directors as *internal monitoring hypothesis.*

3.2.1.3 External monitoring and the market for corporate control

While monitoring by internal mechanisms largely refers to the scale and nature of ownership in absolute terms, external monitoring is essentially based on *changes* in ownership involving outside investors [Manne (1965)]. Earlier studies on corporate governance in Germany have simplistically assumed ownership structures to be constant over time. However, Köke (2002) shows that ownership structures in fact exhibit considerable variation. Changes in ownership and control may result from two sources. First, outside investors may accumulate stakes through block trades of existing shares following voluntary disposals of existing owners. Alternatively, new shares may be issued through private or public placements designed to concentrate voting power in new hands thus deliberately diluting holdings of existing owners.[8]

Outside investors may be attracted by financial distress for several reasons. First, outside investors may seek to actively contribute to the turnaround process if they dispose of the relevant

[8] Of course, this cannot be completed against the will of existing owners. § 186 of the German Companies Act grants existing owners subscription rights to any new issues of stock. I will address this issue further below.

industry and management experience, which is essential to the rescue of an ailing target. In some cases, this experience may well offset the informational advantage typically enjoyed by inside blockholders such as private investors. Thus, the increased monitoring need prevalent during poor performance may be better executed by outsiders, especially corporates and financial firms. Evidence consistent with this view is obtained by Barclay and Holderness (1991) who find that engagements of new outside blockholders are associated with abnormal announcement returns of about 15%. Alternatively, investors could seek a passive investment strategy if they believe that securities are underpriced or that larger blocks of stock engender a more generous consideration under a likely bankruptcy or debt restructuring plan [Gilson (1990)].

Economic theory suggests that changes in ownership and control present bad news for incumbent managers. This follows from considerations that takeovers are most likely to be disciplinary when performance is poor and that different management teams compete with each other on the market for managerial talent [Scharfstein (1988), Jensen and Ruback (1983)]. The empirical evidence for the U.S. offers strong support for the hypothesis that ownership changes, takeovers, and performance related executive replacements are interrelated [Mikkelson and Partch (1997), Denis and Sarin (1999)]. While hostile takeovers have remained a rarity in Germany, disciplining ownership changes in the form of minority block trades occur frequently [Jenksinon and Ljungqvist (2001), Köke (2002)]. However, managerial disciplining by outsiders is not restricted to over-the-counter purchases of existing share blocks but may also occur when distressed firms tap the equity market in order to raise new funds [Franks et al. (2001)]. Under financial distress, equity offerings are likely to occur as a result of creditor pressure since existing owners have little incentive to issue new stock voluntarily [Gertner and Scharfstein (1991)]. For example, the recent equity offering by KarstadtQuelle AG was announced as part of a complex refinancing package imposed by the banks and almost collapsed under the heavy appeal by the firm's shareholders.[9] If subscription rights for the new issue are excluded or existing shareholders refuse to go along, this offers an opportunity for new investors to acquire new blocks of shares, often at a steep discount (in the case of KarstadtQuelle 40%).

In the following, the postulated relation between financial distress, monitoring by outside blockholders and management turnover is labelled *external monitoring hypothesis.*

3.2.1.4 Financial distress and bank monitoring

Under financial distress a third source of managerial control emanates from the firm's creditors. As firm performance deteriorates equity claims decline in value and contractual claims increasingly participate in the firm's underlying business risk. Thus, in the state of crisis, creditors may have incentives to monitor management more actively than shareholders [Jensen (1989)]. In the absence of exhaustive bond financing, this monitoring is mostly attributable to corporate banks, the most prevalent group of lenders in the German domain.

[9] See "KarstadtQuelle einigt sich mit Aktionären", in: *Börsen-Zeitung*, 26 November 2004.

According to Gilson (1990), creditors' contribution to corporate control in financially distressed firms essentially manifests in two ways, (1) explicit ownership of voting stock and (2) restrictive covenants enforced through debt restructurings. Bank ownership of voting stock in German corporations is a common phenomenon [e.g. Gorton and Schmid (2000)]. Moreover, banks often dispose of considerable proxy-votes that they execute on behalf of individual shareholders. Holdings of distressed equity and swaps of debt into equity, however, are restrictively regulated. For example, according to German legislation prior to 1998, banks who take equity in distressed firms deliberately subordinate their remaining debt claims in the firm and thus always fare worse than without the swap in case the restructuring attempt does ultimately fail (Concept of Equitable Subordination, or *Eigenkapitalersatzregeln*). After the enforcement of the German Capital Raising Facilitation Act (KapAEG) the Concept of Equitable Subordination is eased for debt-to-equity swaps, however, banks still face the risk of a subsequent payment obligation if the value of the equity securities received exceeds that of the debt securities given (*Differenzhaftung*). Moreover, the incentive to exchange debt into equity is reduced due to unfavorable taxation rules imposed on the debtor.[10] Nevertheless, banks frequently accept residual claims to resuscitate a distressed debtor, albeit this engagement, at most times, is temporarily and small in size. For example, Westdeutsche Landesbank acquired a minority stake in Gildemeister AG in an out-of-court workout in 1994 and divested the stake upon the firm's return to sustained profitability in 2005.[11]

Banks may also respond to their client's financial distress by claiming (additional) seats in the firm's supervisory board, even without disposing of considerable ownership. While it is difficult to exhaustively identify bank affiliation of all board members especially for small firms, anecdotal evidence suggests that board representation by senior bankers fortifies in response to distress. For example, Dieter Rampl of HypoVereinsbank took a seat in the supervisory board of Elexis AG in 2000, and Alfred Lehner of Bayern Landesbank joined the supervisory board of Walter Bau AG in 2001. At that time, both firms experienced severe financial distress. Most recently, Morgan Stanley announced to delegate a senior banker to head the supervisory board of Borussia Dortmund in order to monitor the firm's recapitalization pursuits.[12]

Finally, and perhaps most effectively, banks may influence corporate control through debt restructurings even without explicit ownership or board representation. When a firm defaults on its debt or is likely to default, its pursuit to avoid bankruptcy typically depends on the mercy of its most powerful lenders. By this means, banks gain considerable control rights and may change the new debt terms in their favor. Consistent with this argument, Gilson (1990) reports that in contrast to ordinary loan agreements renegotiated debt covenants often grant banks explicit veto power over capital expenditures, divestitures, or changes in management. However, banks

---

[10] See Finsterer (1999), pp. 188-191, and Brüchner (1998), pp. 156-176 for a detailed analysis of these issues.

[11] See "WestLB verabschiedet sich von Gildemeister", in: *Handelsblatt*, 07 September 2005.

[12] See "Borussia Dortmund spricht mit Banken über eine Umschuldung", in: *Handelsblatt*, 24 October 2005.

may also make debt concessions contingent on the direct replacement of senior executives. For example, the resignation of KarstadtQuelle's CEO, Christoph Achenbach, subsequent to the firm's recapitalization in 2004, was provoked by the leading creditor banks.[13]

In the following, the assertion that financial distress causes banks to get more involved in corporate control and thereby impose a disciplinary effect on incumbent management is referred to as *bank monitoring hypothesis.*

3.2.2 Propositions

From the preceding analysis, I derive the following non-mutually exclusive propositions on the impact of financial distress on ownership, control, and managerial tenure:

Proposition 1. *Financial distress significantly affects corporate ownership and management turnover. Management turnover is inversely related to operational and financial performance.*

Proposition 2. *Under the internal monitoring hypothesis, ownership by corporate executives and directors increases in financial distress. Management turnover is inversely related to management ownership and positively related to director ownership.*

Proposition 3. *Under the internal monitoring hypothesis, ownership concentration increases in financial distress. Private (inside) blockholders assemble larger ownership stakes. Management turnover is positively related to ownership concentration and holdings by private investors.*

Proposition 4. *Under the external monitoring hypothesis, ownership concentration increases in financial distress. Corporate and financial (outside) blockholders assemble larger ownership stakes. Takeover activity increases. Management turnover is positively related to changes in ownership and holdings by institutional investors.*

Proposition 5. *Under the bank monitoring hypothesis, banks' involvement in corporate control increases. Bank involvement either manifests directly through increased ownership or indirectly through debt renegotiation. Management turnover is positively related to bank involvement.*

[13] See "Gläubigerbanken wollen Vorstände feuern", in: *Spiegel-online*, 25 November 2004.

3.3 Data and measurement

3.3.1 Data structure

In this study I scrutinize the full sample of 267 firms that experienced repeated insufficient interest coverage and steep share price declines between 1996 and 2004. The sample selection process and the structure of the data set are discussed extensively in Chapter 2 of this thesis. Similar to Gilson (1990) and Asquith, Gertner, and Scharfstein (1994) I use the following dating methodology to analyze how firms fare and restructure under persisting financial distress.

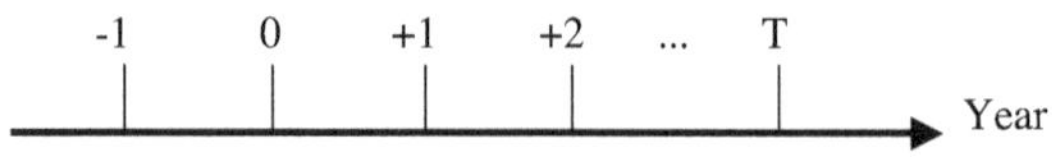

Figure 3.1: Panel structure in event time

Year 0 denotes the year of the initial coverage shortfall. For each firm in the sample financial statement data, ownership information, and data on management and supervisory board composition are tracked from year -1 on, where years -1 and 0 serve as pre-distress benchmarks for changes observed in the subsequent years. In any given year, a firm exits the sample if it either files a formal bankruptcy petition or single-handedly recovers from financial distress. Bankrupt entities are excluded from further inspection because, contrary to most formal reorganizations under Chapter 11 of the U.S Bankruptcy Code, the vast majority of bankruptcy filings in Germany results in the liquidation of the debtor's estate. Formal bankruptcy in Germany, therefore, is mostly equivalent to ultimate failure in the sense that the firm ceases to be an independent legal entity.[14] Conversely, firms that return to financial health are excluded so as to ensure that the observed changes in corporate control and management turnover are correctly attributed to the firms' feeble financial condition. If instead recovering firms were further retained in the sample the impact of distress on corporate restructuring could easily be overstated. By definition, firms are deemed to recover from distress if they fail to meet the underlying distress criterion in any two consecutive years after entering the sample, i.e. experience a sustained period of sufficient interest coverage.[15]

[14] See, for example, Franks, Nyborg, and Torous (1996). Another factors that hampers the scrutiny of firms in bankruptcy is that fact HOPPENSTEDT does not record changes in ownership and control following bankruptcy.

[15] Of course, this is a rather feeble definition of recovery since it does not necessarily imply economic health. A firm may well succeed in overcoming the most perilous financial difficulties and still continue to operate unprofitably. However, for sake of transparency, I prefer using a symmetric definition of a firm's onset of financial distress and its recovery thereof.

Table 3.1: Time series of sample composition

Calender time distribution of sample consisting of 267 German corporations that suffered from financial distress between 1996 and 2004. A firm is classified as financially distressed, if in any two consecutive years—beginning 1996—the firm's earnings before interest and taxes (Ebit) is less than its reported interest expense.

	Firms entering and exiting stratum over sampling interval		
Sample year	Firms entering	Exit due to bankruptcy	Exit due to recovery
1996	37	0	0
1997	12	0	0
1998	22	0	1
1999	53	2	4
2000	77	5	3
2001	45	17	4
2002	21	32	2
2003	0	13	7
2004	0	7	16
Total	267	76	37

The resulting calender time distribution of firms entering and exiting the stratum is depicted in Table 3.1. Evidently, the bulk of the sample entries is centered around the years 1999-2001, which coincides with the zenith of the technology bubble and the onset of the general economic recession shortly afterwards. In consequence, about half of the firms entering the sample are listed on 'Neuer Markt', the former growth segment of the German Stock Exchange, which reflects the recession's relative impact on this particular sector of the economy. Roughly one third of all firms (76 firms) ultimately fail and file for bankruptcy. As can be inferred from Table 3.1, bankruptcies are most common at the height of the recession during the years 2001 and 2002 while most recoveries occur in 2004, the first year of overall economic convalescence. The remaining firms are either acquired somewhere along the distress cycle (54 firms) or are still pending in financial distress at the end of the sampling interval (109 firms).[16] In the final sample firms appear for a mean and median of 3.56 and 4.0 years, respectively. Only three firms appear the maximum number of nine years.

3.3.2 Sample characteristics

Table 4.2 contains selected summary statistics of firm characteristics for the total sample at year 0.[17] Some variables' distributions are highly skewed so that I focus on medians rather than means. The median firm in my sample has total assets worth 54.44 Mio. EUR and a market

[16] Five firms file for bankruptcy after being acquired and four firms are acquired twice. For transparency, these double counts are not eliminated here. Chapter 6 distinguishes more clearly between the different outcomes of distress.

[17] A detailed description of the data sources is contained in Chapter 2 of this thesis.

Table 3.2: Sample summary statistics

Selected mean and median attributes for the sample of 267 German corporations that suffered from financial distress between 1996 and 2004. A firm is classified as financially distressed, if in any two consecutive years—beginning 1996—the firm's earnings before interest and taxes (Ebit) is less than its reported interest expense. Figures relate to year 0 in distress time, i.e. the year of the initial coverage shortfall. Variables are reported on firm-level as well as net of industry effects. *Leverage* is book value of total debt to book value of total capital. *Coverage* presents Ebit over total interest expenses. *Return on assets* is Ebit before depreciation and amortization (Ebitda) over total assets. *Stock return* is the cumulative one-year return of a firm's common stock. Industry-adjusted values are based on the universe of firms with the same two-digit FTSE Global Classification industry code.

	Firm-level data			Industry-adjusted data			
Variable	Mean	Median	Std. dev.	Mean	Median	Std. dev.	N
Assets in Mio. EUR	279.76	54.44	1030.29	-1243.23	-151.51	3054.55	267
Market value equity in Mio. EUR	240.18	49.49	1025.68	-136.78	-2.69	1028.33	267
Coverage	-112.50	-8.34	460.56	-115.63	-9.08	469.39	267
Leverage	0.46	0.42	0.33	0.12	0.01	0.42	267
Return on assets	-0.09	-0.04	0.22	-0.17	-0.11	0.22	267
Stock return	-0.33	-0.48	0.85	-0.21	-0.49	0.73	122

value of common equity of 49.49 Mio. EUR. By comparison, my firms are considerably smaller than the sampled firms in related studies by Asquith, Gertner, and Scharfstein (1994) and Gilson (1990). Corresponding values for total assets in both studies are 234.86 Mio. USD and 74.80 Mio USD, respectively. One reasonable explanation for the observed differences may be the recent sampling period in my study, which deliberately embraces the rise and fall of relatively younger (and smaller) technology firms.[18] Alternatively, small firms in Germany may be more vulnerable to financial distress than their U.S. counterparts. Firms are also considerably smaller than their industry peers. Industry-adjusted data are based on median values of the universe of firms in WORLDSCOPE with the same two-digit FTSE Global Classification industry code. Much of this difference may be due to considerable asset divestitures of my firms in response to a decline in performance prior their initial coverage shortfall. Ofek (1993) reports that asset sales present a frequent response to unexpected declines in operating performance. As noted above, *coverage* is defined as Ebit over interest expenses. By definition, the median firm in my sample exhibits extremely low coverage of -8.34 on a firm level and -9.08 on an industry level, which indicates that my firms are not even close to generating enough cash to meet their debt obligations at year 0.

Median *leverage* defined as book ratio of total debt to capital is 0.42. Perhaps surprisingly, my firms are only slightly higher leveraged than the median firms in their industry. This suggests that my firms' financial trouble may be attributable less to overly rigorous interest obligations but rather to an above industry-average decline in operating profitability. Consistent with this

[18] Indeed, neither Asquith, Gertner, and Scharfstein (1994) nor Gilson (1990) analyze NASDAQ listed firms, the counterparts of German Neuer Markt firms. Further below, I will discuss this issue in more detail.

presumption, median *return on assets* defined by Ebit before depreciation and amortization (Ebitda) over total assets as well as firms' (unadjusted) annual return on their common stock are low at -0.04 and -0.48 on a firm level. Corresponding values on an industry level are also poor at -0.11 and -0.49 , respectively. The representative firm in my sample thus operates at the cusp of unprofitability, which corresponds with Wruck's (1990) argument that financial distress commonly coincides with feeble economic health.

From the figures in Table 4.2 it can be inferred that at least some (it not all) of my sampled firms' poor financial and operational condition is caused by firm-specific rather than industry-wide factors. In consequence, the resolution of financial distress and the return to at least industry-average profitability, to most firms, seems unfeasible without adequate restructuring. In order to detect how firms in my sample cope with their ongoing difficulties I track corporate restructuring activities for each firm through a news research in the BÖRSENZEITUNG (the gazette of all German stock exchanges), LEXIS-NEXIS and the DOWJONES&REUTERS news retrieval (FACTIVA). Collectively, these sources embrace all major German newspapers, electronic news-wires, and trade register filings as well as the most relevant international sources.

Table 3.3 provides a synopsis of selected restructuring activities completed in the years relative to the onset of financial distress. Because the core focus of this chapter is on corporate control I restrict my attention to such measures that directly affect the firm's ownership and capital structures. The most common financial response to distress by the firms in my sample is the infusion of fresh equity capital. In sum, I observe 117 equity issues of which roughly one third (42 cases) are placed via a rights issue while the remaining two thirds (75 cases) present private or public placements under the exclusion of subscription rights for existing owners.[19] Several times fresh equity is issued subsequent to write-offs of the par value of a firm's common stock (29 cases). So called equity write-downs are completed to accommodate previously accumulated losses and often provide a last resort for over-indebted companies. However, they require the convening of an (exceptional) general meeting and are thus very cumbersome (*vereinfachte Kapitalerherabsetzung* according to § 229 AktG).[20]

Firms in my sample also heavily engage in debt restructuring. Following Gilson, John, and Lang (1990), a debt restructuring is defined as a transaction in which a firm obtains relief from its creditors either by a reduction or deferral of contractual payments, a provision of fresh money, or the swap of debt securities against securities with residual or mezzanine claim. In contrast to U.S. evidence, unilateral relief from creditors in Germany is typically provided by house-banks who maintain close ties to their clients and thus incur fewer costs in a workout

[19] § 186 of the German Companies Act (AktG) specifies the conditions under which the exclusion of subscription rights for existing owners is legitimate. According to commentaries, in the state of crisis the exclusion is justified if it offers scope for the engagement of 'distressed investors' (*Sanierungshelfer*) that provide recapitalization services, which existing owners cannot or will not offer. See Buth, Hermanns, and Janus (1998), § 14.

[20] Notably, a firm's decision for the completion of such equity restructurings is not well understood. According to Gertner and Scharfstein (1991), a distressed debtor has little incentive to contribute fresh equity because doing so presents an unsolicited wealth transfer to creditors.

Table 3.3: Corporate restructuring activities in distress time

Selected restructuring measures undertaken relative to the onset of financial distress. Figures are based on a sample of 267 German corporations between 1996 and 2004. Figures may include multiple observations per firm. All data are obtained from text analyses conducted in the BÖRSENZEITUNG, LEXIS-NEXIS, and the DOWJONES&REUTERS news retrieval.

	Corporate restructuring activity in years elapsed relative to onset of financial distress						
	-1	0	+1	+2	+3	≥+4	Total
Equity issue	3	11	29	36	18	26	123
Equity write-down	0	0	2	6	9	12	29
Debt restructuring	0	7	7	15	19	16	64
Block-trades	0	10	11	18	11	9	59
Takeover	0	4	11	10	11	19	55

than, say, dispersed trade creditors. In consequence, the vast majority of debt restructurings in my sample present private renegotiations of bank-debt.[21] Finally, firms in my sample are often subject to direct transfers of control through block investments, i.e. the engagement of new minority shareholders, and outright takeovers. Financial as well as strategic investors are the most active acquirers of substantial minority positions with about 40% of all transactions accounting to each of the two. Other types of investors, i.e. individuals, banks, and institutional investors only play a subordinate role.

From Table 3.3 it is obvious that corporate restructuring tends to proliferate with enduring distress. Provided that such restructuring ultimately affect corporate ownership I am interested in whether ownership structures, too, follow a systematic pattern over the distress cycle. Moreover, I am interested in whether observed changes influence how distressed firms are governed.

3.3.3 Measurement issues

For my empirical analysis several measurement issues need to be addressed. First, I need to construct a measure of concentration of the equity control rights from data on ownership on voting stock. Second, I need to measure discrete changes in ownership and detect in how far they are attributable to different types of owners. Finally, I need a measure for management turnover and a functional specification that captures how turnover is affected by ownership and changes therein.

3.3.3.1 Measurement of ownership

Following earlier studies on corporate ownership in Germany, I use three different measures for the degree of control rights concentration in each firm [e.g. Gorton and Schmid (2000), Köke

[21] With only 4 observations public debt restructurings play a minuscule role in my sample.

(2001)]. First, I use an approximation of the *Herfindahl* index, which measures the absolute level of concentration. The theoretical foundation for the use of the Herfindahl index as a measure for ownership concentration is provided by Demsetz and Lehn (1985). It is defined as $HI = \sum_{i=1}^{N} s_i^2$, where $s_i (i = 1, ..., N)$ is the fraction of common stock owned by the party i. Importantly, the Herfindahl index is based on equity control rights, i.e. on rights that descend from direct holdings of voting stocks. Thus, it does not include proxy votes. Moreover, since I do not have data on all shareholdings (e.g. dispersed shares), the index presents only a lower bound of ownership concentration. Second, I consider the size of the largest share block, *Top blockholder*, as well as the combined stake of the three largest shareholders, *Top 3 blockholder*. Instead of measuring absolute concentration of ownership these measures focus on the upper distribution of a firm's ownership structure. Their use is motivated by Shleifer and Vishny (1986) who argue that single blockholdings (rather than overall concentration) exert the strongest disciplinary effect on management. Finally, I explicitly consider the total *Freefloat* of a firm's shares as plausibility check for the former three measures. It is calculated as the residual from all share blocks reported by HOPPENSTEDT.

In accordance with my analysis in section 3.2.1, I use ownership information in HOPPENSTEDT to further distinguish different types of management and non-management blockholders. Management blockholders are (i) *Management* (members of the board of executives) and (ii) *Directors* (members of the supervisory board). Among non-management blockholders I further distinguish (iii) *Private* investors (family investors and individuals), (iv) *Banks*, (v) *Financial* investors (investment funds, insurance companies), and (vi) *Strategic* investors (non-financial firms and competitors). Further shareholdings by unspecified investors, public institutions, and employees as well as stakes held by the firm itself are commonly classified as (vii) *Miscellaneous* ownership.

Finally, changes in ownership are measured in three ways, (i) variations in the Herfindahl index between years, (ii) block investments and (iii) takeovers. A *Block investment* is defined as the acquisition of a new minority stake of an outside investor, either through a blocktrade or a placement of new equity. By contrast, a *Takeover* is defined as an acquisition of a majority block of common shares. Block investments and takeovers are identified in LEXIS-NEXIS as well as DOWJONES&REUTERS and cross-checked with the annual edition of HOPPENSTEDT Financial Information Stock Guide.

3.3.3.2 Measurement of management turnover

I expect corporate financial distress to be associated with higher rates of management turnover. Following Gilson (1989) and Warner, Watts, and Wruck (1988) management turnover is defined as a change in position of the company's top two executives, i.e. the CEO and the CFO. This is to capture the eminent responsibility of these two individuals for the corporation's development and its financial stability, respectively.[22] In addition, I consider director turnover as replacement of the firm's chairman of the supervisory board, i.e. the chief internal monitor. Turnovers are identified in LEXIS-NEXIS as well as DOWJONES&REUTERS and cross-checked with the annual edition of HOPPENSTEDT Financial Information Stock Guide. While I would expect the majority of management replacements to take place involuntarily, of course there do occur regular changes such as retirements. As Warner, Watts, and Wruck (1988) show, including regular changes can bias the observed relationship between firm performance, ownership and control. Thus I am keen to distinguish between allegedly forced and unforced departures.

Following Warner, Watts, and Wruck (1988), I assign to the sample of unforced departures all changes due to (i) retirement, (ii) change into advisory board, (iii) change into bigger corporation, (iv) health, and (v) death.[23] By contrast, turnovers are classified as forced if they are due to (i) outright dismissal or (ii) resignation or if no official reason was provided but the news coverage clearly indicates a disciplinary background. According to Gilson (1989), firms frequently do not comment management changes that result from dissatisfaction with managers' performance.

For an accurate round-up, Table 3.9 in the Appendix of this chapter summarizes all variable definitions and corresponding data sources.

3.4 Empirical results

3.4.1 Descriptive evidence

3.4.1.1 The impact of financial distress on corporate control

The main objective of this section is to investigate the impact of sustained financial distress on ownership and control of German corporations. Following previous work by Gilson (1990), evidence is organized around changes in the relative monitoring power by the firm's different classes of shareholders. Because the dynamics of ownership and control, especially under the burden of distress, have so far not been exhaustively documented much of the following analysis will deliberately remain descriptive.

Changes in ownership concentration during financial distress are presented in Table 3.4. The results are also illustrated in Figure 3.2. Because firms exit the sample due to recovery or bankruptcy and exhaustive ownership data is not available for all firms at all times the sample

[22] By contrast, Franks and Mayer (2001) consider turnover among all executives not only the firm's top two positions. This approach, however, fails to capture differing sizes of the management board and does not accurately reflect the factual hierarchy among them.

[23] The change of a former CEO into the supervisory board presents a German particularity that is heavily contested by the recently introduced German Corporate Governance Code. See Werder (2002).

Table 3.4: Corporate ownership concentration in distress time

The development of corporate ownership concentration for alternative measures of concentration relative to the onset of financial distress. Figures are based on a sample of 267 German corporations between 1996 and 2004. The *Herfindahl* index represents the mean (median) level of concentration of all of a firm's stakes of common shares larger than 5%. It is defined as $HI = \sum_{i=1}^{N} s_i^2$, where $s_i(i = 1, ..., N)$ is the fraction of common stock owned by the party i. *Top blockholder* represents the mean (median) ownership stake of the firm's single largest blockholder. *Top 3 blockholder* represents the combined mean (median) ownership of the firm's largest three blockholders. All data are obtained from the HOPPENSTEDT Financial Information Stock Guide. Test statistics are based on a simple two-sided t-test of differences in means and on a non-parametric Wilcoxon signed-rank test on differences in medians. *, **, and *** denote the ownership percentage is significantly different from percentage in year -1 at the 10%, 5%, and 1% level, respectively.

	Ownership concentration in years elapsed relative to onset of financial distress					
	-1	0	+1	+2	+3	+4
Herfindahl	0.318	0.256 **	0.261 **	0.253 **	0.238 ***	0.271 *
	(0.262)	(0.199)***	(0.192)***	(0.161)***	(0.161)***	(0.162)***
Top blockholder	0.484	0.417 ***	0.420 **	0.413 ***	0.400 ***	0.420 *
	(0.499)	(0.380)***	(0.380)**	(0.346)***	(0.346)***	(0.360)**
Top 3 blockholder	0.630	0.580 *	0.570 **	0.550 ***	0.540 ***	0.530 ***
	(0.623)	(0.600)*	(0.570)**	(0.540)***	(0.532)***	(0.530)***
Freefloat	0.330	0.340	0.356	0.382 **	0.402 ***	0.414 ***
	(0.332)	(0.310)	(0.342)	(0.370)**	(0.393)***	(0.420)***
N	155	235	248	233	187	93

size decreases substantially over distress time.[24] I thus focus on the six year interval ranging from years -1 to +4 although several firms are tracked for a longer time period.[25] From Table 3.4 it is apparent that ownership concentration substantially decreases in event time. The median Herfindahl index continuously declines from 26% in year -1 over 19% in year +1 to 16% in year +4. Corresponding figures for the share of the top blockholder and the combined share of the top three blockholdings are 50%, 38%, and 36% as well as 62%, 57%, and 53%, respectively. Conversely, firms' freefloat increases by almost 10% over the same interval. Decreases in ownership concentration (relativ to year -1) for all measures are statistically significant using a paired t-test for differences in means and a Wilcoxon signed-rank test for differences in medians.[26] This evidence unmistakably conflicts with my propositions 3 and 4, which claim that ownership concentration increases under distress due to the increased monitoring need in financially distressed

[24] Gilson (1990) reports a similar time-series variation in his sample.

[25] The smaller sample size in year -1 is attributable to the fact that a large number of firms entered the sample in the year following the going-public so that their inclusion could potentially bias the results. In year +5 the number of observations drops to 52, which makes year +4 a more reasonable upper end for the time frame. In my multivariate analysis in the subsequent section all observations are included and attrition is controlled for using a (quasi-) Hausman procedure as suggested by Verbeek and Nijman (1992).

[26] Both tests complete pairwise comparisons between two years and thus allow for different sample sizes over distress time.

Figure 3.2: The development of corporate ownership in distress time

Mean percentage of common stock held by selected inside and outside blockholders relative to the onset of financial distress. Blockholdings include all shares exceeding 5% of all common stock outstanding. Figures are based on a sample of 267 German corporations between 1996 and 2004. All data are obtained from the HOPPENSTEDT Financial Information Stock Guide.

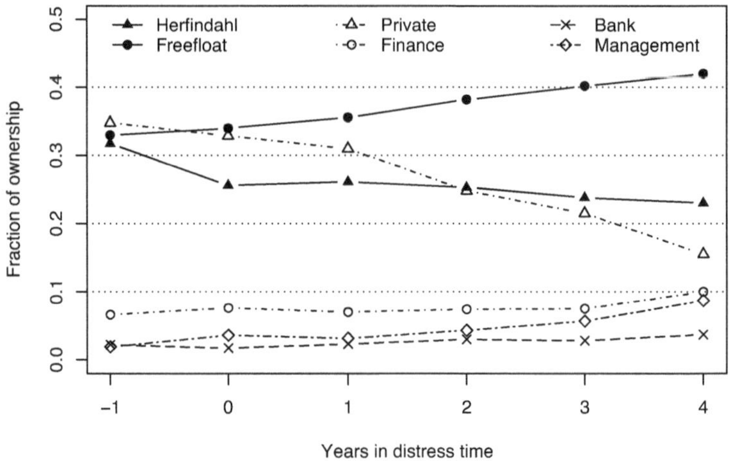

firms. Moreover, the results in Table 3.4 are inconsistent with Gilson's (1990) study who does obtain evidence in line with propositions 3 and 4.

A reasonable explanation for the discrepancy between my results and previous findings may lie in different point of departure for blockholders in the U.S. and Germany. In the U.S. shares are usually held by dispersed owners who need comparatively little stock accumulation in order to obtain a controlling interest in the firm. In Germany, by contrast, firms are typically held by majority owners who may continue to control the firm even after divesting significant fractions of their stakes.[27] Alternatively, the type of blockholders in both countries may explain the difference. In the U.S. the typical blockholder is a well diversified institutional investor (e.g. mutual funds, pension funds, or private equity powerhouses) who deliberately invests in special situations such as distressed equity. German corporations, on the other hand, are frequently owned by individuals and families who are less diversified, more cash constraint and may thus exhibit a higher propensity to selling their stakes in an increasingly troubled company.

Further evidence consistent with this proposition is presented in Table 3.5, which describes the dynamics in the composition of ownership in distress time. For each owner-type, two types

[27] This holds especially in recent years that are characterized by decreasing attendance of general meetings.

of ownership information are provided. The top line values map the fraction of firms in which a particular owner-type represents one of the top five shareholders. The bottom line values, depicted in parentheses, map average ownership shares in percent. The latter are also illustrated in Figure 2. Over the specified distress interval between year -1 and year +4, I observe a substantial shift in the composition of ownership. First and foremost, individual and family owners significantly reduce their investment. While at the time -1 individual and family owners hold substantial shares in more than 76% of all firms in the sample, this frequency declines continuously to about 52% in year +4. In the same manner, their average ownership in my sample's firms declines from 35% to a mere 15%. The observed decline in family representation is statistically as well as economically significant and contradicts proposition 3. However, it is in line with my conjecture that private investors may be less inclined to hold claims of distressed equity over a sustained period of time. Since individual and family investors present the largest beneficial owners in my sample their retreat also presents the most likely cause for the decline in overall ownership concentration illustrated in Table 3.4. Importantly, the decline in private ownership and overall ownership concentration over time is not driven by the firms in my sample that entered distress shortly after their initial public notation. For the sub-sample of firms not formerly listed on Neuer Markt, i.e. so called old economy firms, the analysis yields materially identical results.

Other than blockholdings by private investors, ownership by strategic and financial investors do not exhibit a statistically significant variation over the distress cycle. However, ownership by financial investors constantly increases from around 26% to 37% in relative frequency and from 6% to 10% in mean fraction of shares held. These figures clearly exceed conventional levels of financial ownership in German corporations, which Köke (2001) reports to be around 6% and may present a result of the increasing control transfer activity reported in Table 3.3.

Evidence on bank ownership during financial distress is more ambiguous. While average ownership does not increase significantly in distress time, the average number of firms in which banks become major shareholders more than doubles from about 9% in year -1 to 19% in year +4. This increase in statistically significant at the 5% level. The observation that bank involvement proliferates under continuing distress is consistent with proposition 5, however banks seem to be reluctant to increase their ownership stakes beyond a certain threshold. One reason for this incongruity certainly lies in the legal restrictions concerning bank ownership of distressed equity. Another explanation is that German banks who maintain close ties to their clients do not need large equity holdings in order to obtain a seat in the advisory board and exert pressure on management. Instead, they often use proxy votes for deposit clients as well as frequent renegotiations of debt claims to gain influence on corporate decision making.

Ownership by corporate managers over the distress cycle is described in Panel B of Table 3.5. As expected, ownership by management and directors seems to increase significantly under financial distress. In year +4 corporate insiders hold significant share blocks in more than 34% of all firms, compared with only 4% in year -1. Likewise, the overall fraction of shares held by either

Table 3.5: Corporate ownership composition in distress time

Corporate ownership data by type of blockholder and relative to the onset of financial distress. Figures are based on a sample of 267 German corporations between 1996 and 2004. For each owner-type, two types of ownership information are provided. The top line values represent the fraction of firms in which a particular owner-type belongs to the top five shareholders. The bottom line values, depicted in parentheses, map average ownership shares in percent. All data are obtained from the HOPPENSTEDT Financial Information Stock Guide. Test statistics are based on a simple two-sided t-test of differences in means and on a non-parametric Wilcoxon signed-rank test on differences in medians. *, **, and *** denote the ownership percentage is significantly different from percentage in year -1 at the 10%, 5%, and 1% level, respectively.

	Ownership composition in years elapsed relative to onset of financial distress					
	-1	0	+1	+2	+3	+4
Panel A: Ownership non-management blockholders						
Private	0.763	0.783	0.761	0.706 *	0.689 ***	0.519 ***
	(0.353)	(0.329)	(0.310)	(0.248)***	(0.215)***	(0.155)***
Strategic	0.348	0.311	0.340	0.364	0.407	0.392
	(0.164)	(0.134)	(0.150)	(0.164)	(0.167)	(0.171)
Financial	0.259	0.362	0.324	0.333	0.347	0.367
	(0.066)	(0.076)	(0.070)	(0.074)	(0.075)	(0.100)
Bank	0.089	0.094	0.109	0.140	0.168 *	0.190 **
	(0.022)	(0.017)	(0.023)	(0.030)	(0.028)	(0.037)
Misc.	0.037	0.055	0.040	0.051	0.056	0.036
	(0.012)	(0.013)	(0.009)	(0.009)	(0.013)	(0.019)
Panel B: Ownership by management blockholders						
Management	0.044	0.072	0.065	0.110 **	0.144 **	0.291 ***
	(0.019)	(0.033)	(0.028)	(0.039)*	(0.049)**	(0.075)***
Directors	0.000	0.021	0.016	0.018	0.030 **	0.051 **
	(0.000)	(0.003)	(0.003)	(0.004)	(0.008)**	(0.012)**
Combined	0.044	0.094	0.081	0.127 *	0.174 **	0.342 ***
	(0.019)	(0.036)	(0.031)	(0.043)*	(0.057)**	(0.087)***
N	155	235	248	233	187	93

managers or directors increases from scantly 2% to almost 9%. Most of the increase in inside ownership is attributable to an increasing risk sharing by executive managers whose average stake rises from 2% in year -1 to 7.5% in year +4. This evidence is consistent with proposition 2, which holds that incentive related benefits associated with stock based compensation of managers are greatest when a firms is operating unprofitably.

3.4.1.2 The impact of financial distress on management turnover

Consistent with previous evidence by Ofek (1993) and Gilson (1989) the replacement of top executives is a prevalent response to financial distress in my sample's firms. Table 3.6 contains the time-series distribution of management turnover events for my sample over the period 1996-2004. There is considerable variation in turnover rates over the sampled years, both in terms

Table 3.6: Management turnover during sampling period
Sample distribution of 251 senior management changes in 267 financially distressed firms during the period 1996-2004. Management turnover is defined as a change in position of the company's top two executives, i.e. the CEO and the CFO. Turnovers are identified through a news research in the BÖRSENZEITUNG, LEXIS-NEXIS, and the DOWJONES&REUTERSnews retrieval and cross-checked with the annual edition of HOPPENSTEDT Financial Information Stock Guide.

Year	Number of firms	All management changes	Management changes per firm	Share of forced departures
1996	37	8	0.22	0.88
1997	49	7	0.14	0.86
1998	61	4	0.07	1.00
1999	108	14	0.13	0.93
2000	177	35	0.20	0.77
2001	201	75	0.37	0.76
2002	188	59	0.31	0.85
2003	168	33	0.20	0.91
2004	145	16	0.11	1.00
Total	267	251	0.19	0.88

of management changes per firm and the fraction of forced turnovers. However, amplitudes in both categories may be due to the relatively low number of observations in some years. Average annual turnover in my sample over the entire interval amounts to 19% whereas in five sampling years turnover amounts to at least 20%. The average fraction of forced turnovers in my sample exceeds 80%, which indicates that premature departures of key executives in my sample is the rule rather than the exception. While previous evidence on management tenure in Germany is sparse, observed turnover rates clearly exceed conventional levels of turnover in German firms. For example, Schrader and Lüthje (1995) report average turnover rates of 11% for Germany's largest corporations during 1965-1993, 25%-35% of which occurred involuntarily. To control for differences in the sampling period, I also tracked turnover data for an unconditioned control sample of all Dax 100 corporations during the 1998-2003 interval.[28] Annual turnover rates for the control sample averaged 15%, roughly 50% of which were due to disciplinary departures. While these figures bear more resemblance to my sample of distressed firms, the difference in turnover rates suggests that managers in troubled firms experience significantly shorter tenure than their counterparts in non-distressed entities.[29]

Complimentary evidence on how turnover is affected by financial distress is provided in Figure 3.3. Similar to Gilson (1989), I track the survival of senior managers over the distress cycle. The figure depicts the fraction of Chief Executive Officers (*CEO*) and their monitors,

[28] The Dax 100 comprises the 100 largest corporations in terms of market capitalization and is the most representative cross-section of publicly listed firms in Germany. A detailed description of the data can be obtained in Jostarndt, Rudolph, and Thierauf (2005).

[29] In fact, the observed difference understates abnormal turnover in financially distressed firms if one considers that managers in large corporations usually exhibit longer tenure, ceteris paribus. See Gilson (1989) and my evidence below.

Figure 3.3: Management survival relative to onset of financial distress

Survival rates of senior managers and directors in 267 financially distressed firms during the period 1996-2004. The figure depicts the fraction of Chief Executive Officers and chairmen of the board of directors who were incumbents in year -1 and remain in office over the six-year interval centered around the onset of financial distress. Turnovers are identified through a news research in the BÖRSENZEITUNG, LEXIS-NEXIS, and the DOWJONES&REUTERS news retrieval and cross-checked with the annual edition of HOPPENSTEDT Financial Information Stock Guide.

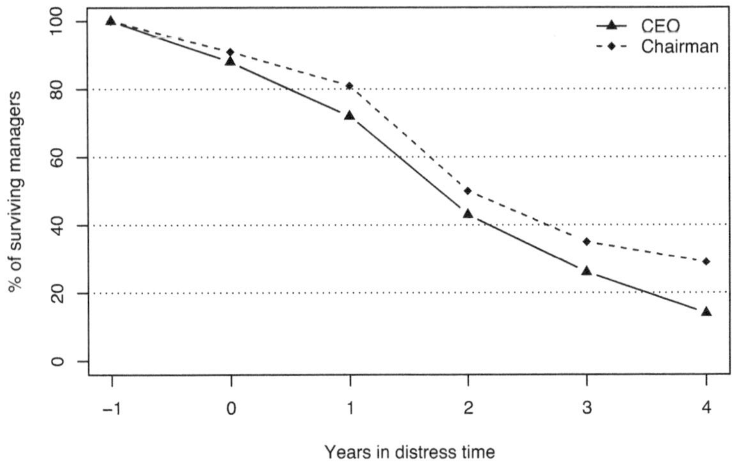

the chairmen of the supervisory board (*Chairman*) who were incumbents in year -1 and remain in office over the six-year interval centered around the onset of financial distress. Two insights are striking: First, survival of managers steeply declines after year +1, with only 43% and 14% of original incumbents remaining in office beyond years +2 and +4, respectively. Increases in turnover are economically as well as statistically significant. Corresponding p-values of paired t-test for differences in mean turnover between years -1 and +4 and between years +1 and +2 are 0.000 and 0.006, respectively. Second, the turnover pattern of directors, while not equally sensitive to performance, very much resembles that of executives. While the causality is not clear, the evidence suggests that in the pursuit of survival CEOs and directors depend on each other. By contrast, CEOs my DAX 100 control sample bear significantly lower job-risks. When tracked over an unconditioned period of 6 years during 1998 and 2003 56% of managers are still in office at the end of the interval. Combined, the evidence in this section is consistent with the proposition that management turnover is significantly affected by the firm's financial condition and that managers suffer large personal costs of financial distress.

3.4.2 Evidence from panel regressions

The above analyses suggest that ongoing financial distress provokes substantial changes in the ownership of firms' equity claims as well as in the allocation of rights to manage corporate operations. What remains unaddressed to this point is the relation between these two. As discussed earlier, theoretical arguments hold that the structure of corporate ownership and changes therein should directly influence managerial tenure. In this section I investigate this relation in a multivariate setting.

3.4.2.1 Econometric specification

To investigate the determinants of management turnover in my sample I estimate ordinary probability models that simultaneously relate the incidence of a forced management departure to measures of performance and ownership as well as several control variables. The dependent variable in the regressions equals one if the defined turnover event is observed in a given firm-year and zero otherwise, i.e. I estimate models of binary choice. Since I dispose of panel data, i.e. there are repeated observations for the same firms over time, I am able to obtain consistent coefficient estimates for my exogenous variables that are uncontaminated by correlations with unobserved firm-specific effects.[30] Crucially, unobserved firm-heterogeneity is a paramount issue in empirical corporate governance studies because it may account for a great deal of the cross-sectional variation in the relation between corporate governance and performance. Its disregard deliberately results in omitted variable problems that produce biased and inconsistent estimation results.[31]

Depending on the perceptions of the firm-specific effects fixed and random effects models (and numerous variations in each of these classes) can be distinguished. Maddala (1987) contains a comprehensive overview of different approaches covering both fixed effects and random effects models. Under the assumption that unobserved firm effects are normally distributed and drawn at random from the underlying population of firms, my econometric model of choice is the random-effects logit model that is estimated via Maximum-Likelihood. Such a model seems to be applicable for this setting since I include time-invariant variables among the regressors [Greene (2003)]. Another argument in favor of this specification is that it solves numerical

[30] In this context, unobserved firm-heterogeneity manifests, for example, in peculiarities in a firm's corporate charter or power struggles among directors that are both obscure from the outside.

[31] For a detailed discussion of econometric issues in empirical corporate governance studies, see Bhagat and Jeffries (2002) and Köke (2002).

problems arising from firms with an observed annual turnover equalling zero for all t.[32] A basic version of this model is discussed in Conaway (1990).[33]

In the turnover equation to be estimated I include firm size and industry affiliation as control variables. Firm size is measured by the natural *logarithm of total assets*. It is explicitly considered because previous studies suggest that management turnover may differ between smaller and larger firms. However, results have been ambiguous and may mostly be attributable to sample particularities. Industry affiliation is considered because my sampling period requires that I distinguish between so-called old and new economy firms. For example, turnover in technology-intensive industries may be lower, *ceteris paribus*, because managers in such firms may be better entrenched due to higher firm-specific human capital [e.g. Shleifer and Vishny (1989)]. To capture the dichotomy between old and new economy firm-types I include into the specification a dummy variable *Neuer Markt* that equals unity if the firm was formerly listed in the growth segment of the German Stock Exchange.

3.4.2.2 Estimation results

A. Management turnover, performance, and corporate ownership

Table 3.7 contains estimation results from random effects logit regressions of management turnover on four different sets of exogenous variables. To facilitate a comparison of my results with previous studies on management turnover, I restrict my attention in Model 1 to my measures for indebtedness and corporate performance as well as my control variables. My results confirm earlier evidence by Gilson (1989) for a stratified sample and Warner et al. (1988) for a random sample. The estimated coefficients of the *stock return* variable and the *return on assets* variable have the predicted negative signs and are highly statistically significant. The same holds if performance is measured by industry adjusted values of the return variables (not reported). Thus, consistent with proposition 1, turnover tends to increase rapidly in response to poor prior performance.[34] Further, an increase in corporate leverage provokes higher rates of management turnover. The effect of the *leverage* variable is positive and statistically significant at the 10% level of confidence. This finding corresponds with proposition 1, which states that turnover increases with the likelihood of default.

---

[32] I choose logit rather than probit models to facilitate comparisons with related studies who all use logit specification. See Gilson (1989), and Warner, Watts, and Wruck (1988). However, as robustness check I also estimate probit specifications, which deliver materially identical results.

[33] Hausman tests conducted with different sets of exogenous variables cannot reject the Null-hypothesis that coefficients from random and fixed effects specifications are different on a 5% level of confidence. Therefore, the choice of a random effects model seems appropriate. See Hausman (1978).

[34] To mitigate the hazard of multicollinearity between market and book measures of performance, I include lagged values of the latter and contemporaneous values of the former. The results, however, are robust to variations in the use of either lagged or contemporaneous as well either firm-level or industry-adjusted measures of performance. Similarly, Warner, Watts, and Wruck (1988).

Regarding the control variables, increasing firm size in terms of total assets increases the likelihood of a forced management departure. The estimated coefficient of the *assets* variable is positive and highly significant (at the 1% level of confidence) in all model specifications. Higher turnover for larger firms in my sample is consistent with previous evidence by Gilson (1989). An ostensible explanation for the positive impact of firm size is that bigger firms have larger internal labor markets and may therefore find it less costly to replace senior executives [e.g. Furtado and Rozeff (1987)]. However, the vast majority of successors for the replaced managers in my sample come from outside the firm suggesting that internal labor markets are less important for successions at the top executive level. Alternatively, replacing management in larger firms may be cheaper because managing larger firms requires less firm-specific human capital and thus offers less scope for entrenchment [e.g. Shleifer and Vishny (1989)]. Other than firm size, the dummy variable, *Neuer Markt*, is insignificant in all models. This results suggest that succession patterns do not differ between so-called old and new economy firms.

Departing from this basic specification, the regression model is gradually expanded by including variables on management ownership (model 2), overall ownership concentration (model 3), and ownership shares held by different types of blockholders (model 4). From the results in Table 3.7, I draw the following inference: First, after controlling for leverage and firm performance, increased holdings by managers and directors do not affect the likelihood of management turnover. The estimated coefficients of the *management ownership* variable and the *director ownership* variable do exhibit the predicted negative and positive signs but are statistically insignificant in all models. Second, turnover is unaffected by increases in overall ownership concentration as well as by increased fractions of private shareholdings (i.e. shares of family investors and individuals). The estimated coefficients for both proxies of ownership concentration, the *Herfindahl* index and the share of the *top blockholder*, in models 3 and 4, exhibit no significant influence on management turnover.[35] Neither does the estimated coefficient of the *Private ownership* variable in model 4, though it does have the predicted positive sign. Third, increased outside ownership by strategic investors, financial investors, and banks significantly affects management turnover of firms in my sample. The estimated coefficients of *strategic ownership*, *financial ownership*, and *bank ownership* are positive and significant at the 10%, 5%, and 1% level of confidence, respectively.

The first result conflicts with the proposition 2, which holds that increased managerial holdings should insulate top executives from disciplinary replacement and that increased shareholdings by directors should fortify their monitoring efforts. Also, this finding is inconsistent with previous results by Denis et al. (1997) and Franks et al. (2001) who observe a significant impact of inside ownership on management turnover. This is even more surprising given that shareholdings by firm insiders were found to increase substantially over the distress interval (Table 3.5). However, the evidence is consistent with Gilson's (1990) argument that under ongoing financial turbulence internal monitoring by the board of directors may no longer suffice to provoke the

[35] This also holds if both variables are tested alone.

required organizational change. Moreover, the insensitivity of turnover to managerial holdings indicates that turnover in beleaguered firms may not solely reflect an incentive problem but also, increasingly, a competence problem.[36]

Result two suggests that there is no positive relation between overall ownership concentration and the likelihood of forced management departures. Evidently, this finding conflicts with proposition 3, which holds that due to improved monitoring incentives, firms with concentrated ownership and powerful blockholders are more likely to experience management changes than firms with dispersed holdings of shares. Also, this finding collides with previous evidence on cross-sections of U.S. and German firms. For example, Denis et al. (1997) and Jostarndt, Rudolph, and Thierauf (2005) both find that ownership concentration significantly increases turnover. Similarly, the observed effect for private ownership on turnover contradicts proposition 3, which states that private investors who traditionally adopt the most powerful monitoring role in German corporations and mostly represent owners at the ultimate ownership level have stronger incentive and ability to discipline management. Prior evidence on the efficiency of privately dominated boards by Wenger and Kaserer (1998) is thus not supported by my findings on distressed companies.

[36] As a practitioner puts it: "[When] you're walking into a room that is characterized by despair, failure, and frustration. With all these people sitting together, the first thing that has to happen is the venting of outrage against the schmucks who got them there in the first place. [...] It's hard to tank a billion dollars of debt and then offer yourself as the savior to your creditors." Sam Zell, Chairman, Equity and Financial Management Company, quoted in the Journal of Applied Corporate Finance Roundtable Discussion on "Bankruptcies, Workouts, and Turnarounds", April 1991.

Table 3.7: Panel regressions I-IV

Random-Effects Maximum-Likelihood estimation of logistic regressions relating senior management changes to a vector of explanatory variables. Regressions are based on a panel of 267 German corporations that suffered from financial distress between 1996 and 2004. The dependent variable equals one if the defined turnover event is observed in a given firm-year and zero otherwise. *Assets* is (lagged) the natural logarithm of book value of total assets. *Leverage* is (lagged) book value of total debt over book value of common equity plus book value of total debt. *Return* represents the (lagged) one-year buy-and-hold return of a firm's common stock. *Return on assets* is earnings before interest taxes depreciation and amortization (Ebitda) over total assets. *Neuer Markt* presents a dummy variable that equals one if the firm was listed on the former growth segment of the German stock exchange, and zero otherwise. Ownership definitions are from Table 3.9. The two columns of each model contain the coefficient estimates and asymptotic standard errors, respectively. *, **, and *** denote the parameters are statistically significant at the 10%, 5%, and 1% level, respectively. The Wald χ^2–statistic tests the hypothesis that all the variables in the model are simultaneously equal to zero. ρ measures the proportion of the total variance contributed by the panel-level (between) variance component.

	Model 1		Model 2		Model 3		Model 4	
	Coeff.	se	Coeff.	se	Coeff.	se	Coeff.	se
Assets (Log)	0.217	(0.071)***	0.219	(0.071)***	0.223	(0.071)***	0.213	(0.069)***
Leverage	0.849	(0.495)*	0.827	(0.492)*	0.735	(0.499)	0.757	(0.496)
Stock return	-0.582	(0.108)***	-0.585	(0.107)***	-0.572	(0.108)***	-0.568	(0.106)***
Return on assets	-0.681	(0.307)**	-0.677	(0.306)**	-0.716	(0.307)**	-0.702	(0.306)**
Management ownership			-0.395	(0.871)	-0.439	(0.874)	0.798	(1.087)
Director ownership			3.040	(2.510)	2.793	(2.492)	3.955	(2.509)
Herfindahl					-1.943	(1.543)	-2.204	(1.639)
Top blockholder					1.657	(1.378)	0.864	(1.492)
Private ownership							0.951	(0.699)
Strategic ownership							1.291	(0.741)*
Financial ownership							1.705	(0.815)**
Bank ownership							2.721	(0.944)***
Neuer Markt	0.286	(0.234)	0.290	(0.233)	0.212	(0.239)	0.273	(0.239)
Constant	-4.957	(0.855)***	-4.971	(0.849)***	-5.124	(0.861)	-5.315	(0.865)***
N(obs.)	914		914		914		914	
N(firms)	267		267		267		267	
Wald-χ^2	42.11	***	43.72	***	45.15	***	53.78	***
ρ	0.085		0.074		0.069		0.032	

The insignificance of both overall concentration of ownership as well as shareholdings by private owners on turnover rates in my sample appears more plausible when considered along with my evidence obtained in the previous section: Private shareholdings and with it total ownership concentration were shown to decrease significantly over the distress interval. Thus, when high ownership concentration is vastly attributable to substantial stakes of private investors but private investors demonstrably decrease their stakes in response to distress, it is not surprising that the commonly expected relation between ownership concentration and disciplinary management turnover no longer holds. Instead, this evanescent relationship provides further support for the hypothesis that financial distress provokes an overall shift from internal to external monitoring. As Jensen and Ruback (1983) and John and Senbet (1998) point out, external mechanisms of control are most active when established forces surrender the job or fail to work effectively.

Result three provides strong support for proposition 4. Amid the retreat of private investors, the comparatively little stakes of corporate (strategic or financial) investors and banks gain more weight, *ceteris paribus*, which in turn increases their monitoring incentives (and ability). Moreover, holdings by corporate investors were shown to remain rather stable in event time, in fact ownership by financial investors was shown to gradually increase with ongoing distress (Table 3.5). This suggests that corporate investors, other than families and individuals, are less averse to holding claims in distressed equity. Finally, the significant influence of increasing bank ownership on turnover is consistent with proposition 5, which asserts that banks get more involved in corporate control when firm value deteriorates and debt claims become increasingly risky.

The χ^2-statistic reported in all regressions ranges between 43.72 in the fist model and 53.78 in the fourth model. The hypothesis that all parameters are simultaneously equal to zero is rejected at the 1 percent level for all models.[37]

B. Management turnover and the market for corporate control

This section provides further support for the external monitoring hypothesis by exploring the relation between management turnover and actual shifts in corporate control of distressed firms. In this manner, explicit changes in ownership, rather than absolute levels are subject to the investigation. As noted earlier, shifts in corporate control of distressed firms may occur in three separate ways: Block investments, takeovers, and debt restructurings. I further distinguish block investments by whether the acquirer is a financial or a strategic investor. I am thus able to asses the relative importance of banks, financial investors, and strategic investors in the external monitoring of distressed firms.

Estimation results are reported in Table 3.8. Point of departure is my basic model that contains measures for leverage, performance and ownership concentration as well as the controls

[37] Table 3.10 in the Appendix contains correlations between the independent variables.

as exogenous variables. In model 5 of Table 3.8 I test the bank monitoring hypothesis. I include dummy variables that indicate whether a forced management departure is forestalled or accompanied by a default or a debt restructuring. Since actual defaults are hard to observe in practice, I use mandatory filings in accordance with § 92 of the German Companies Act (AktG) as proxy for default. According to § 92 I AktG, a firm must publicly announce if it has lost more than half of its equity book value to accommodate its losses. In this respect, the filing marks a discrete increase in leverage and thus a significant control shift to creditors. The evidence in model 5 provides strong support for proposition 5. The estimated coefficients of the default and debt restructuring variables are positive and significant at the 10% and 1% level, respectively. The result is also consistent with evidence in model 4 of Table 3.7. In several instances, banks are not shareholders to begin with but receive equity (and thus direct control rights) under the reorganization plan. However, since only a small fraction of out-of-court workouts in Germany involves debt-to-equity swaps the evidence suggests that debtholders in fact do not require large amounts of equity in order to enforce their will on corporate control.

Model 6 explicitly tests the impact of block investments. I distinguish between strategic and financial bidders. Both coefficients have the predicted positive sign and are significant at the 5% and 1% level, respectively. However, considering the comparatively little stakes acquired by financial investors (Table 3.5), their influence on turnover must be accentuated. Financial investors who deliberately invest in distressed targets and actively engage in the firm's restructuring present a comparatively novel trend on the German capital market, which has garnered considerable attention in the financial press [e.g. Becker (2003)]. Prominent cases included in my sample are Apollo's investment in Primacom AG in 2004 and Wyser-Pratte's investment in Babcock Borsig AG in 2002, both of which were quickly followed by a premature departure of the firm's key executives.[38] In this respect, my results are consistent with recent U.S. evidence by Hotchkiss and Mooradian (1997) who find that so-called "vulture investors" take active monitoring roles in distressed firms and increase firm value by disciplining managers.

[38] See "Babcock Chef Lederer zieht sich zurück" in: *Süddeutsche Zeitung*, 13 March 2002; and "Wechsel an der Primacom-Spitze", in: *Börsen-Zeitung*, 15 June 2004.

Table 3.8: Panel regressions V-VIII

Random-Effects Maximum-Likelihood estimation of logistic regressions relating senior management changes to a vector of explanatory variables. Regressions are based on a panel of 267 German corporations that suffered from financial distress between 1996 and 2004. The dependent variable equals one if the defined turnover event is observed in a given firm-year and zero otherwise. *Assets* is (lagged) the natural logarithm of book value of total assets. *Leverage* is (lagged) book value of total debt over book value of common equity plus book value of total debt. *Return* represents the (lagged) one-year buy-and-hold return of a firm's common stock. *Return on assets* is earnings before interest taxes depreciation and amortization (Ebitda) over total assets. *Neuer Markt* presents a dummy variable that equals one if the firm was listed on the former growth segment of the German stock exchange, and zero otherwise. Remaining variable definitions are from Table 3.9. The two columns of each model contain the coefficient estimates and asymptotic standard errors, respectively. *, **, and *** denote the parameters are statistically significant at the 10%, 5%, and 1% level, respectively. The Wald χ^2–statistic tests the hypothesis that all the variables in the model are simultaneously equal to zero. ρ measures the proportion of the total variance contributed by the panel-level (between) variance component.

	Model 5		Model 6		Model 7		Model 8	
	Coeff.	se	Coeff.	se	Coeff.	se	Coeff.	se
Assets (Log)	0.211	(0.072)***	0.236	(0.072)***	0.244	(0.072)***	0.228	(0.072)***
Leverage	0.500	(0.507)	0.863	(0.494)*	0.900	(0.496)*	0.552	(0.506)
Stock return	-0.554	(0.108)***	-0.583	(0.108)***	-0.587	(0.108)***	-0.569	(0.109)***
Return on assets	-0.576	(0.313)**	-0.709	(0.305)**	-0.726	(0.307)**	-0.615	(0.314)**
Herfindahl	-0.218	(0.450)	-0.228	(0.444)	-0.328	(0.448)	-0.341	(0.451)
Management Ownership	0.259	(0.355)			0.329	(0.358)	0.289	(0.355)
Debt restructuring	1.230	(0.378)***					1.176	(0.375)***
Default	1.163	(0.658)*					1.219	(0.652)*
Block investment (Financial)			1.986	(0.679)***	2.028	(0.682)***	2.098	(0.677)***
Block investment (Strategic)			1.214	(0.545)**	1.215	(0.544)**	1.085	(0.548)**
Takeover					0.792	(0.459)*	0.763	(0.456)*
Neuer Markt	0.260	(0.236)	0.233	(0.235)	0.233	(0.236)	0.221	(0.236)
Constant	-4.824	(0.866)***	-5.161	(0.859)	-5.279	(0.869)	-5.070	(0.872)***
N(obs.)	913		914		914		913	
N(firms)	267		267		267		267	
Wald-χ^2	52.87	***	53.40	***	55.09	***	64.52	***
ρ	0.071		0.063		0.065		0.053	

A similar picture emerges for takeovers. In model 7 I add the *takeover* variable along with the block investment variables. Its estimated coefficient is positive and significant at the 10% level. This result corresponds with proposition 4 and theoretical arguments by Scharfstein (1988), which hold that managers' job risk increases after takeovers. However, the effect is statistically and economically weaker than for block investments. Due to a limited number of takeovers involving financial bidders I cannot distinguish takeovers by the type of acquirer. Competitors and strategic bidders clearly outnumber financial and other investors by accounting for roughly 80% of all acquisitions. The predominance of strategic buyers is consistent with a related argument by Williamson (1988) that strategic bidders should typically be able to outbid financial investors because they face lower uncertainties about the target firm's quality and attach higher reservation values due to feasible post-merger synergies. Moreover, the evidence provides further support for my conjecture that most of my firms' malady is in fact home-made and less attributable to industry wide effects. According to Shleifer and Vishny (1992), industry distress should result in substantially lower numbers of strategic bidders.

In model 8 all four forces on the market for corporate control are tested simultaneously. All results in models 5-7 are confirmed in model 8. The results suggest that in disciplining management, all forces work as compliments rather than substitutes. The χ^2-statistic reported in all regressions ranges between 52.87 in the first model and 64.52 in the fourth model. When compared with the results in Table 3.7, these figures suggest that management turnover in financially distressed firms is better explained if actual shifts in ownership and control rather than absolute levels are inspected.[39]

3.4.2.3 Sensitivity analysis

In order to confirm the robustness of my results several specification tests were performed. In principle, concerns with the robustness of my findings, may stem from (1) my measurement of ownership and its impact on turnover, (2) my definition of management turnover, and (3) attrition resulting from the use of unbalanced panel data. I address these concerns below.

A. Ownership specification

Objection against the application of my ownership variables may surface for two reasons, the omission of interaction terms between ownership and performance and the omission of a potentially non-linear relationship between ownership and turnover. Turnover models that include interaction terms formulated as *turnover=f(performance, ownership, ownership×performance, controls)* are frequently applied so as to test whether ownership matters and whether ownership in combination with poor performance matters.[40] Since, by design, all firms in my sample

[39] A correlation matrix of the independent variables is presented in Table 3.11 in the Appendix.
[40] Powers (2005) surveys this strand of literature.

perform poorly, the difference between both measures should be negligible. However, to ensure the comparability of my results, I amplify my specification in model 4 by, alternately, two sets of interaction terms. I multiply my established ownership variables by (1) *distress duration*, i.e. the number of years spent in distress in a particular firm-year and (2) a dummy variable *loss* that equals one if a firm's Ebitda is negative and zero otherwise. The underlying assumption is that monitoring by blockholders should intensify as performance further deteriorates. Estimation results are reported in Table 3.12 in the Appendix. Evidently, my results obtained in models 1-4 above hold with the inclusion of interaction terms. In particular, my core findings on the insignificance of overall ownership concentration and the significance of ownership by banks and financial blockholders are unaffected by the modifications in the model.

Following, among others, McConnell and Servaes (1990), I further inspect potential non-linearities in the ownership-turnover relation by extending the model by quadratic terms of inside ownership (*management ownership*^{2}), ownership concentration (*top blockholder*^{2}), private ownership (*priv ownership*^{2}), and strategic ownership (*strat ownership*^{2}). The theoretic argument for a non-linear relation between block ownership and turnover is that collusion between management and large blockholders becomes more likely as ownership stakes increase, especially when combined with departures from one-share-one-vote [e.g. Grossman and Hart (1988)]. For example, majority blockholders could enforce wealth redistributions from minority owners and, in return, grant management job security despite poor performance.[41] When added to the regression the quadratic ownership terms do indicate some curve-linearities in the turnover equation (model 3 of Table 3.12). Especially for private ownership, turnover tends to increase at low levels of private holdings and decreases as owners assemble larger blocks. However, the effects are not robust to alternative specifications of the model (not reported). In addition, none of the observed curve-linearities on ownership concentration, strategic ownership and management ownership are statistically significant. This evidence provides further support for my result that ownership concentration as well as insider ownership have no substantial (linear or non-linear) effect on management tenure in financially distressed firms.

B. Turnover definition

My definition of management turnover, although based on findings by Warner, Watts, and Wruck (1988) and Gilson (1989), is admittedly arbitrary. To examine, to what extent my results depend on this definition, I re-estimate each of my logit specifications with three distinct alterations in the dependent variable. First, I include in the analysis all departures of firms' CEOs and CFOs irrespective of an alleged disciplinary background. For example, studies by Franks and Mayer (2001) and Köke (2002) also do not distinguish between voluntary and forced management resignation. Second, I focus on CEO departures only. In cases where the premature

41 Such inter-shareholder conflicts of interest are a common phenomenon in Germany where deviations from one-share-one-vote (through pyramid structures) persist in many corporations, see Köke (2001).

departure of financial officers actually presents a "pawn-sacrifice" of the CEO, including such departures into the management turnover definition could overstate the efficacy of internal and external monitoring mechanisms. However, since only about one fifth of all turnovers in my analysis actually involve departures of CFOs this problem should be less pronounced. Third, I restrict my attention solely on turnover of the chief directors, i.e. the chairmen of the supervisory board. If, as popularly claimed, there exists a widespread "ride together—die together" attitude between key executives and their chief internal monitors, turnover patterns of both should bear some resemblance.

Estimation results for alternative turnover definitions are contained in Tables 3.13-3.15 in the Appendix. The first two alternative definitions (model 2 and 3) produce results that are virtually identical to my original definition of management turnover (model 1). As expected, however, the impact of performance on turnover in both variations is somewhat smaller than reported throughout this text; a result, which is most likely attributable to the deliberate inclusion of voluntary resignations in these models. Also apparent from Tables 3.13-3.15, turnover of directors is only poorly explained by my specifications. Solely takeovers strongly affect turnover of directors. The evidence is consistent with earlier findings on supervisory board turnover in Germany [e.g. Franks and Mayer (2001)] and suggests that turnover of directors occurs less performance-related but mostly within regular successions.

C. Panel attrition and selectivity bias

One crucial feature of my data sample is its unbalanced panel structure, i.e. the number of observations is unequal for all firms. This structure results from two factors. First, the unbalanced structure is a deliberate feature of my research design because I exclude firms from further inspection after bankruptcy and recovery. That is, different firms suffer from distress for different periods of time. Second, my sample is afflicted by missing data points, which is due to incomplete time-series of data in WORLDSCOPE and HOPPENSTEDT for some firms and variables. Incomplete or missing data are a common side-effect of German corporate governance studies [e.g. Köke (2002)].

Crucially, missing observations in panel data can cause serious biases and inconsistencies in the regression estimates if the encountered non-response is endogenously determined. For example, in my context the regression model may under- or overstate the impact of distress on corporate control activities if firms with longer time-series of available data are systematically different from firms that exit early. One computationally convenient approach to check for sample selectivity bias in panel data is to perform an Added-Variable procedure (or Quasi-Hausman test) as suggested by Verbeek and Nijman (1992). I define an indicator variable $response_{it}$ as $response_{it} = 1$ if (y_{it}, x_{it}) is observed and 0 otherwise. Next, I construct the attrition variable as $attrition_i = \sum_{t=1}^{T} response_{it}$, indicating the total number of periods i is observed, and include $attrition_i$ as additional regressor in my random-effects logit model. Under the null-hypothesis of non-selective response in my panel structure, the estimated coefficient for the added variable is statistically insignificant and the applied model is appropriate. Under the alternative hypothesis of sample selectivity, however, the coefficient is non-zero and static panel data models yield biased and inconsistent estimation results [Wooldridge (2002)].

I estimate several models with this modified specification. The estimated coefficient of the attrition variable is negative but statistically insignificant in all specifications.[42] The results suggest that my evidence reported above is not inflicted by biases resulting from endogenous panel data attrition.

3.5 Summary and conclusions

This study provides a first insight into the anatomy of financial distress in German firms. I find a strong indication for an attenuation in internal monitoring efficiency. Private investors, traditionally a bulwark in corporate ownership structures in Germany, substantially reduce their ownership stakes and thereby cease to be an effective source of managerial control. Management turnover, which clearly exceeds conventional levels of turnover in Germany, is insensitive to overall ownership concentration and concentration of private ownership. Moreover, stock-based compensation of insiders, although increasing under distress, neither fosters nor substitutes the disciplinary replacement of key-executives. Conversely, monitoring by external forces fortifies under financial distress. Amid the retreat of private investors, ownership representation by banks and financial investors almost doubles under continuing distress. In consequence, disciplinary management turnover is mostly triggered by banks and outside investors and often occurs subsequent to control transfers through debt restructurings, block investments, and takeovers.

One interpretation of my findings is that protracted distress causes a gradual shift from internal to external mechanisms of corporate control. Alternatively, the observed control changes may be due to a shift from identifiable to non-identifiable control mechanisms. If turnover rates increase despite decreasing ownership concentration, this may be a result of less scope for management for colluding with incumbent blockholders. To my knowledge, this is a genuine finding that has not been documented before. However, several open questions remain. For example, I cannot decipher what exactly induces private investors to sell their ownership in response to distress. My results suggest that liquidity and risk aversion are central issues, however this may be only an ostensible explanation. Furthermore, my results suggests that managers incur high personal costs of financial distress. Yet, I cannot substantiate whether these costs are sufficiently high to have a commensurable impact on day-to-day corporate policy decisions. In this respect, I hope my study can give a fresh impetus for further research on the causes and consequences of corporate financial distress.

[42] For the sake of brevity the results of the Verbeek and Nijman (1992) procedure are not reported in tables. However, the tables can be obtained from the author upon request.

Bibliography for Chapter 3

Asquith, P., R. Gertner, and D. Scharfstein (1994): "Anatomy of Financial Distress: An Examination of Junk-Bond Issuers," *The Quarterly Journal of Economics*, 109, 625–658.

Baker, G. P., M. C. Jensen, and K. J. Murphy (1988): "Compensation and Incentives: Practice Vs. Theory," *The Journal of Finance*, 43, 593–616.

Barclay, M. J., and C. G. Holderness (1989): "Private Benefits from Control of Public Corporations," *Journal of Financial Economics*, 25, 371–395.

——— (1991): "Negotiated Block Trades and Corporate Control," *The Journal of Finance*, 46, 861–878.

Bebchuk, L. A. (1999): "A Rent-Protection Theory of Corporate Ownership and Control," NBER Working Paper No. 7203.

Becker, W. (2003): "Geier oder Notärzte? US-Investoren wittern in deutschen Turnaround-Kandidaten hohe Renditen," *Börsen-Zeitung*, (158 [08.19.03]), 13.

Bhagat, S., and R. H. J. Jeffries (2002): *The Econometrics of Corporate Governance Studies*. MIT Press, Cambridge, MA.

Brüchner, T. (1998): *Reorganisationstrategien für insolvenzbedrohte Unternehmen*. Peter Lang, Frankfurt a.M.

Buth, A., M. Hermanns, and R. Janus (1998): "Finanzwirtschaftliche Aspekte der Fortführung von Krisenunternehmen," in *Restrukturierung, Sanierung, Insolvenz*, ed. by A. Buth, and M. Hermanns, pp. 224–245, München. Beck.

Conaway, M. R. (1990): "A Random Effects Model for Binary Data," *Biometrics*, 46, 317–328.

Demsetz, H., and K. Lehn (1985): "The Structure of Corporate Ownership: Causes and Consequences," *Journal of Political Economy*, 93, 1155–1177.

Denis, D. J., D. K. Denis, and A. Sarin (1997): "Ownership Structure and Top Executive Turnover," *Journal of Financial Economics*, 45, 193–221.

Denis, D. J., and A. Sarin (1999): "Ownership and Board Structures in Publicly Traded Corporations," *Journal of Financial Economics*, 52, 187–223.

Edwards, J., and K. Fischer (1994): *Banks, Finance and Investment in West-Germany Since 1970*. Cambridge University Press, Cambridge, U.K.

Ehrhardt, O., and E. Nowak (2003): "Private Kontrollrenten in Deutschen Familienunternehmen," *Die Betriebswirtschaft*, 63, 363–377.

Fama, E. F., and M. C. Jensen (1983): "Separation of Ownership and Control," *Journal of Law and Economics*, 26, 301–325.

Finsterer, H. (1999): *Unternehmenssanierung Durch Kreditinstitute: Eine Untersuchung unter Beachtung der Insolvenzordnung*. Gabler, Wiesbaden.

Franks, J., and C. Mayer (2001): "Ownership and Control of German Corporations," *The Review of Financial Studies*, 14, 943–977.

Franks, J. R., C. Mayer, and L. Renneboog (2001): "Who Disciplines Management in Poorly Performing Companies?," *Journal of Financial Intermediation*, 10, 209–248.

Franks, J. R., K. Nyborg, and W. Torous (1996): "A Comparison of US, UK, and German Insolvency Codes," *Financial Management*, 25, 19–30.

Franks, J. R., and W. N. Torous (1989): "An Empirical Investigation of U.S. Firms in Reorganization," *The Journal of Finance*, 44, 747–769.

Furtado, E., and M. Rozeff (1987): "The Wealth Effects of Company Initiated Management Changes," *Journal of Financial Economics*, 18, 147–160.

Gertner, R., and D. Scharfstein (1991): "A Theory of Workouts and the Effects of Reorganization Law," *The Journal of Finance*, 46, 1189–1222.

Gibbons, R. S., and K. J. Murphy (1990): "Relative Performance Evaluation for Chief Executive Officers," *Industrial and Labor Relations Review*, 43, 30–51.

Gilson, S. C. (1989): "Management Turnover and Financial Distress," *Journal of Financial Economics*, 25, 241–262.

——— (1990): "Bankruptcy, Boards, Banks, and Blockholders," *Journal of Financial Economics*, 27, 355–387.

Gilson, S. C., K. John, and L. H. Lang (1990): "Troubled Debt Restructurings, An Empirical Study of Private Reorganization of Firms in Default," *Journal of Financial Economics*, 27, 315–353.

Gilson, S. C., and M. R. Vetsuypens (1993): "CEO Compensation in Financially Distressed Firms: An Empirical Analysis," *The Journal of Finance*, 48, 425–458.

Gorton, G., and F. A. Schmid (2000): "Universal Banking and Performance of German Firms," *Journal of Financial Economics*, 58, 29–80.

Gray, P. H. (1998): "A Comment on Wenger and Kaserer," in *Competition and Convergence in Financial Markets*, ed. by S. W. Black, and M. Moersch, pp. 79–84, North-Holland. Elsevier.

Greene, W. H. (2003): *Econometric Analysis*. Prentice Hall, Upper Saddle River, 5th edn.

Grossman, S. J., and O. D. Hart (1988): "One Share - One Vote and the Market for Corporate Control," *Journal of Financial Economics*, 20, 175–202.

Haugen, R., and L. Senbet (1978): "The Insignificance of Bankruptcy Costs to the Theory of Optimal Capital Structure," *The Journal of Finance*, 33, 383–393.

Hausman, J. A. (1978): "Specification Tests in Econometrics," *Econometrica*, 46, 1251–1271.

Hotchkiss, E. S., and R. M. Mooradian (1997): "Vulture Investors and the Market for Corporate Control of Distressed Firms," *Journal of Financial Economics*, 43, 401–432.

Jenksinon, T., and A. Ljungqvist (2001): "Hostile Stakes and the Role of Banks in German Corporate Governance," *Journal of Corporate Finance*, 7, 397–446.

Jensen, M. C. (1988): "Takeovers: Their Causes and Consequences," *Economic Perspectives*, 2, 21–48.

——— (1989): "Active Investors, LBO's and Privatization of Bankruptcy," *Journal of Applied Corporate Finance*, 2, 35–44.

JENSEN, M. C., AND W. MECKLING (1976): "Theory of the Firm: Managerial Behavior, Agency Costs, and Ownership Structure," *Journal of Financial Economics*, 3, 305–360.

JENSEN, M. C., AND R. S. RUBACK (1983): "The Market for Corporate Control: The Scientific Evidence," *Journal of Financial Economics*, 11, 5–50.

JOHN, K., AND L. W. SENBET (1998): "Corporate Governance and Board Effectiveness," *Journal of Banking and Finance*, 22, 371–403.

JOSTARNDT, P., B. RUDOLPH, AND M. THIERAUF (2005): "Unternehmenskontrolle und Management-Disziplinierung in Deutschland: Neue Ergebnisse," in *Handbuch Mergers and Acquisitions Management*, ed. by B. Wirtz, pp. 203–228, Wiesbaden. Gabler.

KÖKE, J. (2001): "New Evidence on Ownership Structures in Germany," *Kredit und Kapital*, 14, 257–292.

——— (2002): *Corporate Governance in Germany: An Empirical Investigation.* Physica, Heidelberg.

MADDALA, G. S. (1987): "Limited Dependent Variable Models Using Panel Data," *The Journal of Human Resources*, 22, 307–338.

MANNE, H. G. (1965): "Mergers and the Market for Corporate Control," *The Journal of Political Economy*, 73, 110–120.

MCCONNELL, J. J., AND H. SERVAES (1990): "Additional Evidence on Equity Ownership and Corporate Value," *Journal of Financial Economics*, 27, 595–612.

MIKKELSON, W. H., AND M. M. PARTCH (1997): "The Decline of Takeovers and Disciplinary Managerial Turnover," *Journal of Financial Economics*, 44, 205–228.

OFEK, E. (1993): "Capital Structure and Firm Response to Poor Performance," *Journal of Financial Economics*, 34, 3–30.

POWERS, E. A. (2005): "Interpreting Logit Regressions with Interaction Terms: An Application to the Management Turnover Literature," *Journal of Corporate Finance*, 11, 504–522.

ROSS, S. (1977): "The Determinants of Financial Structure: The Incentive-Signalling Approach," *Bell Journal of Economics*, 8, 23–40.

RUDOLPH, B. (2003): "Unternehmensfinanzierung und Corporate Governance - Entwicklungen und weiterer Anpassungsbedarf," *Betriebs-Berater*, 58, 2053–2060.

SCHARFSTEIN, D. S. (1988): "The Disciplinary Role of Takeovers," *Review of Economic Studies*, 55, 185–200.

SCHRADER, S., AND C. LÜTHJE (1995): "Das Ausscheiden der Spitzenführungskraft aus dem Unternehmen," *Zeitschrift für Betriebswirtschaftslehre*, 65, 468–492.

SENBET, L. W., AND J. K. SEWARD (1995): "Financial Distress, Bankruptcy and Reorganization," in *Finance*, ed. by R. A. Jarrow, V. Maksimovic, and W. T. Ziemba, pp. 921–957, Amsterdam, N.H. Elsevier.

SHLEIFER, A., AND R. W. VISHNY (1986): "Large Shareholders and Corporate Control," *Journal of Political Economy*, 94, 461–488.

——— (1989): "Management Entrenchment: The Case of Manager-Specific Investments," *Journal of Financial Economics*, 25, 123–139.

——— (1992): "Liquidation Values and Debt Capacity: A Market Equilibrium Approach," *The Journal of Finance*, 47, 1343–1366.

——— (1997): "A Survey of Corporate Governance," *The Journal of Finance*, 52, 737–783.

SMITH, C. W., AND R. M. STULZ (1985): "The Determinants of Firms' Hedging Policies," *The Journal of Financial and Quantitative Analysis*, 20, 391–405.

TE WILDT, C. (1996): *CEO Turnover and Corporate Performance*. Wissenschaftsverlag Vauk, Kiel.

VERBEEK, M., AND T. NIJMAN (1992): "Testing for Selectivity Bias in Panel Data Models," *International Economic Review*, 33, 681–703.

VON THADDEN, E.-L. (1990): "On the Efficiency of the Market for Corporate Control," *Kyklos*, 43, 635–658.

WARNER, J. B., R. L. WATTS, AND K. H. WRUCK (1988): "Stock Prices and Top Management Changes," *Journal of Financial Economics*, 20, 461–492.

WEISBACH, M. S. (1988): "Outside Directors and CEO Turnover," *Journal of Financial Economics*, 20, 431–460.

WENGER, E., AND C. KASERER (1998): "The German System of Corporate Governance: A Model Which Should Not Be Imitated," in *Competition and Convergence in Financial Markets*, ed. by S. W. Black, and M. Moersch, pp. 41–78, Amsterdam. Elsevier.

WERDER, A. V. (2002): "Der Deutsche Corporate Governance Kodex: Grundlagen und Einzelbestimmungen," *Der Betrieb*, 55, 801–810.

WILLIAMSON, O. E. (1988): "Corporate Finance and Corporate Governance," *The Journal of Finance*, 43, 567–592.

WOOLDRIDGE, J. M. (2002): *Econometric Analysis of Cross-Section and Panel Data*. MIT Press, Cambridge, MA.

WRUCK, K. H. (1990): "Financial Distress, Reorganization, and Organizational Efficiency," *Journal of Financial Economics*, 27, 419–444.

Appendices

1. Summary of variable definitions and data sources
2. Correlation matrices for independent variables
3. Supplementary panel regressions

Table 3.9: Summary of variable definitions and data sources

Variable	Definition	Data source
Panel A: Ownership data		
Herfindahl	Herfindahl index across all blocks of common voting stock defined as $HI = \sum_{i=1}^{N} s_i^2$, where $s_i (i = 1, ..., N)$ is the fraction of common stock owned by the party i.	HOPPENSTEDT Financial Information Stock Guide
Top blockholder	Size of the largest share block of common voting stock	HOPPENSTEDT Financial Information Stock Guide
Top 3 blockholder	Sum of the three largest share blocks of common voting stock	HOPPENSTEDT Financial Information Stock Guide
Management ownership / Director ownership	Share of common voting stock held by members of the executive board / members of the supervisory board	HOPPENSTEDT Financial Information Stock Guide
Private ownership	Share of common stock held by families or individual investors (shares held by different family members were aggregated)	HOPPENSTEDT Financial Information Stock Guide
Strategic ownership	Share of common voting stock held by non-financial corporates	HOPPENSTEDT Financial Information Stock Guide
Financial ownership	Share of common voting stock held by investment funds, private equity funds, and insurance companies	HOPPENSTEDT Financial Information Stock Guide
Bank ownership	Share of common voting stock held by corporate and investment banks	HOPPENSTEDT Financial Information Stock Guide
Panel B: Restructuring data		
Debt restructuring	Out-of-court reduction or deferral of contractual payments, provision of fresh money, or swap of claims	LEXIS-NEXIS, and DOWJONES&REUTERS
Default	Mandatory filing in accordance with § 92 I of the German Companies Act (AktG)	LEXIS-NEXIS, and DOWJONES&REUTERS
Block investment	Acquisition of minority stake of common voting stock by outside investor through blocktrade or placement of new shares	LEXIS-NEXIS, DOWJONES&REUTERS and HOPPENSTEDT
Takeover	Acquisition of majority block of common voting stock by outside investor	LEXIS-NEXIS, DOWJONES&REUTERS, and HOPPENSTEDT

Table 3.10: Correlation matrix of independent variables in panel regressions I-IV

Correlation matrix of independent variables used in Table 3.7. Variable definitions are from Table 3.7 and 3.9. Each column contains correlation coefficients and and their respective p-values in parentheses below.

		(1)	(2)	(3)	(4)	(5)	(6)	(7)	(8)	(9)	(10)	(11)	(12)	(13)
(1)	Assets (log)	1.000												
(2)	Leverage	0.066	1.000											
		(0.024)												
(3)	Stock return	0.056	0.076	1.000										
		(0.087)	(0.016)											
(4)	Return on assets	0.150	-0.043	-0.023	1.000									
		(0.000)	(0.106)	(0.457)										
(5)	Neuer Markt	-0.243	-0.108	-0.169	-0.075	1.000								
		(0.000)	(0.000)	(0.000)	(0.004)									
(6)	Herfindahl	0.249	-0.017	0.093	0.029	-0.198	1.000							
		(0.000)	(0.532)	(0.002)	(0.254)	(0.000)								
(7)	Top blockholder	0.272	-0.012	0.050	0.024	-0.143	0.953	1.000						
		(0.000)	(0.643)	(0.093)	(0.343)	(0.000)	(0.000)							
(8)	Management ownership	0.001	-0.003	-0.056	0.008	0.012	0.134	0.173	1.000					
		(0.965)	(0.917)	(0.059)	(0.753)	(0.614)	(0.000)	(0.000)						
(9)	Director ownership	-0.009	-0.002	0.017	0.002	0.031	-0.011	0.021	0.041	1.000				
		(0.739)	(0.936)	(0.564)	(0.951)	(0.194)	(0.654)	(0.372)	(0.085)					
(10)	Private ownership	0.006	0.013	-0.087	0.055	0.137	0.233	0.356	-0.148	-0.060	1.000			
		(0.825)	(0.637)	(0.004)	(0.033)	(0.000)	(0.000)	(0.000)	(0.000)	(0.011)				
(11)	Strategic ownership	0.201	-0.050	0.070	-0.005	-0.140	0.600	0.546	-0.080	-0.043	-0.235	1.000		
		(0.000)	(0.057)	(0.020)	(0.833)	(0.000)	(0.000)	(0.000)	(0.001)	(0.072)	(0.000)			
(12)	Financial ownership	0.042	0.002	0.003	-0.018	-0.058	0.140	0.178	-0.029	-0.001	-0.089	-0.077	1.000	
		(0.133)	(0.936)	(0.918)	(0.479)	(0.015)	(0.000)	(0.000)	(0.222)	(0.981)	(0.000)	(0.001)		
(13)	Bank ownership	0.189	0.051	0.047	0.019	-0.133	0.100	0.118	-0.034	-0.024	-0.058	0.003	-0.021	1.000
		(0.000)	(0.054)	(0.113)	(0.471)	(0.000)	(0.000)	(0.000)	(0.151)	(0.319)	(0.015)	(0.888)	(0.369)	

Table 3.11: Correlation matrix of independent variables in panel regressions V-VIII

Correlation matrix of independent variables used in Table 3.8. Variable definitions are from Tables 3.8 and 3.9. Each column contains correlation coefficients and and their respective p-values in parentheses below.

		(1)	(2)	(3)	(4)	(5)	(6)	(7)	(8)	(9)	(10)	(11)	(12)
(1)	Assets (log)	1.000											
(2)	Leverage	0.066	1.000										
		(0.024)											
(3)	Stock return	0.056	0.076	1.000									
		(0.087)	(0.016)										
(4)	Return on assets	0.150	-0.043	-0.023	1.000								
		(0.000)	(0.106)	(0.457)									
(5)	Neuer Markt	-0.243	-0.108	-0.169	-0.075	1.000							
		(0.000)	(0.000)	(0.000)	(0.004)								
(6)	Herfindahl	0.249	-0.017	0.093	0.029	-0.198	1.000						
		(0.000)	(0.532)	(0.002)	(0.254)	(0.000)							
(7)	Management ownership	-0.064	-0.026	-0.088	-0.033	-0.017	0.053	1.000					
		(0.023)	(0.335)	(0.003)	(0.205)	(0.466)	(0.025)						
(8)	Debt restructuring	0.161	0.079	-0.072	0.017	-0.052	0.004	0.015	1.000				
		(0.000)	(0.003)	(0.016)	(0.517)	(0.029)	(0.877)	(0.538)					
(9)	Default	-0.041	0.043	0.026	-0.071	-0.075	0.034	0.029	0.032	1.000			
		(0.158)	(0.107)	(0.384)	(0.007)	(0.002)	(0.162)	(0.232)	(0.191)				
(10)	Block investment	0.013	-0.002	-0.014	-0.009	0.048	-0.008	0.011	0.008	-0.017	1.000		
	(Financial)	(0.633)	(0.933)	(0.646)	(0.724)	(0.044)	(0.740)	(0.654)	(0.756)	(0.489)			
(11)	Block investment	0.019	-0.003	0.013	0.021	-0.032	0.012	-0.011	0.118	0.017	-0.012	1.000	
	(Strategic)	(0.505)	(0.925)	(0.671)	(0.425)	(0.178)	(0.606)	(0.644)	(0.000)	(0.488)	(0.623)		
(12)	Takeover	0.001	-0.014	0.043	-0.015	-0.001	0.122	-0.001	0.017	0.059	-0.019	0.010	1.000
		(0.965)	(0.592)	(0.150)	(0.568)	(0.981)	(0.000)	(0.967)	(0.483)	(0.016)	(0.420)	(0.662)	

Table 3.12: Panel regressions of model IV with interaction terms and non-linearities
Random-Effects Maximum-Likelihood estimation of logistic regressions that simultaneously relate senior management changes to a vector of explanatory variables. Regressions are based on a panel of 267 German corporations that suffered from financial distress between 1996 and 2004. The dependent variable equals one if the defined turnover event is observed in a given firm-year, and zero otherwise. Interaction terms are formed with two performance measures: *Distress* is a count variable that captures the number of years spent in distress in a particular firm-year. *Loss* is a dummy variable that equals one if a firm's Ebitda is negative and zero otherwise. All other variable definitions are from Tables 3.7 and 3.9. The two columns of each model contain the coefficient estimates and asymptotic standard errors, respectively. *, **, and *** denote the parameters are statistically significant at the 10%, 5%, and 1% level, respectively. The Wald χ^2 statistic test the hypotheses that all the variables in the model are simultaneously equal to zero. ρ measures the proportion of the total variance contributed by the panel-level (between) variance component.

	Model 1		Model 2		Model 3	
	Distress duration		Loss making		Non-linearities	
	Coeff.	se	Coeff.	se	Coeff.	se
Assets (Log)	0.236	(0.075)***	0.251	(0.073)***	0.221	(0.072)***
Leverage	0.737	(0.526)	0.851	(0.509)*	0.851	(0.510)*
Stock return	-0.612	(0.110)***	-0.513	(0.108)***	-0.555	(0.107)***
Return on assets	-0.563	(0.331)*	-0.628	(0.322)*	-0.706	(0.313)**
Herfindahl	-2.593	(2.134)	-2.770	(1.874)	-6.247	(5.689)
Herfindahl×Distress	0.166	(0.457)				
Herfindahl×Loss			0.881	(1.447)		
Largest block	0.841	(1.608)	1.069	(1.532)	-1.267	(2.164)
Largest block^2					6.164	(5.985)
Mgmt ownership	2.402	(1.950)	0.619	(1.547)	6.795	(3.645)*
Mgmt ownership^2					8.299	(5.755)
Mgmt ownership×Distress	-0.779	(0.829)				
Mgmt ownership×Loss			0.428	(1.831)		
Director ownership	4.090	(2.656)	3.871	(2.571)	-12.237	(16.128)
Director ownership^2					52.871	(48.692)
Priv ownership	0.389	(0.863)	0.248	(0.938)	3.979	(1.936)**
Priv ownership^2					3.300	(2.459)
Priv ownership×Distress	0.529	(0.303)*				
Priv ownership×Loss			1.171	(0.855)		
Strat ownership	1.354	(1.060)	0.978	(1.050)	3.205	(2.100)
Strat ownership^2					-1.679	(2.240)
Strat ownership×Distress	0.012	(0.376)				
Strat ownership×Loss			0.385	(1.164)		
Fin ownership	2.000	(1.142)*	1.414	(1.149)	2.497	(1.301)*
Fin ownership×Distress	-0.118	(0.389)				
Fin ownership×Loss			0.425	(1.291)		
Bank ownership	3.646	(1.585)**	2.785	(1.211)**	3.407	(1.367)**
Bank ownership×Distress	-0.377	(0.464)				
Bank ownership×Loss			0.109	(1.819)		
Neuer Markt	0.316	(0.254)	0.239	(0.245)	0.262	(0.244)
Constant	-5.676	(0.935)***	-5.766	(0.918)***	-5.522	(0.905)***
N(obs.)	914		914		914	
N(firms)	267		267		267	
Wald-χ^2	54.68	***	58.22	***	56.17	***
ρ	0.08		0.052		0.052	

Table 3.13: Panel regressions of model I with alterations in the dependent variable

Random-Effects Maximum-Likelihood estimation of logistic regressions relating senior management changes to a vector of explanatory variables. Regressions are based on a panel of 267 German corporations that suffered from financial distress between 1996 and 2004. The dependent variable equals one if the defined turnover event is observed in a given firm-year and zero otherwise. In model 1 dependent variable equals the turnover definition applied in Tables 3.7 and 3.8. In model 2 the dependent variable embraces all turnover events irrespective of an alleged disciplinary background. In model 3 the dependent variable includes only CEO turnovers. In model 4 the dependent variable includes only turnovers in the chair of the supervisory board. *Assets* is (lagged) the natural logarithm of book value of total assets. *Leverage* is (lagged) book value of total debt over book value of common equity plus book value of total debt. *Return* represents the (lagged) one-year buy-and-hold return of a firm's common stock. *Return on assets* is Earnings before interest taxes depreciation and amortization (Ebitda) over total assets. *Neuer Markt* presents a dummy variable that equals one if the firm was listed on the former growth segment of the German stock exchange, and zero otherwise. Remaining variable definitions are from Table 3.9. The two columns of each model contain the coefficient estimates and asymptotic standard errors, respectively. *, **, and *** denote the parameters are statistically significant at the 10%, 5%, and 1% level, respectively. The Wald χ^2 statistic test the hypotheses that all the variables in the model are simultaneously equal to zero. ρ measures the proportion of the total variance contributed by the panel-level (between) variance component.

	Model 1 Default		Model 2 All turnovers		Model 3 CEO turnover		Model 4 Director turnover	
	Coeff.	se	Coeff.	se	Coeff.	se	Coeff.	se
Assets (Log)	0.217	(0.071)***	0.201	(0.063)***	0.094	(0.075)	-0.006	(0.058)
Leverage	0.849	(0.495)*	0.909	(0.437)**	0.974	(0.506)*	0.181	(0.418)
Stock return	-0.582	(0.108)***	-0.565	(0.097)***	-0.541	(0.113)***	-0.102	(0.087)
Return on assets	-0.681	(0.307)**	-0.401	(0.283)	-0.462	(0.321)	-0.352	(0.274)
Neuer Markt	0.286	(0.234)	0.441	(0.225)*	0.179	(0.240)	-0.220	(0.187)
Constant	-4.957	(0.855)***	-4.480	(0.756)***	-3.797	(0.873)***	-5.315	(0.865)
N(obs.)	914		914		914		766	
N(firms)	267		267		267		259	
Wald-χ^2	42.11	***	50.53	***	29.32	***	4.10	
ρ	0.085		0.029		0.025		0.000	

Table 3.14: Panel regressions of model IV with alterations in the dependent variable

Random-Effects Maximum-Likelihood estimation of logistic regressions relating senior management changes to a vector of explanatory variables. Regressions are based on a panel of 267 German corporations that suffered from financial distress between 1996 and 2004. The dependent variable equals one if the defined turnover event is observed in a given firm-year and zero otherwise. In model 1 dependent variable equals the turnover definition applied in Tables 3.7 and 3.8. In model 2 the dependent variable embraces all turnover events irrespective of an alleged disciplinary background. In model 3 the dependent variable includes only CEO turnovers. In model 4 the dependent variable includes only turnovers in the chair of the supervisory board. *Assets* is (lagged) the natural logarithm of book value of total assets. *Leverage* is (lagged) book value of total debt over book value of common equity plus book value of total debt. *Return* represents the (lagged) one-year buy-and-hold return of a firm's common stock. *Return on assets* is Earnings before interest taxes depreciation and amortization (Ebitda) over total assets. *Neuer Markt* presents a dummy variable that equals one if the firm was listed on the former growth segment of the German stock exchange, and zero otherwise. Remaining variable definitions are from Table 3.9. The two columns of each model contain the coefficient estimates and asymptotic standard errors, respectively. *, **, and *** denote the parameters are statistically significant at the 10%, 5%, and 1% level, respectively. The Wald χ^2 statistic test the hypotheses that all the variables in the model are simultaneously equal to zero. ρ measures the proportion of the total variance contributed by the panel-level (between) variance component.

	Model 1 Default		Model 2 All turnovers		Model 3 CEO turnover		Model 4 Director turnover	
	Coeff.	se	Coeff.	se	Coeff.	se	Coeff.	se
Assets (Log)	0.213	(0.069)***	0.199	(0.062)***	0.085	(0.077)	-0.039	(0.061)
Leverage	0.757	(0.496)	0.797	(0.441)*	0.945	(0.529)*	0.384	(0.436)
Stock return	-0.568	(0.106)***	-0.547	(0.095)***	-0.543	(0.115)***	-0.141	(0.089)
Return on assets	-0.702	(0.306)**	-0.447	(0.286)	-0.522	(0.332)	-0.329	(0.278)
Management ownership	0.798	(1.087)	0.769	(0.931)	0.180	(1.124)	0.324	(0.818)
Director ownership	3.955	(2.509)	2.747	(2.239)	5.230	(2.412)**	3.312	(2.173)
Herfindahl	-2.204	(1.639)	-2.169	(1.543)	-1.949	(1.768)	1.015	(1.306)
Largest block	0.864	(1.492)	1.124	(1.335)	1.268	(1.629)	-0.316	(1.307)
Private ownership	0.951	(0.699)	0.846	(0.615)	0.923	(0.757)	0.010	(0.574)
Strategic ownership	1.291	(0.741)*	0.805	(0.650)	1.044	(0.795)	0.512	(0.560)
Financial ownership	1.705	(0.815)**	1.108	(0.729)	1.364	(0.879)	-0.011	(0.669)
Bank ownership	2.721	(0.944)***	2.138	(0.860)***	2.059	(1.035)**	0.618	(0.821)
Neuer Markt	0.273	(0.239)	0.382	(0.214)*	0.180	(0.259)	-0.024	(0.204)
Constant	-5.315	(0.865)***	-4.836	(0.769)***	-4.310	(0.936)***	-1.102	(0.749)
N(obs.)	914		914		914		766	
N(firms)	267		267		267		259	
Wald-χ^2	53.78	***	60.49	***	37.56	***	17.05	
ρ	0.032		0.002		0.002		0.000	

Table 3.15: Panel regressions of model VIII with alterations in the dependent variable

Random-Effects Maximum-Likelihood estimation of logistic regressions relating senior management changes to a vector of explanatory variables. Regressions are based on a panel of 267 German corporations that suffered from financial distress between 1996 and 2004. The dependent variable equals one if the defined turnover event is observed in a given firm-year and zero otherwise. In model 1 dependent variable equals the turnover definition applied in Tables 3.7 and 3.8. In model 2 the dependent variable embraces all turnover events irrespective of an alleged disciplinary background. In model 3 the dependent variable includes only CEO turnovers. In model 4 the dependent variable includes only turnovers in the chair of the supervisory board. *Assets* is (lagged) the natural logarithm of book value of total assets. *Leverage* is (lagged) book value of total debt over book value of common equity plus book value of total debt. *Return* represents the (lagged) one-year buy-and-hold return of a firm's common stock. *Return on assets* is Earnings before interest taxes depreciation and amortization (Ebitda) over total assets. *Neuer Markt* presents a dummy variable that equals one if the firm was listed on the former growth segment of the German stock exchange, and zero otherwise. Remaining variable definitions are from Table 3.9. The two columns of each model contain the coefficient estimates and asymptotic standard errors, respectively. *, **, and *** denote the parameters are statistically significant at the 10%, 5%, and 1% level, respectively. The Wald χ^2 statistic test the hypotheses that all the variables in the model are simultaneously equal to zero. ρ measures the proportion of the total variance contributed by the panel-level (between) variance component.

	Model 1		Model 2		Model 3		Model 4	
	Default		All turnovers		CEO turnover		Director turnover	
	Coeff.	se	Coeff.	se	Coeff.	se	Coeff.	se
Assets (Log)	0.228	(0.072)***	0.211	(0.063)***	0.088	(0.077)	-0.006	(0.617)
Leverage	0.552	(0.506)	0.718	(0.444)	0.830	(0.527)	0.502	(0.433)
Stock return	-0.569	(0.109)***	-0.557	(0.097)***	-0.537	(0.115)***	-0.148	(0.090)*
Return on assets	-0.615	(0.314)**	-0.346	(0.286)	-0.386	(0.331)	-0.352	(0.286)
Herfindahl	-0.341	(0.451)	-0.260	(0.394)	0.164	(0.249)	0.813	(0.356)**
Management Ownership	0.289	(0.355)	0.260	(0.315)	0.135	(0.376)	-0.016	(0.294)
Debt restructuring	1.176	(0.375)***	0.901	(0.352)***	0.763	(0.390)**	-0.777	(0.467)
Default	1.219	(0.652)*	1.027	(0.618)*	1.131	(0.645)*	0.238	0.607
Block investment (Financial)	2.098	(0.677)***	2.131	(0.672)***	1.600	(0.664)**	0.408	(0.719)
Block investment (Strategic)	1.085	(0.548)**	1.295	(0.502)***	0.477	(0.659)	0.258	(0.544)
Takeover	0.763	(0.456)*	0.765	(0.415)*	0.843	(0.464)*	1.055	(0.365)***
Neuer Markt	0.221	(0.236)	0.405	(0.206)*	0.164	(0.249)	-0.054	(0.200)
Constant	-5.070	(0.872)***	-4.630	(0.762)***	-3.847	(0.907)***	-1.460	(0.713)**
N(obs.)	913		910		913		765	
N(firms)	267		267		267		259	
Wald-χ^2	64.52	***	76.06	***	43.65	***	22.89	**
ρ	0.053		0.002		0.002		0.0287	

Chapter 4

Of bail-outs and bankruptcies: An empirical study of distressed debt restructurings in Germany*

4.1 Introduction

A firm that needs to restructure its debt in order to avoid or remedy a default essentially faces a choice between two alternatives. It may privately renegotiate the affected debt claims in a workout or file a formal bankruptcy petition to resolve financial distress through an in-court proceeding. Financial scholars have long been engaged in discussing the relative merits and shortfalls of both alternatives. Bankruptcy, in general, has the advantage that it protects a distressed debtor from the 'harassment' of creditors and mitigates hold-out and information problems among different classes of claimholders [e.g. Jackson (1982), Gertner and Scharfstein (1991)]. In a private workout, on the other hand, firms are likely to avoid much of the direct and indirect costs associated with a formal proceeding [e.g. Jensen (1989), Wruck (1990)]. This suggests that a firm will choose the workout option if settling this way leaves the firm appreciably more valuable and if unanimous consent among all claimants is feasible. If, however, the affected parties

* I would like to thank Wolfgang Bühler, Dietmar Harhoff, Christoph Kaserer, Colin Mayer, Ken Okamura, Luis Rodrigues, Bernd Rudolph, Gerhard Schröck, Oren Sussman, and Hannes Wagner for helpful discussions. The study in this chapter has also benefited from conference and doctoral seminar presentations at the 9th Conference of the Swiss Society for Financial Market Research, Zürich 2006, the Annual Conference on Corporate Strategy (ACCS), Berlin 2006, the 4th Portoguese Finance Network International Conference, Porto 2006, the European Finance Association Meeting, Zürich 2006, the German Finance Association (DGF) Annual Meeting, Oestrich-Winkel 2006, the University of Munich (2005), the Technical University of Munich (2005), and the University of Oxford (2006). I would like to thank two anonymous referees for their thoughtful comments.

cannot agree on how to share the alleged benefits associated with settling out-of-court, then formal bankruptcy may be the dominant option even though the combined wealth of all parties is ultimately lower [e.g. Giammarino (1989), Brown (1989)]. Yet, despite these relatively precise predictions provided by theory, empirical results have remained sparse and inconclusive. In particular, there exists little evidence on how firms actually choose between an in- and out-of-court resolution of distress, and to what extend firm value is affected by that choice. Moreover, we currently know little about how the choice between workout and bankruptcy is affected by the design of national bankruptcy legislation. Much of this lack of evidence is attributable to the difficulty to obtain exhaustive data.[1] This holds especially for corporate Germany where, until fairly recently, most of the restructuring activity occurred without public disclosure.[2]

This study empirically investigates debt restructurings of a sample of financially distressed companies in Germany. For several reasons using German data may yield some interesting insights into the corporate bankruptcy decision. First, German bankruptcy legislation provides clear-cut incentives for the affected parties to avoid or seek a formal bankruptcy process. In Germany a bankruptcy filing typically results in the loss of control for the debtor and a strong tendency towards liquidation. A distressed debtor seeking a going concern, therefore, usually attempts to settle the case in a private workout. In this non-interventionist setting a bankruptcy filing directly reflects the institutional constraints of private bargaining and conveys information about the claimant's perception of the firm's viability. The U.S. Chapter 11 bankruptcy code, by contrast, provides incentives for firms to enter bankruptcy for other, more ambiguous motives, such as protection against large uncertain liabilities [Franks and Torous (1989)] or entrenchment of incumbent managers [Bradley and Rosenzweig (1992) and Bolton and Scharfstein (1996)]. Second, the unprecedented rise in bankruptcy cases in recent years among which were some of the biggest in the nation's history, such as Philipp Holzmann or Babcock Borsig, along with the substantial reform of German bankruptcy legislation that came into effect in 1999, provides a database that was previously not obtainable. I am thus not only able to provide evidence on the bankruptcy decision in general, but I can also make some inference about the specific costs of formal bankruptcy in Germany. This allows me to contribute to the growing literature on comparative bankruptcy legislation [e.g. Franks, Nyborg, and Torous (1996), Davydenko and Franks (2004)].

My analysis is based on a sample of 116 distressed debt restructuring attempts in Germany between 1997 and 2004. Of the sampled firms about half successfully restructure

[1] I am only aware of two studies that more or less directly address this issue, see Gilson, John, and Lang (1990) and Asquith, Gertner, and Scharfstein (1994).

[2] See Kaiser (1996), pp. 73-74 and references quoted therein.

their debt in a private workout while the other half fail and file an insolvency petition under the new bankruptcy code. I provide detailed summary statistics on both sub-samples that describe the most commonly observed features of private workouts and shed a first light on how firms that file for bankruptcy choose between alternative bankruptcy triggers. My multivariate analysis suggests that firms more likely to succeed in their restructuring attempt are, on average, higher leveraged and exhibit higher going concern values. Bankruptcy, on the other hand, is more likely for firms with deficient lender coordination and high fractions of collateralized debt. Analysis of stock returns suggests that the market uses similar information to predict which firms will ultimately succeed at completing a private workout. Abnormal stock price performance over the entire restructuring interval reveals that shareholders fare significantly better if the firm manages to avoid bankruptcy, with overall leverage and debt structure being the core valuation drivers. Moreover, I find substantially lower stock returns for my sub-sample of bankrupt firms than reported in related studies on U.S. Chapter 11 filings.

The remainder of this study is organized as follows. Section 2 discusses the economics of financial distress and debt restructuring and gives a brief introduction to Germany's bankruptcy legislation. Section 3 provides the details of the sample selection and formulates the hypotheses. The main results, their interpretations, and robustness checks are contained in section 4. Section 5 concludes. In the Appendix I describe the methodology for my empirical analyses and report supplementary statistics as well as the results of the robustness checks.

4.2 The economics of bankruptcy and debt restructuring

4.2.1 Key elements of the German bankruptcy code

4.2.1.1 The 1994 bankruptcy reform

Until 1999 German bankruptcy legislation provided for two separate forms of court proceedings, composition following the Forced Settlement Act of 1935 (*Vergleichsordnung*) and mandatory liquidation following the Bankruptcy Act of 1877 (*Konkursordnung*). While the former aimed at reorganizing economically viable firms, the latter was to ensure efficient processing of a non-viable entity. In 1994 new legislation was passed and came into effect in 1999 to combine both procedures into a unified code (*Insolvenzordnung*). The necessity for a revamped bankruptcy legislation was primarily triggered by two long criticized inefficiencies associated with the pre-1999 bankruptcy system. First, there existed no automatic stay for secured creditors, which often resulted in a piecemeal liquidation of all collateralized assets prior to the opening of formal proceedings. In consequence, more than 70% of all bankruptcy petitions were declined due to insufficient coverage of the administrative expenses [Breuer (2003)]. Second, due to the overly rigorous eligibility criteria imposed on a debtor seeking composition proceedings, in-court reorganization of a debtor's operations became a virtual impossibility. German bankruptcy law, therefore, was considered highly non-interventionist: Distressed firms were either resuscitated through a private workout or liquidated under court supervision.[3] Yet, in cases where claimholders could not agree upon a plan to ensure the going concern of a viable debtor, the firm was doomed, because this dichotomy could provide no in-court alternative to a private workout. As a result, corporate financial distress frequently resulted in the inefficient liquidation of an economically viable debtor.

While the new bankruptcy code resembles the existing one in many ways, the 1994 bankruptcy reform confronted the lamented shortcomings of the existing code in several ways. The main innovations were:

- Liquidation and reorganization are considered as equally important mechanisms to achieve the collective satisfaction of all creditors' claims.
- There is an automatic stay of secured claims for three months.

[3] Franke (1983) estimates that more than 50% of potential bankruptcy cases were averted via pre-bankruptcy restructuring.

- All non-secured insolvency creditors are treated by the rule of *par conditio creditorum*. There are thus no longer preferred creditors.[4]

By definition, formal proceedings under the new code do no longer automatically trigger liquidation. A bankruptcy filing, therefore, may present a worthwhile alternative also to economically viable debtors. The following section briefly describes the fundamental rules and proceeding of the new bankruptcy code.

4.2.1.2 Rules and proceeding of the new bankruptcy code

Under the 1994 code the bankruptcy proceeding is divided into three distinct phases; a first phase between bankruptcy filing and opening, a second phase between bankruptcy opening and information hearing, and a third phase subsequent to the information hearing. The opening of bankruptcy procedure occurs pursuant to and within a period of normally three months after a bankruptcy petition, which may be filed by the debtor herself or one of her creditors. Unlike the U.S. Chapter 11 bankruptcy code, German bankruptcy legislation traditionally requires proof of a bankruptcy trigger for the filing to be valid. Bankruptcy triggers are over-indebtedness, insolvency, and imminent insolvency. The former two have already been in place under the old code and oblige the debtor to file a petition, while the latter was introduced by the reform and offers an unsolicited option for the debtor to file a (pre-packaged) bankruptcy petition. During the period between bankruptcy filing and the onset of proceedings, the court usually stops payments to creditors and appoints a preliminary administrator.

If the court finds that (1) a bankruptcy trigger is in place and (2) the debtor's asset base suffices to cover the administrative expenses, it will formally open the procedure in which the appointed administrator assumes control over the debtor's assets. Additionally, a creditor assembly is installed with the task of supervising the administrator. The court also specifies the dates for the information hearing (*Berichtstermin*) and the examination hearing (*Prüfungstermin*) until which all creditors must file their claims. At the information hearing, the administrator expresses a recommendation to creditors on the value-maximizing way of processing the debtor's estate. As noted above, this presents either a shutdown and liquidation of the business or a reorganization pursuant to an insolvency plan, which may be proposed by the debtor or the administrator. In case of the latter, creditors effectively consent to an exchange of their impaired claims in

[4] Above all, preferred creditors included pension funds, social security agencies and tax authorities whose claims were assigned priority status in the bankruptcy process, see § 61 I Konkursordnung. Harhoff, Stahl, and Woywode (1998) show that a majority of alleged premature liquidations were triggered by such lenders.

the bankrupt firm against a package of new securities in the going concern. The creditors decide by means of majority vote between both alternatives, frequently following the administrator's recommendation.

In case of liquidation, payments to creditors stem from the liquidation proceeds of the debtor's assets. The value of a specific creditor's reimbursement is in principle determined by the rule of absolute priority under which a certain creditor class is compensated for the face value of its pre-bankruptcy claim only after all other classes designated as senior are paid in full. In principle, the code distinguishes creditor-classes according to the following hierarchy: (1) estate creditors (mostly administrative claims), (2) secured creditors (of which statutory liens and mortgages rank highest followed by assignments over plant and equipment and assignments over accounts receivable), (3) insolvency creditors (includes all unsecured creditors such as trade creditors, employees, and social-security agencies), and (4) subordinated creditors (all creditors whose claims are subordinated by law or by contract). In case the debtor is to be reorganized pursuant to an insolvency plan, the acceptance of the plan requires an affirmative vote of the claimholders in each impaired class. To break deadlocks, the court can unilaterally enforce the plan on a dissenting class if the value of the new securities it receives under the plan at least equals what the class would receive as share in a liquidation.[5] Finally, the bankruptcy procedure is formally consummated if either all liquidation proceeds are distributed to creditors (§200 InsO) or the insolvency plan successfully passes the creditor assembly (§258 InsO).

4.2.1.3 The effects on finance and control

The ramifications of default and bankruptcy on finance and control of the affected firm have been subject to an ongoing academic debate.[6] Under German bankruptcy legislation, two effects stand out: The loss of control of the debtor and the intricacy to obtain financing with superiority to existing claims. The debtor's loss of control over the firm's operations manifests in the court-appointment of the administrator who solely acts on behalf of creditors. This also holds in the event of resuscitation of the firm pursuant to an insolvency plan reorganization. The only exception to this rule occurs if the debtor successfully applies for self-management according to § 270 InsO.[7] As courts and creditor

[5] This so called *Obstruktionsverbot* (§245 InsO) strongly resembles the 'cram down' procedure that solves voting deadlocks in a Chapter 11 bankruptcy process.

[6] Senbet and Seward (1995) and Chen, Weston, and Altman (1995) provide reviews of the theoretic literature, Franks and Torous (1989) and Gilson (1990) empirically study changes in finance and control during Chapter 11 reorganizations. The economic ramification of German bankruptcy legislation is discussed, among others, by Franks, Nyborg, and Torous (1996), Brüchner (1998) and Ritter (2000).

[7] Under self-management, the debtor is supervised by a court-appointed trustee. However, the trustee has a significantly weaker standing than an insolvency administrator because all operative control remains in the hands of the debtor.

assemblies are relatively reluctant to grant self-management to debtors, however, this provision has little practical merit. The loss of control for the debtor sharply contrasts with the debtor-in-possession (DIP) provision of the U.S. Chapter 11 bankruptcy code under which the debtor remains in control and is assigned the exclusive right to propose a plan of reorganization within the first three months of the process.

The hassle to obtain senior finance in the state of crisis results from the concept of equitable subordination (*Eigenkapitalersatzrecht*), which forbids the provision of loans or de facto contributions of assets in a situation where a 'prudent and reliable' financier would instead provide equity. In fact, senior claims fraudulently provided to the firm antecedent to a bankruptcy filing will be subordinated by the court *ex post* and may even be subject to prosecution as a criminal offense. During the proceedings, estate credit with priority over existing claims may be provided, however the mere purpose of such credit is to avoid the deadlock of the debtor's operations prior to the information hearing. Any additional funds, e.g. to finance sustainable investment opportunities, are usually not provided by lenders.[8] In this respect also, the German code substantially differs from Chapter 11 reorganizations in which high amounts of DIP financing with supra priority status are frequently accommodated even if doing so violates against existing seniority covenants.[9]

Considering their expected loss of control and the difficulty to obtain senior finance, debtors have little incentive to file a pre-packaged bankruptcy petition. In this respect, German bankruptcy legislation keeps much of its pre-reform non-interventionist character. If, however, as Jensen (1989) argues, a pre-installed onset of the proceeding is essential for a successful reorganization, debtors' incentive to protract distress until obligatory bankruptcy is triggered will have adverse efficiency implications. Amid the shift in control from debtor to creditors and the abolishment of preferred lenders classes, secured creditors (especially holders of liens), in turn, are likely to emerge as most powerful class of claimants. Even though their rights are reduced compared to the old code, they have the exclusive right to force the sale of their collateral and demand immediate reimbursement after the three months moratorium imposed on all creditors (§§ 50, 170 InsO.).

8 "Such credits never serve as sustainable financing for the bankrupt entity, and thus cannot be interpreted as credible signal for its prospect solvency. Instead, the funds are frequently provided to accelerate the debtor's shutdown." Jürgen Röthig of Bankhaus Metzler commenting on the EUR 50 Mio. estate credit granted to Philipp Holzmann, one of the nation's biggest bankruptcy cases [as quoted in *Berliner-Zeitung*, 25 November 1999].

9 See Chatterjee, Dhillon, and Ramirez (2004), Franks, Nyborg, and Torous (1996). In addition, unlike in the U.S., there are no German banks specializing in DIP financing. Instead, German banks would consider DIP financing more as necessary evil rather than a form of business they are willing to promote.

4.2.2 Determinants of successful debt restructurings

As the previous section has shown, an insolvent debtor, in most cases, prefers an out-of-court settlement with its creditors to a formal bankruptcy proceeding. To the firm's creditors, the ones actually in charge upon default, the decision is more subtle. According to financial theory, their choice between private renegotiation and bankruptcy essentially depends on two factors.[10] First, creditors, like the debtor, will prefer a private workout if settling this way presents the lower-cost alternative to a bankruptcy proceeding. In this case, firm value will be higher and the firm's debt can be restructured in a way that leaves each of the original claimholders better off. Creditors' incentive to allow an out-of-court restructuring of the debtor will thus increase with the size of the potential cost savings from avoiding formal bankruptcy. Second, the lower-cost alternative will be pursued if and only if all different claimholders can agree on how to share the realized surplus. Provided that individual creditors are likely to receive more favorable treatment in a court-supervised restructuring (or liquidation), a private workout attempt may fail even if the combined proceeds of all claimants in bankruptcy is ultimately lower.

In the following I delve deeper into financial theory on the determinants of successful debt restructurings and the incentives of claimholders to recontract privately rather than in-court. The analysis will serve as foundation for the formulation of my hypotheses and the derivation of proxy variables in the subsequent sections.

4.2.2.1 Bankruptcy costs and firm value

Corporate financial distress and bankruptcy affect a firm's operations in cases where it is not cheap, quick, and painless as presumed by neoclassical theory, but rather costly and dissipative. By standard, costs of financial distress are distinguished between direct and indirect costs. While the former comprise all legal and administrative expenses that accrue during financial restructurings, the latter primarily constitute underinvestment in valuable investment opportunities resulting from the fact that financially troubled firms are hampered from conducting business as usual. If creditors are able to anticipate these costs and account for them in the initial contract, these costs will essentially manifest in a loss of shareholder wealth [Jensen and Meckling (1976)]. In the past, numerous studies have attempted to measure the direct costs of distress for workouts as well as Chapter 11 bankruptcies. While differing in magnitude, the obtained results suggest that

[10] See Gilson, John, and Lang (1990). Much of the theoretic literature views the corporate bankruptcy decision as a strategic game played (1) between stockholders and bondholders, e.g. Bulow and Shoven (1978), Brown (1989), White (1980) or, as more appropriate for the German case where stockholders' bargaining power is dismal, (2) among different classes of creditors, e.g. Longhofer and Peters (1999).

direct costs of recontracting are significantly higher under formal bankruptcy.[11] Most likely, it is argued, this difference is due to the more administrative nature of bankruptcy and the higher number of parties involved. As for the indirect cost component, hard evidence is not as easily obtained. However, it is reasonable to argue that for the same reason as above indirect costs, also, are higher under bankruptcy. Consistent with this assumption, empirical studies show that financially distressed companies, prior to filing a formal bankruptcy petition, often vainly attempt to restructure their debt privately.[12]

While there yet exists no related evidence for Germany, two factors tempt me to argue that the cost-rift between in- and out-of-court restructurings is glaringly deeper under German bankruptcy legislation. First, debt finance of German corporations is mainly restricted to bank-loans often provided by house-banks that maintain a close relationship to their debtors. A workout with such private lenders is likely to produce significantly lower direct costs, *ceteris paribus*, than tender-offers to public bondholders frequently observed in U.S. reorganizations.[13] Second, it appears reasonable to assume that the peril of underinvestment is much more pronounced in a German bankruptcy case. This stems from the non-interventionist character of German bankruptcy legislation, which tends to provoke a delayed onset of proceedings and thus a premature extinction in going-concern value. Underinvestment may be aggravated by the appointment of an administrator under German law as opposed to a debtor-in-possession situation under Chapter 11. However honorable their intentions, administrators lack firm-specific management skills that are often essential for a fast and efficient processing. Moreover, they are compensated from the debtor's estate with supra priority and therefore have little financial interest in the firm. In deciding what to propose at the information hearing, they may thus insufficiently consider the impact of their doing on total firm value (debt as well as residual claims). Naturally, the costs associated with the foregoing of valuable investments in bankruptcy are particularly high for firms with relatively higher profitability and higher going concern value in terms of intangible synergies and idiosyncratic future growth opportunities [e.g. Myers (1977)]. In this line of reasoning, claimholders of such firms have stronger incentives to avoid bankruptcy.

Upon default, the value of the going concern largely depends on how quickly the firm was able to respond to initial shortfalls in liquidity and profitability. According to Jensen

---

[11] Median out-of-pocket costs of recontracting are found to amount up to 0.32% of total assets for workouts [Gilson, John, and Lang (1990)] and to range between 3.1% and 7.5% of market value for bankruptcies [Weiss (1990), Altman (1984), Ang, Chua, and McConnell (1982), Warner (1977)]. Comparing all studies, Wruck (1990) concludes that in bankruptcy these costs exceed those in workouts almost by factor 10.

[12] See Gilson, John, and Lang (1990), and my evidence below.

[13] For example, a tender offer often requires the engagement of additional intermediaries, such as investment banks and lawyers.

(1989), highly-leveraged firms are likely to respond faster to a decline in performance than their less-leveraged counterparts because a small decline in firm value is sufficient to trigger default, and along with it the onset for value enhancing operative change. This argument implies that high leverage will hasten a firm's attempts to restructure its operating business as well its financial claims, thereby preserving higher fractions of its firm value. In case leverage is low, by contrast, default occurs only after a protracted period of operating deficiency. By the time they hit the workout stage, low-leveraged firms will have lost high fractions of their going-concern value and thus have comparatively little to gain by avoiding a formal bankruptcy procedure. Empirical support for this thesis is provided by Ofek (1993). She finds that high leverage significantly increases the speed with which a firm restructures its assets and liabilities in response to sharp declines in operating performance. It follows that if high-leverage is deemed a catalyst for efficient organizational change, I should expect the likelihood of a successful workout attempt to be positively related with the level of a firm's pre-default leverage.

4.2.2.2 Information asymmetry

The relative cost disadvantage of a formal bankruptcy proceeding is (in part) offset by several factors that impede an out-of-court agreement among all claimholders. First, the imposed automatic stay provision under bankruptcy protects the debtor's estate from harassment by individual creditors. In a distress situation, individual creditors have an incentive to "run on the debtor" to collect reimbursement or seize collateral. In the extreme, such activity results in the famous common-pool problem that may only be resolved by court-interference. Moreover, bankruptcy may be preferable to a private workout in cases where high asymmetric information prevents fair bargaining between the debtor and creditors. As argued by Giammarino (1989) and Heinkel and Zechner (1993), a poor debtor, in a state of distress, has the incentive to avoid liquidation and disguise the firm's true condition. In doing so, the debtor may influence creditors' perception of the firm in her favor and thereby realize more favorable terms in the restructuring plan.[14] Even worse, a debtor may seek to expropriate wealth from creditors by excessively increasing the risk of the firm's operations. In a court-supervised process, by contrast, additional disclosure rules, such as a detailed inventory and a valuation of all assets, mitigate informational disadvantages of outsiders. Moreover, the appointment of the administrator eliminates the debtor's discretion for over-investment on creditors' expense. Firms with higher informational opacity between owners and creditors may therefore be

[14] For example, evidence shows that the management of troubled firms has incentives to manage earnings upwards, mainly to avoid debt covenant violation. See DeAngelo, DeAngelo, and Skinner (1994) DeFond and Jiambalvo (1994).

more likely to resolve financial distress by means of bankruptcy, even if the incurred costs exceed those accruing in a private workout.[15]

4.2.2.3 Creditor conflicts

Even if creditors can easily verify a debtor's true economic condition and control for perilous risk-shifting *ex post*, a private workout attempt may break down due to deficient coordination and conflicting interests among creditors. In a financially distressed firm, creditor conflicts predominantly arise for two non-mutually exclusive reasons, namely (1) coordination problems among claimants of a given class of debt and (2) wealth transfers between different classes of debt. The coordination problem results from the fact that if the restructuring of a certain debt class involves multiple lenders, individual claimants have the incentive to 'hold-out' or free-ride in the expectation that the concessions that ensure the success of the restructuring will be provided by others. Since all claimants have similar incentives (depending on their relative stake in the class) and mutual monitoring can be excessively costly, the restructuring is likely to fail [Gertner and Scharfstein (1991), Roe (1987)]. Typically, the coordination problem is more severe in a private workout because the adoption of a restructuring plan usually requires the unanimous consent among all lenders whose claims are in default.[16] In a formal bankruptcy process, on the other hand, the problem is less severe because the decisions of how to process the debtor's estate and how to construct the features of a reorganization plan require only a specified majority of the creditors in each class of claims. Moreover, dissenting classes can be forced to comply with the plan under the code's '*Obstruktionsverbot*' provision.

It is intuitive that the coordination problem increases with the number of creditors participating in the restructuring plan [e.g. Bolton and Scharfstein (1996)]. This holds in particular for public debt contracts, which are often placed in the hands of a dispersed number of bondholders.[17] In practice, direct renegotiation of public debt is often impeded by prohibitive legislation. For example, the U.S. Trust Indenture Act of 1939 prohibits any voting mechanism, other than unanimity, to alter any features of its outstanding public debt. Similarly, the German Debenture Law (*Schuldverschreibungsgesetz*) of 1899 prohibits any modification of an outstanding bond's principal unless explicitly ordered by a bankruptcy judge. As a result, private restructuring of publicly traded debt mostly

[15] In fact, Giammarino (1989) shows that poorly informed creditors may prefer bankruptcy even in the extreme case where private renegotiation is completely costless.

[16] It may even require the consent of those creditors who are not directly affected. This is because the adoption of the plan could in principle expropriate wealth from non-affected creditors who, in turn, could threaten to sue the firm (and other creditors). See Gilson, John, and Lang (1990), p. 321.

[17] For that reason, earlier models on debt restructuring explicitly rule out the possibility that a debtor renegotiates with public bondholders. See Bulow and Shoven (1978) and White (1980).

occurs indirectly in form of voluntary exchange offers where bondholders are offered to tender their old claims against a package of new securities with lower seniority, reduced principal, or deferred payments.[18] However, due to individual creditor's incentive to hold out for a more favorable treatment, the outcome of exchange offers is very risky. In fact, anecdotal evidence suggests that exchange offers frequently result in bargaining deadlocks that can only be resolved through bankruptcy.[19] A similar argument refers to the heterogeneity of the firm's financial claims. Trade credit in particular is hard to renegotiate because it is not only widely held but also relatively heterogeneous with respect to amount, term-structure and other features. This intricacy precludes the use of exchange offers to restructure trade credit in the same manner as publicly traded bonds. Moreover, securing a consensus among trade creditors is also thought to be more difficult because they tend to be 'acrimonious' and 'unsophisticated' [Gilson, John, and Lang (1990)].

In this line of argument, out-of-court restructuring of debt will be easier when much of the firm's debt is owed to banks [e.g. Smith and Warner (1979)]. Especially in Germany banks are more sophisticated lenders and maintain closer relationships to their clients, which makes them more amenable to restructuring their impaired claims out-of-court [e.g. Kaiser (1996)]. Moreover, bank-debt is usually more concentrated and less heterogenous than other forms of debt, which reduces hold-out problems and facilitates the coordination of claims in a state of distress. In fact, bank lenders in Germany frequently form bank-pools to control for possible coordination problems *ex ante*. A standard pool contract establishes a binding commitment for every member to coordinate its client-related actions with all other pool banks. Furthermore, the contract usually specifies a sharing rule concerning the cost of renegotiation in case of default as well as the distribution of proceeds from a liquidation or the going concern of the client [Brunner and Krahnen (2002)]. As a consequence, a bank pool may improve coordination among multiple lenders in case their common debtor falls short of any contractual duty and thus enhance the odds for a successful workout.

In addition to hold-out and coordination problems, achieving an agreement among creditors outside of bankruptcy will be hampered by the peril of wealth transfers that could

[18] While public debt restructurings in Germany have remained very sparse in general, the few that did occur were completed as exchange offers. The most prominent transactions are Augusta Technologie EUR 75 Mio. convertible bond in February 2005, Vereinigte Deutsche Nickelwerke EUR 104 Mio. straight bond in December 2004, and EM. TV EUR 469 Mio. convertible bond in April 2004.

[19] For example, in 2001 the exchange offer pursued by Brokat Technologies for its defaulted EUR 125m bond failed because the required quota for the acceptance of the plan was not achieved. In consequence, Brokat had to file for Bankruptcy under which the bondholders received a dismal recovery rate below 30% of par value [See *Börsenzeitung*, 5 February 2002.] Similarly, the exchange offers by EM.TV and Augusta Technologies were very close to fail and could only be completed because shareholders made extremely generous concessions to dissenting bondholders [See *Handelsblatt*, 16 February 2004].

surface if a firm borrows from different classes of debt. This is because allocations under any given restructuring plan can always be increased at the expense of a separate claimant class. Picture, for example, the co-existence of secured and unsecured credit-claims in a firm's debt structure. As Bulow and Shoven (1978) and Gertner and Scharfstein (1991) show, a distressed debtor will find it difficult to obtain a maturity extension or debt-relief from an unsecured lender because more senior lenders receive most of the benefits due to the reduced riskiness of their claims.[20] The incentives for a secured creditor to offer relief are more difficult to predict. If the creditor is only moderately well secured (i.e. the pledged collateral is worth notably less than the par value of the owed principal), bailing out the debtor is likely to enhance the value of the secured claim since it is the first to benefit from any future appreciations of the firm's assets. If, on the other hand, the secured claim is likely to be paid in full under formal bankruptcy, rescuing the debtor will have little effect on the creditor's position. In this case, secured creditors are harmed the least by a piecemeal liquidation of the firm's assets and thus bear only little or none of the costs accruing under bankruptcy.[21] Instead, offering unilateral relief adds risk and makes secured creditors most vulnerable to coalition forming among more junior claimants [e.g. Bulow and Shoven (1978) and Bigus (2002)]. In sum, a firm with greater debt secured by tangible collateral is more likely to file for bankruptcy than a firm with unsecured debt.

4.2.3 Prior empirical evidence

My study contributes to the strand of literature that examines the *ex post* perspective of corporate financial distress. While few studies have directly addressed the issue of this chapter, some related evidence has been generated. Gilson, John, and Lang (1990) study the characteristics of firms that are forced to restructure their debt after a sustained period of extremely poor stock price performance. Consistent with Jensen's (1989) bankruptcy costs hypothesis, they find that firms are more likely to restructure privately, rather than in-court, when they have more intangible assets and thus are particularly vulnerable to the dissipative nature of bankruptcy. This intuition is also reflected in their analysis of stock returns around the outcome of debt restructurings. They find that shareholders fare significantly worse in bankruptcy than in a workout. Gilson (1997), on the other hand, finds that transaction costs are higher in private workouts than under Chapter 11, which suggests that bankruptcy may offer some neglected benefits for the debtor. Most likely, the ambiguity of the obtained evidence is due to some of the uniquely debtor-friendly features

[20] This prediction is a variant of the debt-overhang problem introduced by Myers (1977), which suggests that it is difficult to raise new financing when at least some of the proceeds go to pay off existing creditors.

[21] This holds especially under German bankruptcy legislation, which offers secured ('absonderungsberechtigt') creditors reimbursement prior to all common insolvency creditors.

of Chapter 11 that may induce some debtors to actually seek bankruptcy.[22] Asquith, Gertner, and Scharfstein (1994) study the restructuring activities for a sample of high-yield bond issuers that became distressed. Among their key findings is that conflicts of interests and coordination problems between private and public lenders impede successful private workouts. In their sample, banks never unilaterally forgive debt when the firm has subordinated bonds outstanding. The hold-out problem is elaborated upon by James (1995) who finds that banks are more likely to forgive principal and take equity if less of the outstanding debt is owed to public lenders or if public debt claims are impaired in the same manner. Collectively, these results are consistent with the assertion of Gertner and Scharfstein (1991) that the existence of public debt issues in a firm's capital structure presents the most severe impediment to efficient debt restructuring.

In Germany, public debt plays only a very limited role in the financing of corporations. Therefore, creditor conflicts involving public debt claims are less likely to significantly affect the bankruptcy decision. Instead, it is likely that creditor conflicts in Germany restrict to coordination problems among bank lenders and conflicts of interest between different classes of private debt. Consistent with this argument, Brunner and Krahnen (2002) find that banks of distressed lenders often engage in pool formation to avoid bargaining deadlocks *ex post*. In addition, they find bank-pools to significantly enhance the chances of a successful workout and to effectively shorten the length of the restructuring interval. However, bank-pools only work effectively if the overall number of banks participating in the pool is small. Their evidence is in line with the prediction by Bolton and Scharfstein (1996) that coordination *ex post* is hampered as the number of votes required to reach a consensus increases. Using a previously not obtainable data set, my own empirical analysis in this chapter builds on and and significantly extends the previous work by Gilson, John, and Lang (1990) and Brunner and Krahnen (2002). To my knowledge, I provide the first comprehensive examination of the corporate bankruptcy decision in a strongly creditor-friendly institutional setting. I study the impact of firm value, capital structure, and coordination of different types of creditors. Moreover, I examine market valuation effects of the different outcomes of debt restructuring attempts and relate my findings to the microstructure of Germany's revised bankruptcy legislation.

[22] Evidence by Hotchkiss (1995) also point in the direction that insolvent firms may use Chapter 11 bankruptcy as an entrenchment device. She finds that the majority of firms emerge from bankruptcy as stand alone entities but continue to perform poorly.

4.3 Data and hypotheses

4.3.1 Sampling procedure

Identifying firms that seek to restructure all or part of their outstanding debt claims is not a straightforward procedure because there exist hardly any legal or institutional indicators as to what constitutes a debt restructuring attempt. Moreover, my research question demands that I restrict my attention to defaulting or close-to-defaulting firms and thus preclude from my analysis debt restructuring activities undertaken by non-distressed entities. To meet these requirements I conduct a news research in the BÖRSENZEITUNG (the gazette of all German stock exchanges), LEXIS-NEXIS, and the DOWJONES&REUTERS news retrieval (FACTIVA) for all firms in the initial distress sample.[23] A firm is assigned to the sub-sample of debt restructurings if it can be inferred from the news research that the firm faces an actual or imminent default and attempts to restructure all or part of its outstanding debt.

Following Gilson, John, and Lang (1990), I define a debt restructuring as a transaction in which a firm modifies the structure of its debt with one of the following consequences: (1) required interest or principal payment on a specific debt contract are waived or reduced, (2) the maturity of a specific debt contract is extended, (3) a firm receives an entirely new contract (fresh money) which helps it remedy the default on another, or (4) creditors are given securities with residual or mezzanine claim in exchange for their fixed claim. This categorization is not without difficulties: As Kiefer (2003) points out, 'hard' evidence of a debt restructuring can only be found in cases of debt forgiveness for this is the only measure that has to be reported as exceptional item in the firm's profit and loss account. Beyond the amount forgiven neither banks nor firms have to report the details of a restructuring. For any further information about creditors modifying their claims I have to rely on the aforementioned sources. Therefore, the relative frequencies of the observed restructuring outcomes may not be entirely accurate.[24]

A restructuring attempt is classified as successful if, through the consummation of the transaction, the firm manages to avoid bankruptcy. Importantly, this solely implies that the *current default* is resolved privately and does not rule out the possibility that the firm encounters financial distress again in the future. Conversely, a restructuring attempt is classified as unsuccessful if the firm fails to obtain the desired debt relief and in consequence files for formal bankruptcy proceedings. By this means, I identify a total

[23] The selection process for the initial distress sample, the structure of the data set, and the used data sources are discussed extensively in Chapter 2 of this thesis.

[24] I also sample attempts of public debt restructurings. However, with only 4 observations public debt restructurings play a minuscule role in my sample.

Table 4.1: Composition of distressed debt restructurings over sampling period

Time series of observed distressed debt restructuring attempts between 1997 and 2004. A debt restructuring attempt is defined as any effort undertaken by the debtor to rearrange its debt structure in response to an actual or imminent default. If the firm fails in this pursuit and consequently files for bankruptcy the attempt is classified as unsuccessful. Information on debt restructuring attempts is obtained from text analyses conducted in the BÖRSENZEITUNG, LEXIS-NEXIS, and the DOWJONES&REUTERS news retrieval.

Year	Number of debt restructuring attempts	Number of successful restructurings	Number of bankruptcy filings
1997	4	4	0
1998	1	1	0
1999	3	3	0
2000	4	2	2
2001	22	10	12
2002	41	14	27
2003	21	10	11
2004	20	13	7
Total	116	57	59

of 123 debt restructuring attempts of which I have to eliminate seven transactions due to missing balance sheet information for the years prior to the restructuring. My final sample thus consists of 116 debt restructuring attempts undertaken by 98 firms between 1997 and 2004 of which 57 are classified as successful and 59 are classified as unsuccessful. Multiple restructuring attempts per firm are included if they are at least six months apart and if the initial attempt was classified as successful. In the following analysis of this chapter I restrict my attention to this sub-sample of firms.

Table 4.1 contains the time series of the observed debt restructuring attempts over the sampling period between 1997 and 2004. Evidently, the bulk of the debt restructuring activity is concentrated in the years 2000-2003. This coincides with the collapse of technology, telecoms, and media stock and the onset of the general economic recession early in the new decade. Table 4.1 also partitions the total sample into successful and failed transactions. The total sample is almost evenly divided between the two subsets. Except for the first three years (when the absolute number of transactions is small) there seems to be no time trend in the observed failure rate.[25]

[25] I cannot rule out that this trend in the beginning of the sampling period is influenced by the legislative reform in 1999. However, due to the extremely small sample size in these years, I cannot inspect this issue statistically.

Table 4.2: Sample summary statistics

Selected mean and median attributes for the sample of 116 distressed debt restructurings between 1997 and 2004. Figures are based on the last available business year predating the onset of restructuring. All variables are reported on firm-level as well as net of industry effects. Industry-adjusted values are based on the universe of firms in the same two-digit FTSE Global Classification industry code. *Leverage* is book value of total liabilities over market value of common equity plus book value of total liabilities. *Coverage* is Ebit over total interest expenses. *Return on assets* is Ebit before depreciation and amortization (Ebitda) over total assets. *Stock return* is the (unadjusted) buy-and-hold return of the firm's common stock during the 250 trading days preceding the onset of the restructuring attempt. Figures are obtained from WORLDSCOPE.

	Firm-level data			Industry adjusted data			
	Mean	Median	Std. dev.	Mean	Median	Std. dev.	N
Assets in Mio. EUR	508.29	86.98	1423.67	-1300.74	-146.49	3923.82	116
Market value equity in Mio. EUR	25.5	2.83	60.15	-5.59	-11.89	61.62	116
Leverage	0.62	0.72	0.29	0.25	0.18	0.42	116
Coverage	-37.21	-4.96	122.73	-31.04	-3.33	117.74	112
Return on assets	-0.17	-0.02	0.49	-0.21	-0.09	0.48	116
Stock return	-0.36	-0.59	0.70	-0.51	-0.43	0.78	115

4.3.2 Sample characteristics

For my subsequent analysis stock price and balance sheet data are obtained from DATASTREAM and WORLDSCOPE.[26] Detailed information on debt structure and collateralization are directly taken from the firms' annual reports. In 18 cases there was no annual report published in the year of the restructuring. For these firm's I use data from two business years prior to the restructuring attempt.[27]

Table 4.2 provides selected summary statistics on firm characteristics for the entire sample. Although I report both means and medians, I focus on the medians due to the skewed distribution of some variables, which causes the medians to be the more appropriate representation of the typical sample firm. The median firm in my sample has total assets worth 86.98 Mio. EUR and a market value of its common equity of 2.83 Mio. EUR. By comparison, my firms are considerably smaller than the sampled firms in the Asquith, Gertner, and Scharfstein (1994) study of distressed junk-bond issuers and somewhat bigger than in the Kiefer (2003) sample of bankrupt German firms, the latter being most likely due to the fact that I restrict my study exclusively to publicly traded corporations.

[26] A detailed description of the data sources is contained in Chapter 2 of this thesis.

[27] Brunner and Krahnen (2002) mention that for financially distressed firms publication of financial statements sometimes becomes irregular. However, since I focus exclusively on publicly traded corporations that are subject to more rigorous disclosure rules, this problem is less pronounced for my sample.

Median *leverage* as defined by book value of total liabilities over market value of common equity plus book value of total liabilities is 0.72.[28] The sampled firms thus exhibit the common German trait of high indebtedness that is also found, among others, by Brunner and Krahnen (2002). As noted above, *coverage* is defined as Ebit over interest expenses. By definition, the median firm in my sample exhibits extremely low coverage of -4.96, which indicates firm's disability to fulfill the debt obligations out of its operating business. *Stock return*, measured as (unadjusted) buy-and-hold return of the firm's common stock during the 250 trading days preceding the onset of the restructuring attempt, amounts to a median of -59%. Notably, this deterioration in stock value is considerably higher than the corresponding figure reported by Gilson, John, and Lang (1990) for their sample of Chapter 11 filings. The difference may be due to the more creditor-friendly setting of the German insolvency code, which often makes debt restructurings a measure of last resort. Finally, median *return on assets* as defined by Ebit before depreciation and amortization (Ebitda) over total assets is low at -0.02 suggesting that the representative firm in my sample operates at the cusp of unprofitability. This is consistent with Wruck's (1990) argument that financial distress commonly coincides with feeble economic health.

Industry-adjusted data are based on median values of the universe of firms in WORLDSCOPE with the same two-digit FTSE Global Classification industry code. The figures show that my sampled firms are considerably smaller than the median firm in their respective industry, both in terms of book and market values. Much of this difference may be due to considerable divestitures of assets of my firms in response to their ongoing financial difficulty. Ofek (1993) reports that asset sales frequently occur in response to performance declines. Moreover, my firms are more highly leveraged than their immediate peers and under-perform in terms of financial health (coverage), profitability (return on assets), and stock return. The evidence suggest that the firms in my sample are distressed not only in absolute terms but also relative to the typical firm in their industry.

4.3.3 Hypotheses and variables

In this section I translate my theoretic predictions in several (not mutually exclusive) testable hypotheses and elaborate on how I intend to operationalize the relevant independent variables. This task bears some considerable difficulty because theoretical models usually contain constructs that are impossible to observe empirically. For example, Bolton and Scharfstein (1996) and Berglöf and Von Thadden (1994) explicitly model costs of coordination among multiple creditors—an important factor in a firm's reorganization whose

[28] Note that in contrast to the previous chapter *leverage* comprises all liabilities (also non-interest bearing) to stress the importance of bank-debt in workouts.

true magnitude is never observable. Likewise, Heinkel and Zechner (1993) model *ex ante* information asymmetry as key element of financial contracting, while in reality the degree of such opacity can (if at all) only be measured *ex post*. Formulating hypotheses on the basis of theoretical models must also consider data availability and empirical feasibility. For these reasons, possible distortions arising from suboptimal approximation of latent variables—though hardly ever avoidable—are a potential caveat that should be kept in mind throughout the analysis. I formulate the following hypotheses on the determinants of a successful debt restructuring attempt:

- H1: Higher going concern values of a firm's assets and higher profitability increase the likelihood of successful debt restructuring.
- H2: Higher pre-default leverage increases the likelihood of successful debt restructuring.
- H3: Higher informational asymmetry between debtors and creditors decreases the likelihood of successful debt restructuring.
- H4: Conflicts among creditors and deficient lender coordination decrease the likelihood of successful debt restructuring.

Hypotheses H1 and H2 are applications of Jensen's (1989) argument that higher leveraged firms will trigger financial distress with only little decline in profitability and thus experience slighter corrosion of firm value prior to their default. The relative costs of formal bankruptcy are higher for these firms and thus claimholders have more to gain in a private workout. I measure leverage in two separate ways: I calculate *total leverage* as the ratio of book value of total liabilities to the sum of market value of common equity and book value of total liabilities.[29] This is to capture the effect of overall indebtedness. I also calculate a *relative leverage* measure as the share of total liabilities owed to bank-lenders, i.e. the ratio of book value of total bank-debt to book value of total liabilities.[30] This latter definition pays tribute to the argument that institutional creditors such as banks engage as more active monitors than others. Finding an adequate proxy variable for a firm's going concern value is disproportionately harder. A frequently applied proxy variable is *Tobin's Q*, which presents the ratio of the market value of a firm's assets to their piecemeal liquidation value and is measured by total market value of equity plus book value of total debt divided by book value of total equity plus book value of total debt. One problem typically associated with the application of *Tobin's Q* is that it may reflect

[29] A similar measure is applied by Ofek (1993).

[30] My relative leverage measure corresponds with the bank-debt ratio applied by Gilson, John, and Lang (1990).

some or all of the market's assessment about how well the firm will deal with its financial difficulty. In this case, *Tobin's Q* inadequately captures a firm's true *ex ante* going concern value. Alternatively, the time spent in financial distress prior to a debt restructuring may be an appropriate proxy. The panel structure of my data allows the calculation of this variable. While such a measure cannot grasp the absolute value of a firm's going concern, it may nonetheless be able to reflect how much of it has been absorbed under the burden of protracted distress. In the sense of Jensen (1989), a comparatively shorter distress duration should be directly associated with a higher remaining proportion of firm value and thus stronger incentives to rescue the firm in a private workout. Since none of the variables alone is likely to fully capture a firm's actual going concern value, I will revert to both *Tobin's Q* and *distress duration*, throughout the analysis.

Hypothesis H3 arises from the models by Giammarino (1989) and Heinkel and Zechner (1993). Because insiders have superior information about firm quality and like to gamble on creditors' expense creditors may find it in their best interest to use a court-supervised solution even if private renegotiation is less costly. As noted earlier, measuring information asymmetry *ex ante* is difficult. I therefore apply two different proxies, i.e. *firm-age* and the *volatility* of a firm's stock returns. The use of the former is mainly driven by the fact that younger firms have a shorter corporate track record, which hampers valuation of the firm's assets and aggravates sound predictions about its future development. In the same manner, high stock return volatility is an indicator of frequent and unexpected adjustments of the market's perception of a stock's value. This is more likely to occur in firms whose quality is more difficult to asses by outside investors.

The prediction in hypothesis H4 draws upon the theoretical literature on the *ex post* inefficiency of a complex capital structure [e.g. Bolton and Scharfstein (1996), Gertner and Scharfstein (1991)]. I measure creditor conflicts and lender coordination in three separate ways. First, I will again explore the impact of my *fraction of bank-debt* variable, which is motivated by the fact that bank-debt is usually more concentrated and homogenous than, say, trade credit. Thus, higher fractions of bank-debt should facilitate coordination among creditors and increase the likelihood of a successful workout. Second, I apply a measure for the share of a firm's collateralized debt (*collateral*). This is justified by the presumption that under the German insolvency code, secured lenders have a higher incentive than unsecured lenders to enforce their rights in a formal proceeding as opposed to a private workout.[31]. Finally, I account for the existence of bank-pools. A *bank-pool*

[31] I calculate to measures of collateralization. The first is the *overall fraction secured* and the second is restricted to the fraction of debt secured by *tangible collateral* (defined as debt secured by liens and assignments over plant and equipment)

is considered an effective mechanism against the hold-out problem among creditors and should therefore promote private rather than formal reorganization.

Under the prevailing legal and institutional setting in Germany, the successful outcome of a distressed debt restructuring can be assumed to have an unambiguously positive effect on shareholder wealth. I try to capture this effect by examining the impact of the choice between workout and bankruptcy on the value of a firm's common stock. Moreover, I am interested in knowing whether the market is able to predict the likelihood of a successful workout and to appreciate the cost saving associated with it. If so, my hypotheses on the determinants of a successful outcome can be directly translated into assertions about their expected impact on the observable market reactions around the onset of a restructuring. For example, if the market expects that a higher pre-default leverage ratio increases the likelihood of a successful workout and thus reduces the total costs of recontracting, higher levered firms should *ceteris paribus* experience more favorable market reactions around the initial announcement of their restructuring attempt. Likewise, if high fractions of collateralized debt signal poor survival chances, firms with relatively high amounts of collateralized debt should experience less favorable stock returns during their restructuring attempt. For an accurate round-up, Table 4.10 in the Appendix sums up the hypotheses and their expected impact on the restructuring's outcome and the corresponding stock market reaction.

4.4 Descriptive statistics and estimation results

4.4.1 Descriptive statistics

4.4.1.1 Success and failure in distressed debt restructurings

The following section further explores the anatomy of distressed debt restructurings. Because in the German domain the incidence of default, debt restructuring, and bankruptcy has not yet undergone exhaustive scrutiny the analysis in this section will deliberately remain descriptive.

Financial theory has long recognized that the timing of initiating the in-court proceedings for a bankrupt firm may have a great impact on how efficiently it is ultimately processed. How bankrupt firms actually choose between these alternative motives, however, has not yet been subject to empirical research. In my sample of 116 debt restructurings 59 firms ultimately fail in their pursuit of a private workout and in consequence file a formal bankruptcy petition. Table 4.3 contains a summary description of this subset of

Table 4.3: Summary description of sub-sample of unsuccessful debt restructurings

Summary description of the sub-sample of 59 unsuccessful debt restructurings. A debt restructuring is classified as unsuccessful if the firm is unable to privately renegotiate its debt-terms with creditors and in consequence files for in-court bankruptcy proceedings. According to the German insolvency code firms must file for bankruptcy in the events of insolvency (§ 17 InsO) and over-indebtedness (§ 19 InsO) and may voluntarily file for bankruptcy if insolvency is imminent (§ 18 InsO). *Leverage* is book value of total liabilities over market value of common equity plus book value of total liabilities. *Tobin's Q* is total market value of equity plus book value of total debt divided by book value of total equity plus book value of total debt. *Distress duration* captures the number of years the firm has spent financially distressed until the onset of the restructuring. Median values are reported in parentheses. Figures are obtained from WORLDSCOPE.

	Motive for bankruptcy filing			
Variable	Insolvency	Imminent insolvency	Over-indebtedness	All bankruptcies
Leverage	0.45	0.61	0.80	0.62
	(0.44)	(0.70)	(0.80)	(0.65)
Tobin's Q	1.26	0.84	1.19	1.10
	(0.75)	(0.77)	(0.66)	(0.73)
Distress Duration	3.20	3.00	4.30	3.50
	(3.00)	(3.00)	(4.00)	(3.33)
N	41	12	6	59

firms depending on their respective type of filing. The vast majority of firms (70%) file a bankruptcy petition upon an actual default, i.e. use the insolvency criterion as trigger for their filing. Only 6 of 59 firms report over-indebtedness as primary bankruptcy motive. Two factors possibly explain this low figure: First, over-indebtedness presents a stock-based distress criterion in the sense of Wruck (1990) that is not based on actual cash flows but requires intricate valuation tasks, which makes the fulfillment of this criterion harder to measure. Second, the incidence of over-indebtedness is usually forestalled by cash flow based insolvency, which per se obliges the firm to file a bankruptcy petition. Consistent with this argument, insolvent firms, upon the onset bankruptcy, have spent less time in financial distress (3.2 years) and exhibit a higher going concern value (median *Tobin's Q* of 0.75) than over-indebted firms (4.3 years and median *Tobin's Q* of 0.66, respectively). Only 12 firms file for bankruptcy upon an imminent default. Firms choosing this novel criterion are considerably higher leveraged (0.70), have spent a slightly shorter time in distress (3.0), and exhibit a somewhat higher value for *Tobin's Q* (0.77) than the bulk of firms who delay their filing until actual insolvency. This result is consistent with Jensen (1989) who argues that higher leveraged firms reorganize more quickly thus allowing more of the firm's value to be preserved. Given the observed more favorable prospects of debtors using the voluntary motive of imminent insolvency, their number, at first glance, seems surprisingly low. However, their rare occurrence is consistent with the argument derived in section 4.2.1 that the expected loss of control for the debtor in a formal proceeding keeps her from filing an early bankruptcy petition in cases where it would be of most value. Most likely, this is due to the prevailing stigma of bankruptcy in Germany, which views formal reorganization as ultimate retribution rather than a chance and thus prevents the majority of debtors from filing a premature, albeit more promising, bankruptcy petition. The reported figures shed some light on the bankruptcy decision in Germany. However, since the new Insolvency Code has only been in effect since 1999 and there exists no related evidence, it is yet to be determined whether these results are specific to my sample or actually mirror a systematic pattern.

Of my sampled 116 restructuring attempts 57 were classified as successful. As noted before, an attempt is classified as successful if there exists an official announcement or news account declaring the successful consummation of a debt restructuring. While this definition a successful outcome of a restructuring, by design, is easy to verify, an exhaustive description of all contractual rearrangements often is not. The reason being is that press releases or news accounts often refer only to the key features of a restructuring regardless of its true complexity. For an exhaustive sampling of the latter, confidential bank data would be necessary.[32] Panel A of Table 4.4 provides summary statistics on my sub-sample of successful debt restructurings. I distinguish between six essential—non mutually exclusive—outcomes of debt restructurings: Outright forgiveness (waiver), the extension of a debt's maturity, the swap of debt into equity, the provision of fresh money, the subordination of claims, and the embedment of a recovery agreement.[33] The latter is not in itself a restructuring device but rather an optional feature that specifies under which conditions the credit claims that are impaired by the restructuring may reinstate in the future (i.e. *Besserungsvereinbarung*).

Evidently, not all outcomes are equally common. For my sample, debt forgiveness is the most frequently observed outcome closely followed by the provision of fresh money and the extension of maturity. This result contradicts with Asquith, Gertner, and Scharfstein (1994) who find only one case out of 59 private restructurings in which a bank forgives some or all of its principal. This discrepancy is most likely due to the differing relevance of public debt financing in both samples. Asquith, Gertner, and Scharfstein (1994) exclusively sample high-yield bond issuers for which conflicting interests between private and public lenders are pronounced. In such a setting, a unilateral forgiveness of principal by a private lender constitutes an unsolicited wealth transfer to subordinate public bond-

[32] Brunner and Krahnen (2002) sample their firms relying on internal bank data only. In line with Asquith, Gertner, and Scharfstein (1994) they argue that bank-concessions are frequently accompanied by bank-tightenings, such as increases in interest rates or shortenings of maturity. I find that the latter is less frequently subjected to public reporting. Thus, while public sources may very well be sufficient to classify a restructuring attempt as ultimately successful, the reported details of a restructuring may be overly optimistic.

[33] A debt-equity swap may also contain equity-linked securities, such as bonus shares (i.e. *Genußscheine*).

Table 4.4: Summary description of sub-sample of successful debt restructurings

Summary description of the restructuring outcomes for the sub-sample of 57 successful debt restructurings. A debt restructuring is classified as successful if the firm is able to privately renegotiate its debt-terms with creditors and thereby avoids in-court bankruptcy proceedings. Multiple outcomes per transactions are possible. Panel A comprises means and frequencies of six debt restructuring outcomes identified from the firms' restructuring agreement published upon formal consummation. Panel B exhibits observed correlations among all six outcomes. Figures are obtained from LEXIS-NEXIS, DOWJONES&REUTERS, and firms' annual reports

Panel A: Means and frequencies of successful debt restructuring outcomes

Outcome	N	Fraction of affected debt	Fraction of total 57 restructurings
Principal waiver	28	0.57	0.49
Maturity extension	19	0.47	0.33
Debt-to-equity swap	6	0.45	0.11
New contract (Fresh money)	22	0.75	0.39
Subordination	7	0.40	0.12
Recovery agreement	9	0.43	0.16

Panel B: Correlation matrix of successful debt restructuring outcomes

	1.	2.	3.	4.	5.	6.
1. Principal waiver	1.00					
2. Maturity extension	0.14	1.00				
3. Debt-to-equity swap	0.20	0.15	1.00			
4. New contract (Fresh money)	0.09	0.20	0.06	1.00		
5. Subordination	0.25	0.29	-0.01	0.27	1.00	
6. Recovery agreement	0.46	-0.19	-0.14	-0.32	0.05	1.00

holders [Gertner and Scharfstein (1991)]. If, by contrast, public debt plays no or only a minor role—as for my sample—the peril of such intra-creditor wealth transfers is less pronounced.[34] Moreover, as sketched by the correlation matrix in Panel B of Table 4.4, the incidence of debt forgiveness is frequently escorted by other measures especially the embedment of a recovery agreement, which moderates the impact of outright forgiveness. The high absolute number of debt forgiveness in my sample is thus not, in itself, a puzzle. According to Table 4.4, debt-to-equity swaps only play a minor role in rescuing distressed companies. A reasonable explanation for this phenomenon lies in the legal and regulatory restrictions of commercial banks taking equity claims in distressed firms. According to German legislation, banks who take equity in distressed firms deliberately subordinate their remaining debt claims in the firm and thus always fare worse than without the swap in case the restructuring attempt does ultimately fail. Moreover, banks face the risk of a subsequent payment obligation if the value of the equity securities received exceeds that

[34] Consistent with this argument, James (1995) finds that banks are more likely to forgive principal and take equity when less of the outstanding debt is owed to public lenders.

of the debt securities given (*Differenzhaftung*).[35] Economically related measures such as forgiveness or maturity extension of some parts of the claims, by contrast, do not impair the seniority of the others.

4.4.1.2 Univariate analysis

This section contains a univariate analysis that sheds a first light on how firms in my sample choose between private workout and formal bankruptcy. Table 4.5 contrasts selected performance and capital structure characteristics of my firms by whether or not they succeed in restructuring their debt outside of formal bankruptcy.[36] Panel A contains general firm characteristics, Panel B contains performance characteristics and Panel C contains capital structure characteristics. Again, I focus on median values. To begin with, my sampled firms that succeed in restructuring their debt privately are considerably larger than firms ending up bankrupt. The median firm in the former sub-sample has a value of total assets of 149 Mio. EUR while the median firm in latter sub-sample only holds assets worth 56 Mio. EUR. This difference is statistically significant at the 1 percent level of confidence using a simple Wilcoxon rank-sum test. I also test differences in firm-age and market-segment, however both sub-samples appear to be fairly similar in these categories.

[35] See Finsterer (1999), pp. 188-191, and Brüchner (1998), pp. 156-176 for a detailed analysis of these issues.

[36] All accounting measures in Table 4.5 are taken from the fiscal year most closely predating the onset of the restructuring. Table 4.11 in the Appendix contains a supplementary analysis of firm and capital structure characteristics for year 0 in distress time.

Table 4.5: Univariate analysis of distressed debt restructurings

Selected mean and median attributes for the sample of 57 successful and 59 unsuccessful distressed debt restructuring attempts between 1997 and 2004. Figures are based on the last available business year predating the onset of restructuring. Variable definitions are from Table 4.6. Test statistics between both sub-samples are based on a simple two-sided t-test of differences in means, and on a non-parametric Wilcoxon signed rank test of differences in medians. *, **, and *** denote the differences between sub-samples are statistically significant at the 10%, 5%, and 1% level, respectively. Figures are obtained from WORLDSCOPE, LEXIS-NEXIS, DOWJONES&REUTERS, and firms' annual reports.

Panel A: Firm characteristics								
	57 Successful restructurings			59 Unsuccessful restructurings			Difference	
	Mean	Median	Std. dev.	Mean	Median	Std. dev.	t-test	Wilcoxon
Assets in Mio. EUR	724.07	149.11	1080.83	304.82	56.13	1696.63	-1.58	-3.29***
Age in years	42.05	18.00	35.71	36.87	16.00	46.81	-1.35	-0.76
Neuer Markt	0.41	0.00	0.50	0.54	1.00	0.49	1.49	1.49
Panel B: Performance characteristics								
	57 Successful restructurings			59 Unsuccessful restructurings			Difference	
	Mean	Median	Std. dev.	Mean	Median	Std. dev.	t-test	Wilcoxon
Return on assets	-0.03	-0.01	0.60	-0.28	-0.07	0.22	-3.03***	-2.55**
Tobin's Q	1.00	0.79	0.78	1.22	0.78	0.96	0.66	1.15
Stock return	-0.22	-0.38	0.47	-0.49	-0.68	0.65	-2.54**	-2.78***
Stock return variance	0.06	0.05	0.03	0.07	0.07	0.03	3.26***	3.75***
Distress duration	2.59	3.00	1.48	3.25	3.00	1.68	2.22**	1.78*
Panel C: Capital structure characteristics								
	57 Successful restructurings			59 Unsuccessful restructurings			Difference	
	Mean	Median	Std. dev.	Mean	Median	Std. dev.	t-test	Wilcoxon
Leverage	0.72	0.79	0.33	0.52	0.54	0.22	-3.72***	-2.85***
Fraction of bank-debt	0.68	0.72	0.31	0.47	0.46	0.23	-4.07***	-3.72***
Fraction of public debt	0.14	0.00	0.35	0.08	0.00	0.28	-0.91	-0.91
Fraction of secured debt	0.41	0.27	0.45	0.56	0.74	0.38	1.98**	1.41
Fraction of tangible collateral	0.25	0.01	0.47	0.47	0.27	0.35	2.75***	1.98**
Bank-pool	0.85	1.00	0.48	0.36	0.00	0.35	-6.41***	-5.52***

I also find some notable differences between both sub-samples with respect to firm performance. Firms that restructure privately exhibit higher operating profitability and higher stock returns in the year preceding the default. Both differences are significant at the 1 percent level and are consistent with the hypothesis that relatively more profitable firms will find bankruptcy more costly than private negotiation. Furthermore, I find no statistical difference in *Tobin's Q* despite my hypothesizing that firms in the workout-sample should exhibit significantly higher values for *Tobin's Q*. However, the lack of significance may be due to the aforementioned shortcomings of the *Q* variable as proxy for a company's going concern value. In fact, my firms do significantly differ with respect to my alternative proxy for going concern value, *distress duration*, i.e. the time spent financially distressed prior to the actual default. On average, firms in the bankruptcy sub-sample suffer almost one year longer from insufficient interest coverage (*distress duration* of 2.59 vs. 3.25 years), the difference being statistically significant for both means and medians. Firms in the bankruptcy sub-sample also exhibit significantly higher stock return *volatility* during the year prior to the restructuring attempt. This difference also is significant at the 1 percent level of confidence and supports the hypothesis that firms with higher informational asymmetry (proxied by stock return volatility) are more vulnerable to creditor-owner conflicts and thus more likely to restructure in bankruptcy.

Both sub-samples also differ considerably with respect to their capital and debt structure. Firms that restructure privately exhibit significantly higher pre-default *leverage* than bankrupt firms, both in absolute terms as well as in the fraction of debt owed to bank lenders. The median firm in the workout sub-sample has a total *leverage* of almost 80% and owes about 70% of its debt to banks. The corresponding figures for the firms in the bankruptcy sub-sample are 54% and 46%, respectively, all differences being statistically significant at the 1 percent level of confidence. The observed differences are consistent with my theoretic predictions. Higher levels of pre-default leverage help the firm preserve value prior to a restructuring and thus increase the incentive of claimholders to settle the case privately. In addition, firms with more bank-debt can more easily renegotiate their debt contracts because banks are more sophisticated lenders and less numerous, making hold-outs less perilous. Public debt, by contrast, plays a minuscule role in the financing of all sampled firms. Only 8 percent of all firms going bankrupt have public debt outstanding. For firms who restructure their debt in a workout, the proportion of public debt is higher at 14%, however, the difference is statistically insignificant. Finally, I find substantial variation in collateralization and lender coordination between both sub-samples. In the median, bankrupt firms have significantly higher fractions of secured debt than firms in the workout sub-sample (74% vs. 27%). The difference is similar when only tangible *collateral* (defined as debt secured by liens and assignments over plant and equipment) is considered (27% vs. 1%). Conversely, firms that choose the workout option owe considerably more debt to a lender consortium. I find that *bank-pools* are in place in more than 80% of all workouts while for all bankrupt firms this figure averages only 36%. All differences in the debt structure are statistically significant at the 1 percent level and are consistent with hypothesis H4, which proposes that well-secured and unilaterally acting lenders are less amenable to a private renegotiation.

4.4.2 Prediction of successful debt restructurings

4.4.2.1 Model specification

The evidence in the preceding section suggests that firms in both sub-samples significantly differ with regard to my empirical proxies for firm value, capital structure, and informational opacity. In many ways the observed differences are consistent with my hypotheses formulated earlier. The obtained evidence could be spurious, however, if the bankruptcy decision is in fact driven by other perhaps more decisive factors that are highly correlated with the mentioned variables but were not controlled for in the univariate analysis. If, for example, workout success is higher for firms with bank-pools solely because these firms are inherently more profitable, I cannot argue that lender coordination *per se* significantly affects the way a firm's financial distress is resolved.

To identify the *ceteris paribus* impact of my empirical proxies on the likelihood of bankruptcy, I estimate probit regression models that simultaneously relate the outcome of a firm's debt restructuring attempt to my measures of interest as well as several control variables. The dependent variable in the regressions equals one if the firm successfully restructures its debt out-of-court and zero if the firm instead files a formal bankruptcy petition. Because initial sampling is based on a variable that potentially causes default and bankruptcy (low interest coverage), ordinary Maximum-Likelihood yields consistent parameter estimates even though the sample contains more defaulting firms than the general population. This presents exogenous stratified sampling [Manski and McFadden (1983)], which allows more powerful testing of my probit specifications than would be possible using a random sample. As right-hand side variables in my regressions I prefer using firm and capital structure characteristics that most closely predate the onset of the firm's restructuring attempt. These values essentially dictate the terms under which the restructuring takes place. However, I thereby also face the possibility of an endogeneity problem. Endogeneity may result from the fact that some of my firms, by design, have spent several years in financial distress prior to the actual default. This could produce a 'meltdown' in some of the independent variables, which could cause them to be correlated with the error term in the original equation. I will confront this issue further below using a two-step augmented regression procedure as suggested by Davidson and MacKinnon (1993).

4.4.2.2 Multivariate analysis

Table 4.6 contains the maximum-likelihood estimates of several probit regression models. The coefficients for the independent variables are reported as marginal effects. Column 1 shows the results from the full model, i.e. when all hypotheses are tested simultaneously. Column 2 focuses on leverage and firm value in order to explicitly test hypotheses H1 and H2. Column 3 isolates hypotheses H1 and H3 by including the proxies for informational asymmetry. Finally, column 4 isolates hypotheses H1 and H4 by controlling for lender coordination and debt heterogeneity. As control variables, I use *firm size* measured as the logarithm of total assets, a dummy variable *Neuer Markt* indicating whether the firm was formerly listed on the growth segment of the German Stock Exchange, and a dummy variable *back-to-back restructuring* that equals one if the respective restructuring attempt results from a repeated default within the sampling period. Under the hypothesis that creditors, in deciding whether to bankrupt or resuscitate the debtor, solely focus on expected payoffs, the back-to-back dummy will remain insignificant.

From the results in Table 4.6 the following inference can be drawn: First, higher pre-default *leverage* significantly improves the chances of a successful workout attempt. The *leverage* variable has the predicted positive sign in all four regressions and is statistically significant at the 10% and 5% level of confidence, respectively.[37] Second, a successful workout is significantly more likely, the shorter the time a firm has been burdened with distress prior to defaulting. The variable *distress duration* is negative and significant in all regressions at a minimum of the 5% level of confidence. These first two results are consistent with the hypotheses H1 and H2, which predict that high leverage may serve as catalyst for value-preserving reorganization and that firms with relatively higher going-concern value are more likely to restructure privately.

[37] The decrease in statistical significance in models 1 and 4 is most likely due to the inclusion of the bank-pool variable in these regressions. Both variables are positively and significantly correlated (0.53, with a p-value of 0.000), see Appendix.

Table 4.6: Multivariate analysis of distressed debt restructurings

Maximum-Likelihood estimation of probit regressions that simultaneously relate the outcome of a debt restructuring attempt to a vector of explanatory variables. The dependent variable takes the value of one if a firm successfully restructures its debt with creditors, and the value of zero if it files for bankruptcy under the new insolvency code. Regressions are based on a sample of 116 distressed debt restructurings by publicly listed corporations in Germany between 1997 and 2004. All accounting measures are from the last available business year ending before the onset of the restructuring. *Leverage* is book value of total liabilities over market value of common equity plus book value of total liabilities. *Fraction of bank-debt* is total bank-debt over total liabilities. *Return on assets* is Ebitda over total assets. *Distress duration* captures the number of years the firm has suffered from insufficient interest coverage ratios prior the onset of the restructuring. *Collateral* is the fraction of total debt secured by statutory liens or assignments over tangible assets. *Bank-pool* is a dummy variable that equals one if the firm borrows from a pool of concerted lenders, and zero otherwise. *Age* presents a dummy variable that assumes the value of one if the firm is older than the median firm in the sample, and the value of zero otherwise. *Neuer Markt* presents a dummy variable that equals one if the firm was listed on the former growth segment of the German stock exchange, and zero otherwise. *Volatility* captures the standard deviation of a firm's stock return during the 250 days preceding the onset of the restructuring. Finally, *Back-to-back restructuring* is a dummy variable assuming the value of one if the firm pursues a restructuring for a repeated time within the sampling period, and the value of zero if the observed attempt is the first of its kind within the sampling period. Each model contains the coefficient estimates reported as marginal effects for all continuous variables and as discrete changes for all dummy variables from 0 to 1. Robust asymptotic standard errors are reported in parentheses. *, **, and *** denote the parameters are statistically significant at the 10%, 5%, and 1% level, respectively. The reported R^2 is the McFadden (1973) measure. The Wald χ^2 statistic tests the hypothesis that all coefficients in the model are simultaneously equal to zero.

	Model 1		Model 2		Model 3		Model 4	
	dF/dx	se	dF/dx	se	dF/dx	se	dF/dx	se
Log (Assets)	0.013	(0.043)	0.059	(0.038)	0.055	(0.041)	-0.023	(0.037)
Leverage	0.536	(0.318)*	0.590	(0.239)**	0.597	(0.248)**	0.542	(0.312)*
Fraction of bank-debt	1.122	(0.341)***	0.609	(0.208)***	0.604	(0.216)***	1.088	(0.329)***
Return on assets	0.078	(0.097)	0.228	(0.128)*	0.205	(0.121)*	0.088	(0.095)
Distress duration	-0.135	(0.047)***	-0.089	(0.039)**	-0.084	(0.039)**	-0.132	(0.049)***
Collateral	-0.733	(0.214)***					-0.705	(0.219)***
Bank-pool	0.561	(0.111)***					0.564	(0.106)***
Age	-0.097	(0.187)			-0.083	(0.149)		
Volatility	-1.598	(2.874)			-2.320	(2.421)		
Neuer Markt	0.284	(0.185)	0.091	(0.133)	0.081	(0.162)	0.227	(0.155)
Back-to-back restructuring	-0.272	(0.129)**	-0.346	(0.125)**	-0.339	(0.124)**	-0.274	(0.128)*
N	116		116		116		116	
Adjusted-R^2	0.344		0.183		0.173		0.371	
χ^2	32.74	***	41.56	***	44.37	***	27.92	***

Third, the amount of bank-debt significantly affects the bankruptcy decision. The estimated coefficient on the *fraction of bank-debt* variable has the predicted positive sign and his highly significant (at the 1% level) in all model specifications. Other things being equal, an increase of the bank-debt fraction of one half standard deviation around the sample's mean increases the likelihood of a successful private agreement by more than 30%. As hypothesized, the positive coefficient has two non-mutually exclusive interpretations. For one, it is consistent with hypothesis H2 because higher levels of bank-debt fortify the monitoring role of leverage. In addition, it corresponds with hypothesis H4, which suggests that hold-outs among creditors are less common when relatively more debt is placed in the hands of banks. Fourth, consistent with hypothesis H4, well secured lenders and insufficient lender-coordination strongly foster formal bankruptcy. The estimated coefficients of the *collateral* variable and the *bank-pool* variable have the predicted signs and are statistically significant at the 1% level of confidence.

Fifth, informational asymmetry does not seem to increase the likelihood of bankruptcy. My proxy variables for information asymmetry, *age* and *volatility*, are not significant in any of the regressions. This result contradicts with my hypothesis H3. I offer two possible explanations for this result. First, I may simply have used the wrong empirical proxies. Alternatively, the merit of a formal procedure in diminishing informational barriers for efficient bargaining may not be sufficiently appreciated by the firm's claimants. This may be due to relatively short "track record" of the new bankruptcy code and a longer transition period needed for investors in order to acquaint themselves with the new regulatory setting. If so, creditors may indeed prefer a bail-out over bankruptcy when in doubt about the firm's true prospects. The estimated coefficient of my *back-to-back* control dummy may be in line with this intuition. In all four model specifications the coefficient is statistically significant and indicates that, other things being the same, the sole fact of a repeated default reduces the probability of a private agreement by at least 27%. If creditors were indeed inclined to prefer a bail-out at an initial default, a repeated default may provide the right occasion to revise their initial decision and bankrupt the debtor "no matter what". This line of argument corresponds with prior research by Gilson (1990) who finds that upon an initial default, creditors become increasingly involved in corporate control, which allows them to better assess the firm's true viability.

The results in Table 4.6 hold with the addition of additional control variables. Firms' stock return as well as interest coverage remain insignificant when added to the regression model without changing the explanatory power of the other variables. Similarly, a time variable controlling for the effect of the stock-market boom between 1999 and 2000 has no impact on the regression results. Finally, the Pseudo-R^2 reported in all regressions is the McFadden (1973) measure and ranges from 0.17 in the third model to 0.37 in the fourth model. The hypothesis that all parameters are simultaneously equal to zero (χ^2-test) is rejected at the 1 percent level for all models.

4.4.2.3 Robustness checks

As noted earlier, one important concern with my cross-sectional regression results is that they depend on the applied right-hand side variables being exogenous, i.e. not jointly determined with the actual outcome of the restructuring.[38] The exogeneity assumption can be justified by the actual progress of a debt-restructuring; firms choose a certain debt structure first and then, upon a default, renegotiate the pre-determined terms. However, firm and capital structure characteristics could be determined by claimants' *expectations* about a firm's restructuring prospects in case of a future default. In that case my ordinary cross-section regressions will yield biased and inconsistent estimation results.

To address this concern I perform an augmented regression test (Durbin-Wu-Hausman) that explicitly tests for exogeneity of my explanatory variables.[39] Essentially, my test for exogeneity involves a two-step procedure. First, I estimate the reduced-form equation for each allegedly endogenous right-hand side variable as a function of all exogenous variables and suitable instruments. Second, I obtain the residuals from all first-step regressions and include them as additional regressors in my original model. If these additional regressors are jointly significantly different from zero, I must reject the exogeneity assumption. The crucial aspect in this approach is the identification of appropriate instruments.[40] The panel structure of my data allows me to use firm and capital structure characteristics from year 0 in distress time, i.e. the first year of the coverage shortfall, as instruments for most of my regressors in the original equation. The rationale behind this is that if there is an endogeneity problem inherent in my model-setup, it will be remedied or at least mitigated by the use of pre-distress values of my regressors.[41] Unfortunately, I do not have panel data for my collateral and bank-pool variables, which forces me to employ other than past-value instruments. I instrument *bank-pool* by using the total number

---

[38] Several studies simply assume away the endogeneity problem by explicitly claiming the explanatory variables to be exogenous. For example, see Gilson, John, and Lang (1990) or Chatterjee, Dhillon, and Ramírez (1996).

[39] A detailed discussion of this approach for linear as well as non-linear models is provided by Davidson and MacKinnon (1993), pp. 237-242 and Pindyck and Rubinfeld (1998), pp. 353-355. Nakamura and Nakamura (1981) show that all three specification tests correspond.

[40] I assume the variables *age*, *volatility*, and *Neuer Markt* to be exogenous. All other firm and capital structure characteristics are checked for endogeneity.

[41] See Maddala (1992), p. 357. I would have preferred using $t = -1$ values, however a large fraction of my firms was still held privately at that time and experienced distress during the first years after going public.

of borrowing relationships and a bank-ownership variable. Furthermore, I instrument *collateral* by using the year 0 value of a firm's liquidity ratio.[42]

The results of my two-step procedure are documented in Tables 4.13 and 4.14 in the Appendix. Models 1-7 contain the reduced form equations for each of the endogenous variables and model 8 contains the estimates for the augmented regression of my original model, which includes the residuals obtained from models 1-7. It is apparent that, while all applied instruments have a significant impact in the respective reduced-form regressions in models 1-7, none of the residuals included in model 8 has a significant impact on the outcome of the debt restructuring attempt. The χ^2-statistic testing whether the coefficients of all residuals are simultaneously equal to zero is 10.71 (p-value of 0.1519). I thus cannot reject the hypothesis that my regressors are uncorrelated with the error term in the original equation. From this evidence I conclude that my results reported earlier are not fraught with an endogeneity problem.

4.4.3 Evidence from stock returns

4.4.3.1 Event classification

In the following I perform two related examinations of stock returns. First, I partition the sample by whether or not a firm ultimately succeeds in its private workout attempt and apply event-study methodology [e.g. Brown and Warner (1985)] to see whether market valuations during the restructuring interval vary between both subsets. Second, I employ a cross-sectional regression analysis to relate the observed announcement returns to variables that I previously used in the probit regressions to predict the success of private renegotiation.

By detecting the impact on firm value, the investigation of stock returns may yield several complementary insights into firms' incentives to choose between in- and out-of-court resolution of financial distress. First, given the evidence in the preceding section that certain firm and capital structure characteristics can be used to predict a successful private workout, I am interested in whether the market, too, forms such a prediction.

By examining abnormal stock returns around the initial announcement of a workout attempt, I can assess whether the market uses similar information to predict the likelihood

[42] I use these instruments for the *bank-pool* variable with the identifying assumption being that the need for a bank-pool increases in the total number of borrowing relationships [e.g. Bolton and Scharfstein (1996)] and decreases in the event where a firm's creditors are also large shareholders. As for the *collateral* variable, I use liquidity as instrument assuming that lenders of cash-constraint firms are likely to demand more collateral in exchange for offering debt.

Table 4.7: Events that approximate the onset of debt restructurings

Frequency distribution of events used to approximate the onset of 116 private debt restructuring attempts undertaken to avoid formal bankruptcy. Transactions take place between 1997 and 2004. Reported numbers are based on data obtained from text analyses conducted in the BÖRSENZEITUNG, LEXIS-NEXIS, and the DOWJONES&REUTERS news retrieval.

Event	Number of occurrences	Successful debt restructurings	Bankruptcy filings
Reference to a default or imminent default	15	6	9
Firm announcement of onset of debt restructuring	15	8	7
Press reference to an ongoing debt restructuring	16	10	6
Firm announcement of liquidity problem	7	3	4
Press reference to a liquidity problem	14	7	7
Filing in accordance with § 92 I AktG	16	7	9
Unknown	33	16	17
Total	116	57	59

of successful private renegotiation. Second, by analyzing cumulative stock returns over the entire restructuring interval I am able to make an inference about the relative cost of financial distress. While I so far have simply assumed (with good reason) that fewer total costs are incurred under private renegotiation than in bankruptcy, this approach allows me to actually compare the costs of both alternatives without having to measure these costs directly [see also Gilson et al. (1990)]. Finally, comparing the abnormal returns upon the announcement of a bankruptcy filing with the corresponding returns for bankruptcy filings under other legislations offers the opportunity to compare cross-country variations of formal bankruptcy costs. Lower announcement returns for German bankruptcies than for U.S. Chapter 11 companies, for example, correspond with the argument for the more debtor-friendly setting of the U.S. bankruptcy code.

My approach requires that I identify not only the outcome but also the onset of a firm's debt restructuring. Ideally, this would mark the starting date of renegotiations between a firm and its creditors. However, the precise date of this event is only rarely disclosed to the public. I therefore conduct a news research in order to identify the first public reference to my firms' debt restructuring activity. My primary sources include the BÖRSENZEITUNG, LEXIS-NEXIS, and the DOWJONES&REUTERS news retrieval. In order to meet my requirements, such an event must refer to either an actual or expected default, an ongoing or commencing restructuring, or a severe liquidity problem. I also include mandatory filings in accordance with § 92 I of the German Companies Act (AktG) as a legally binding forerunner of many formal and informal debt restructurings in Germany.[43] By this means, I believe that I have come reasonably close to identifying the relevant dates for 83 firms (72% of the sample). As is apparent from Table 4.7, each of my classified events is about evenly divided between eventually successful and unsuccessful restructurings. For 33 observations, I could not identify a date that earmarks the likely onset of the transaction. For these restructurings the initial public reference in fact pertain to their final outcome. In some of the subsequent analysis I am therefore forced to restrict my attention to this sub-sample of 83 firms.

4.4.3.2 Analysis of market reactions during distressed debt restructurings

Abnormal common stock returns around the initial announcement and final outcome of a debt restructuring attempt as well as during the interval in-between are reported in Table 4.8. Event window abnormal returns present simple market model residuals calculated over an estimation window from 230 trading days to 31 trading days before the respective event. Since thin and infrequent trading is a commonly observed phenomenon of financially distressed firms, abnormal returns are based on Scholes and Williams (1977) estimates of the market model parameters. The used market model index is the Composite Dax (CDAX) performance index.[44]

Panel A contains the abnormal average returns upon the onset of the debt restructurings. Separate results are reported for the total sample and both sub-samples. Not surprisingly, valuation effects are negative and significant for the entire sample indicating that (imminent) defaults, *per se*, mean bad news for shareholders. Negative abnormal returns range between -3.40% at the announcement day and -26.20% during the 20 day window surrounding the announcement day. There is, however, a considerable difference in the market reactions for both subsets of firms. Irrespective of the defined event window, firms that ultimately fail in their workout attempt under-perform firms that ultimately succeed by a minimum of factor two. For the three-day and twenty-one-day announcement windows the difference in returns is statistically significant and corresponds with the assumption that the market is able to distinguish in advance, which of the firms are more likely to be successful in avoiding formal bankruptcy.

[43] According to § 92 I AktG, a firm must publicly announce if it has lost more than half of its equity book value to accommodate for its losses.

[44] The reported results are robust with respect to different indices or estimation windows.

Table 4.8: Stock price reactions during distressed debt restructurings

Stock price reactions around the onset and outcome of 116 distressed debt restructuring attempts in Germany between 1997 and 2004. Abnormal returns are based on Scholes and Williams (1977) regression estimates of the market model parameters calculated over an [-230;-30] trading day estimation window. Buy-and-hold abnormal returns are calculated following the Ritter (1991) approach. Announcement dates are obtained from the BÖRSENZEITUNG, LEXIS-NEXIS, and the DOWJONES&REUTERS news retrieval. Test statistics are based on a simple two-sided t-test of differences in means between both sub-samples. *, **, and *** denote the returns and their differences are statistically significant at the 10%, 5%, and 1% level, respectively.

Panel A: Average abnormal returns upon onset of debt restructuring attempt							
	(1) Full sample (N=83)		(2) Successful attempts (N=41)		(3) Unsuccessful attempts (N=42)		Difference in means
Event window	AAR	Fraction> 0	AAR	Fraction> 0	AAR	Fraction> 0	t-statistic of (3)-(2)
[0]	-0.034**	0.43	-0.023**	0.53	-0.045*	0.34	-0.82
[-1;0]	-0.066***	0.37	-0.04**	0.43	-0.092***	0.29	-1.382
[-1;1]	-0.118***	0.31	-0.058***	0.41	-0.178***	0.22	-2.575***
[-10;10]	-0.262***	0.22	-0.117**	0.29	-0.406***	0.14	-3.118***
Panel B: Average abnormal returns upon outcome of debt restructuring attempts							
	(1) Full sample (N=116)		(2) Successful attempts (N=57)		(3) Unsuccessful attempts (N=59)		Difference in means
Event window	AAR	Fraction> 0	AAR	Fraction> 0	AAR	Fraction> 0	t-statistic of (3)-(2)
[0]	-0.101***	0.37	0.060**	0.56	-0.259***	0.19	-7.980***
[-1;0]	-0.102***	0.43	0.097**	0.70	-0.298***	0.17	-8.251***
[-1;1]	-0.164***	0.31	0.078**	0.54	-0.402***	0.08	-9.034***
[-10;10]	-0.202***	0.34	0.117**	0.56	-0.515***	0.13	-7.385***
Panel C: Cumulative abnormal returns over entire restructuring interval							
	(1) Full sample (N=83)		(2) Successful attempts (N=41)		(3) Unsuccessful attempts (N=42)		Difference in means
Event window	CAAR	Fraction> 0	CAAR	Fraction> 0	CAAR	Fraction> 0	t-statistic of (3)-(2)
[onset;outcome]	-0.203**	0.34	0.145	0.46	-0.552***	0.21	-4.155***
Panel D: Buy-and-hold abnormal returns over entire restructuring interval							
	(1) Full sample (N=83)		(2) Successful attempts (N=41)		(3) Unsuccessful attempts (N=42)		Difference in means
Event window	BHAR	Fraction> 0	BHAR	Fraction> 0	BHAR	Fraction> 0	t-statistic of (3)-(2)
[onset;outcome]	-0.334***	0.13	-0.100	0.24	-0.568***	0.02	-5.170***

Abnormal returns for both sub-samples upon the announcement of the final outcome of the restructuring attempt are reported in Panel B of Table 4.8. As predicted, firms announcing a filing of a bankruptcy petition as consequence of a failed workout attempt experience significantly negative market valuations; average abnormal returns for the bankruptcy sub-sample amount to up to -51.5% during the 20 day window around the bankruptcy filing. For the announcement of a successful private agreement, corresponding figures are significantly better. In fact, firms announcing a successful workout attempt exhibit significantly positive abnormal returns ranging between 6% and 11.7% around the announcement.

When these results are combined with the returns at the onset of the restructuring attempts in Panel A it appears that shareholders, all in all, fare considerably better when their firms achieve a private agreement with creditors. This impression is confirmed by the evidence contained in Panel C of Table 4.8 that contrasts cumulative abnormal returns for both subsets over the entire restructuring interval. From the onset to the end stockholders of ultimately bankrupt firms suffer an aggregate loss of -55% (p-value of 0.000) while stockholders of ultimately successful firms experience cumulative abnormal returns that are insignificantly different from zero. As robustness check, I also calculate buy-and-hold abnormal returns [Ritter (1991)] over the entire interval for all firms, which produces virtually identical results (Panel D). This evidence corresponds with my prediction that firm value deteriorates more under formal bankruptcy than in a workout. In fact, when compared with corresponding returns reported in earlier studies on Chapter 11 bankruptcies, shareholder losses in German bankruptcies are considerably higher. For example, Altman (1984) finds that shareholders of bankrupt firms suffered an average capital loss of 26% during the period from one month before to one month after bankruptcy announcements. Similarly, bankrupt firms in the Gilson, John, and Lang (1990) sample experience two-day average abnormal returns of approximately -17% around the announcement of a Chapter 11 filing. The exceedingly negative market reaction for my sample's bankruptcies is consistent with my argument derived earlier, that in Germany survival chances of firms in bankruptcy are particularly low.

4.4.3.3 Analysis of cross-sectional regression results

I consecutively conduct a cross-sectional regression analysis in which I relate the observed market model residuals to my established set of explanatory variables. Ordinary least squares estimation results are reported in Table 5.6. My regressions are performed for two different sets of abnormal returns. In columns one and two estimates are based on cumulative abnormal announcement returns around the onset of debt restructurings.

Table 4.9: Cross-sectional analysis of stock price reactions

Ordinary least squares estimates of cross-sectional regressions of cumulative abnormal returns on a vector of explanatory firm-specific variables. Abnormal returns are based on Scholes and Williams (1977) regression estimates of the market model parameters calculated over an [-230;-30] trading day estimation window. Models 1 and 2 are based on returns at the [-10,10] event window around the approximated onset of the debt restructuring attempt. Models 3 and 4 are based on returns during the entire restructuring interval. All accounting measures are from the last available business year ending before the onset of the restructuring. *Outcome* is a dummy variable that equals one if the firm ultimately succeeds in its restructuring attempt, and zero otherwise. All other variable definitions are from Table 4.6. Robust asymptotic standard errors are reported in parentheses. *, **, and *** denote the parameters are statistically significant at the 10%, 5%, and 1% level, respectively. The F-statistic tests the hypothesis that all coefficients in the model are simultaneously equal to zero. The reported Mean *VIF* is the Chatterjee, Hadi, and Price (2000) measure for the model's average variance inflation factor calculated from regressions of each independent variable x on the the other x variables.

	Onset of restructuring				Entire restructuring interval			
	Model 1		Model 2		Model 3		Model 4	
	$\widehat{\beta}$	se	$\widehat{\beta}$	se	$\widehat{\beta}$	se	$\widehat{\beta}$	se
Log (Assets)	-0.066	(0.037)*	-0.066	(0.029)**	-0.241	(0.069)***	-0.232	(0.060)***
Leverage	0.471	(0.252)*	0.466	(0.212)**	0.848	(0.448)*	0.938	(0.465)**
Return on assets	0.057	(0.117)	0.047	(0.112)	0.104	(0.122)	0.087	(0.132)
Tobin's Q	-0.021	(0.071)			-0.168	(0.055)***	-0.142	(0.056)**
Distress duration	-0.016	(0.031)			0.066	(0.057)		
Collateral	-0.271	(0.124)**	-0.240	(0.120)**	-0.383	(0.175)**	-0.526	(0.179)***
Bank-pool	-0.056	(0.144)	-0.072	(0.133)	0.087	(0.236)	0.057	(0.233)
Volatility	3.003	(1.895)			1.211	(4.187)		
Age	0.042	(0.115)			-0.292	(0.203)		
Back-to-back restructuring	0.149	(0.145)			0.195	(0.219)		
Outcome	0.283	(0.115)**	0.253	(0.093)***	0.703	(0.173)***	0.588	(0.179)***
Constant	0.075	(0.535)	0.242	(0.349)	1.968	(0.941)**	1.881	(0.674)***
N	83		83		83		83	
R^2	0.256		0.220		0.464		0.337	
F-Statistic	2.33	**	3.10	***	10.26	***	6.41	***
Mean *VIF*	1.70		1.44		1.69		1.55	

This is to explain the stock market's reaction at the time when the restructuring effort initially becomes known.[45] As the restructuring proceeds and the ultimate outcome is revealed, the market can form a more accurate assessment of the total costs incurred by a specific firm. In models 3 and 4 I therefore use cumulative abnormal returns over the entire restructuring interval as relevant dependent variable. This allows me to inspect the full valuation effect accruing during a distressed debt restructuring.

The evidence in Table 5.6 suggests that most of the relevant valuation effects are already reflected in the market reaction around the initial onset of the restructuring. The estimated coefficient of the *leverage* variable has the expected positive sign and is statistically significant (at least at the 10% level) in all models. This result is consistent with my hypothesis H2, which states that higher pre-default leverage increases the prospects of a successful workout and thus reduces the total cost of financial distress. Moreover, I find evidence consistent with hypothesis H4 stating that high fractions of collateralized debt foster formal bankruptcy at the expense of total firm value. The estimated coefficient of the *collateral* variable has the predicted negative sign and is highly significant in all regressions at the 5% and 1% level of confidence, respectively. Pool formation, by contrast, does not seem to significantly impact the market reaction during the restructuring. However, this may be due to the fact that in many cases the existence of a lender consortium is publicly disclosed only *ex post*. Consistent with this argument, the coefficient of the *bank-pool* variable does exhibit the expected positive sign in models 3 and 4. I also find strong support for the assumption that the market anticipates much of the benefits associated with a successful workout before it is formally consummated. The coefficient of my dummy variable *outcome*, which equals one if the restructuring is successful and zero if the firm ends up in bankruptcy, is positive and statistically significant in all regressions.

Surprisingly, none of my proxies for going-concern value are significant in models 1 and 2. In models 3 and 4, the estimated coefficient of *Tobin's Q* is highly significant (at the 1% and 5% level) but it has a negative impact on a firm's market valuation during the restructuring. An increase in *Tobin's Q* by 0.01 decreases the cumulative abnormal return by 0.16%. This result seems to conflict with my hypothesis H1 and my finding earlier, both of which propose a positive relationship between going-concern value and abnormal stock return. However, a negative impact of *Tobin's Q* is plausible if the market does not use the going-concern value to predict the likelihood of a successful workout, but rather to assess what is at peril if the restructuring fails. Firm's with higher going concern value

[45] I use the large event window [-10,10] for three reasons. First, stocks of distressed firms are often suspended from trading when major news such as a default or § 92 AktG filings surface. Second, I cannot rule out the possibility that some of the news on a debt restructuring leaked into the market prior to my first identified public reference to it. Third, distressed securities are exposed to infrequent trading, which results in a longer time period needed for the full valuation effect to settle in.

are most vulnerable to protracted financial restructurings so that the observed negative relation between *Tobin's Q* and a firm's abnormal return during the restructuring interval is not, in itself, a puzzle.

Consistent with my earlier results, none or my proxies for informational asymmetry seems to influence the observed market reactions. In models 1-4 neither *age* nor *volatility* enter at any level of significance. This sheds some further doubt on my hypothesis H3, which proposes that higher informational asymmetry should hamper private renegotiation and thus produce higher overall costs of distress. Finally, abnormal returns around the onset and during the entire interval of the restructuring are negatively influenced by firm size. The estimated coefficient of the *log (assets)* variable is negative and significant in all models. While the overall magnitude is negligible, one explanation for the observed relation could be that large firms, in general, are higher valued than small firms and thus exhibit stronger deteriorations of value when unexpected events occur. Alternatively, larger organizations and conglomerates may find it harder to deal with financial distress and thus suffer higher losses in firm value as the firm defaults on some of its debt payments.

In all models the hypothesis that all coefficients are simultaneously equal to zero is rejected at the 5% and 1% level, respectively. Multicollinearity inspected by the mean variance inflation factor does not distort the results [Chatterjee, Hadi, and Price (2000)]. Not surprisingly, the overall fit of the model is considerably better for models 3 and 4, which is consistent with assumption that the market needs the entire restructuring interval in order for the full valuation effect of the restructuring to be reflected in the stock price.

4.5 Summary and conclusions

This study empirically analyzes how firms fare in distressed debt restructurings. Using a hitherto not obtainable data set of 116 workout attempts in Germany between 1997 and 2004 I investigate firms' economic incentives to choose between private renegotiation and formal bankruptcy as alternative mechanisms for resolving default. Moreover, I investigate the effect of the respective choice on firm-value. My sample is about evenly divided between successful workouts and bankruptcies. Taking explicitly into account the particularities of the revised German bankruptcy legislation I review the relevant literature and condense the theoretic predictions into four main testable hypotheses. The key findings of my study can be summarized as follows:

1. Workout attempts are more likely to succeed when firms are more highly leveraged and owe more of their debt to banks. In addition, firms with higher going-concern value are more likely to be bailed-out by their creditors.

2. Debt structure and conflicts among creditors also have a strong impact. High amounts of secured debt and insufficient lender coordination strongly foster formal bankruptcy.

3. There is no evidence that higher informational asymmetry between debtor and creditors increases the likelihood of bankruptcy. Instead, creditors seem to prefer a bail-out when in doubt about the firm's prospects and to deliberately bankrupt the debtor in case of a repeated default.

4. In advance of the outcome the stock market seems to be able to predict successful workout attempts and to use similar information to form that prediction. In particular, firms with higher leverage and less secured debt experience considerably more favorable stock returns at the initial announcement of a workout attempt.

5. Over the entire restructuring interval, shareholders fare significantly better if bankruptcy is avoided. Around the announcement of a successful workout, firm value appreciates by up to 11% while the announcement of a bankruptcy filing is associated with a loss in shareholder value of up to 56%. The reported loss in shareholder value of bankrupt firms is significantly higher than the corresponding loss in firm value of U.S. Chapter 11 bankruptcies.

My evidence is consistent with the theoretic prediction that formal bankruptcy is excessively more costly than an informal workout and that firms will prefer the workout option if a private bargain is feasible. One implication of my findings is that, despite increasing efforts by the legislative, formal bankruptcy in Germany is often still equivalent to corporate death. Of my 59 bankruptcies, only one firm (Herlitz AG) has so far emerged from proceedings as a stand alone entity. The corresponding figure for Chapter 11 cases is incomparably larger. Summarizing related U.S. evidence, Wruck (1990) finds that around 60%-95% of all bankrupt firms emerge from Chapter 11 under reorganization plans. The extremely poor survival chances for a bankrupt debtor in Germany are consistent with my finding that distressed firms only rarely make use of their option to file a voluntary (prepackaged) bankruptcy petition. If the prospects of participating in the benefits associated with a forestalled bankruptcy filing are dismal, a distressed debtor has no self-interest to pursue such a filing. This is an adverse incentive effect inherent in the new legislation, which aims at triggering formal restructurings early in the distress cycle. In any event, with an increasing number of bankruptcies under the new Code and longer time-series of data available, the analysis of reorganization and survival of German firms in formal bankruptcy as well as the distribution of proceeds to a firm's various claimholders should be a promising avenue for empirical research to come.

Bibliography for Chapter 4

ALTMAN, E. I. (1984): "A Further Empirical Investigation of the Bankruptcy Costs Question," *The Journal of Finance*, 39, 1067–1089.

ANG, J. S., J. H. CHUA, AND J. J. MCCONNELL (1982): "The Administrative Costs of Bankruptcy: A Note," *The Journal of Finance*, 37, 219–226.

ASQUITH, P., R. GERTNER, AND D. SCHARFSTEIN (1994): "Anatomy of Financial Distress: An Examination of Junk-Bond Issuers," *The Quarterly Journal of Economics*, 109, 625–658.

BERGLÖF, E., AND E.-L. VON THADDEN (1994): "Short-Term Versus Long-Term Interests: Capital Structure with Multiple Investors," *The Quartlerly Journal of Economics*, 109, 1055–1084.

BIGUS, J. (2002): "Bankruptcy Law, Asset Substitution Problem, and Creditor Conflicts," *International Review of Law and Economics*, 22, 109–132.

BOLTON, P., AND D. S. SCHARFSTEIN (1996): "Optimal Debt Structure and the Number of Creditors," *The Journal of Political Economy*, 104, 1–25.

BRADLEY, M., AND M. ROSENZWEIG (1992): "The Untenable Case for Chapter 11," *The Yale Law Journal*, 101, 1043–1095.

BREUER, W. (2003): *Insolvenzrecht. Eine Einführung*. Beck, München.

BROWN, D. T. (1989): "Claimholder Incentive Conflicts in Reorganization: The Role of Bankruptcy Law," *The Review of Financial Studies*, 2, 109–123.

BROWN, S., AND J. WARNER (1985): "Using Daily Stock Returns in Event Studies," *Journal of Financial Economics*, 14, 3–31.

BRÜCHNER, T. (1998): *Reorganisationstrategien für insolvenzbedrohte Unternehmen*. Peter Lang, Frankfurt a.M.

BRUNNER, A., AND J. P. KRAHNEN (2002): "Multiple Lenders and Corporate Distress: Evidence on Debt Restructuring," Working Paper, Goethe University Frankfurt.

BULOW, J. I., AND J. B. SHOVEN (1978): "The Bankruptcy Decision," *The Bell Journal of Economics*, 9, 437–456.

CHATTERJEE, S., U. S. DHILLON, AND G. G. RAMÍREZ (1996): "Resolution of Financial Distress: Debt Restructurings Via Chapter11, Prepackaged Bankruptcies, and Workouts," *Financial Management*, 25, 5–18.

CHATTERJEE, S., U. S. DHILLON, AND G. G. RAMIREZ (2004): "Debtor-in-Possession Financing," *Journal of Banking and Finance*, 28, 3097–3111.

CHATTERJEE, S., A. HADI, AND B. PRICE (2000): *Regression Analysis by Example*. John Wiley and Sons, New York, 3rd edn.

CHEN, Y., J. F. WESTON, AND E. I. ALTMAN (1995): "Financial Distress and Restructuring Models," *Financial Management*, 24, 57–75.

DAVIDSON, R., AND J. G. MACKINNON (1993): *Estimation and Inference in Econometrics*. Oxford University Press, New York. N.Y.

DAVYDENKO, S. A., AND J. R. FRANKS (2004): "Do Bankruptcy Codes Matter? A Study of Defaults in France, Germany, and the UK," Working Paper, London Business School.

DEANGELO, H., L. DEANGELO, AND D. J. SKINNER (1994): "Accounting Choice in Troubled Companies," *Journal of Accounting and Economics*, 17, 113–143.

DEFOND, M. L., AND J. JIAMBALVO (1994): "Debt Covenant Violation and Manipulation of Accruals," *Journal of Accounting and Economics*, 17, 145–176.

FINSTERER, H. (1999): *Unternehmenssanierung Durch Kreditinstitute: Eine Untersuchung unter Beachtung der Insolvenzordnung*. Gabler, Wiesbaden.

FRANKE, G. (1983): "Ökonomische Überlegungen zur Gestaltung eines gerichtlichen Sanierungsverfahrens," *Konkurs-, Treuhand- und Schiedsgerichtswesen*, 44, 35–37.

FRANKS, J. R., K. NYBORG, AND W. TOROUS (1996): "A Comparison of US, UK, and German Insolvency Codes," *Financial Management*, 25, 19–30.

FRANKS, J. R., AND W. N. TOROUS (1989): "An Empirical Investigation of U.S. Firms in Reorganization," *The Journal of Finance*, 44, 747–769.

GERTNER, R., AND D. SCHARFSTEIN (1991): "A Theory of Workouts and the Effects of Reorganization Law," *The Journal of Finance*, 46, 1189–1222.

GIAMMARINO, R. M. (1989): "The Resolution of Financial Distress," *The Review of Financial Studies*, 2, 25–47.

GILSON, S. C. (1990): "Bankruptcy, Boards, Banks, and Blockholders," *Journal of Financial Economics*, 27, 355–387.

——— (1997): "Transaction Costs and Capital Structure Choice: Evidence from Financially Distressed Firms," *The Journal of Finance*, 52, 161–196.

GILSON, S. C., K. JOHN, AND L. H. LANG (1990): "Troubled Debt Restructurings, An Empirical Study of Private Reorganization of Firms in Default," *Journal of Financial Economics*, 27, 315–353.

HARHOFF, D., K. STAHL, AND M. WOYWODE (1998): "Legal Forms, Growth and Exit of West German Firms—Empirical Results for Manufactoring, Construction, Trade and Service Industries," *The Journal of Industrial Economics*, 46, 453–488.

HEINKEL, R., AND J. ZECHNER (1993): "Financial Distress and Optimal Capital Structure Adjustments," *Journal of Economics & Management Strategy*, 2, 531–565.

HOTCHKISS, E. S. (1995): "Postbankruptcy Performance and Management Turnover," *The Journal of Finance*, 50, 3–21.

JACKSON, T. (1982): "Bankruptcy, Non-Bankruptcy Entitlements, and the Creditors Bargain," *Yale Law Journal*, 91, 857–907.

JAMES, C. (1995): "When Do Banks Take Equity in Debt Restructurings?," *The Review of Financial Studies*, 8, 1209–1234.

JENSEN, M. C. (1989): "Active Investors, LBO's and Privatization of Bankruptcy," *Journal of Applied Corporate Finance*, 2, 35–44.

JENSEN, M. C., AND W. MECKLING (1976): "Theory of the Firm: Managerial Behavior, Agency Costs, and Ownership Structure," *Journal of Financial Economics*, 3, 305–360.

KAISER, K. M. (1996): "European Bankruptcy Laws: Implications for Coporations Facing Financial Distress," *Financial Management*, 25, 67–85.

KIEFER, R. (2003): "Essays on Corporate Distress and the German Financial System," Ph.D. thesis, European University Institute Florence.

LONGHOFER, S. D., AND S. R. PETERS (1999): "Protection for Whom? Creditor Conflicts in Bankruptcy," Working Paper 9909, Federal Reserve Bank of Cleveland.

MADDALA, G. S. (1992): *Introduction to Econometrics*. Macmillan, New York, N.Y.

MANSKI, C., AND D. MCFADDEN (1983): "Alternative Estimators and Sample Designs for Discrete Choice Analysis," in *Structural Analysis of Discrete Data with Econometric Applications*, ed. by C. Manski, and D. McFadden, pp. 2–50. MIT Press, Boston, MA.

MCFADDEN, D. (1973): "Conditional Logit Analysis in Qualitative Choice Behavior," in *Frontiers in Econometrics*, ed. by P. Zarembka, pp. 105–142. Academic Press, New York, N.Y.

MYERS, S. C. (1977): "Determinants of Corporate Borrowing," *Journal of Financial Economics*, 5, 147–175.

NAKAMURA, A., AND M. NAKAMURA (1981): "On the Relationships Among Several Specification Error Tests Presented by Durbin, Wu, and Hausman," *Econometrica*, 49, 1583–1588.

OFEK, E. (1993): "Capital Structure and Firm Response to Poor Performance," *Journal of Financial Economics*, 34, 3–30.

PINDYCK, R. S., AND D. L. RUBINFELD (1998): *Econometric Models and Economic Forecasts*. McGraw-Hill, Boston, MA.

RITTER, J. R. (1991): "The Long-Run Performance of Initial Public Offerings," *The Journal of Finance*, 46, 3–27.

RITTER, W. (2000): *Unternehmenssanierung im Neuen Insolvenzrecht*. Verlag Wissenschaft und Praxis, Kaiserslautern.

ROE, M. (1987): "The Voting Prohibition in Bond Workouts," *Yale Law Review*, 97, 232–279.

SCHOLES, M., AND J. WILLIAMS (1977): "Estimating Betas from Nonsynchronous Data," *Journal of Financial Economics*, 5, 309–327.

SENBET, L. W., AND J. K. SEWARD (1995): "Financial Distress, Bankruptcy and Reorganization," in *Finance*, ed. by R. A. Jarrow, V. Maksimovic, and W. T. Ziemba, pp. 921–957, Amsterdam, N.H. Elsevier.

SMITH, C., AND J. WARNER (1979): "On Financial Contracting: An Analysis of Bond Covenants," *Journal of Financial Economics*, 7, 117–161.

WARNER, J. B. (1977): "Bankruptcy Costs: Some Evidence," *The Journal of Finance*, 32, 337–347.

WEISS, L. A. (1990): "Priority of Claims and Ex-Post Recontracting in Bankruptcy," *Journal of Financial Economics*, 27, 285–314.

WHITE, M. J. (1980): "Public Policy Toward Bankruptcy: Me-First and Other Priority Rules," *The Bell Journal of Economics*, 11, 550–564.

WRUCK, K. H. (1990): "Financial Distress, Reorganization, and Organizational Efficiency," *Journal of Financial Economics*, 27, 419–444.

Appendices

1. Summary of hypotheses and testable prediction
2. Univariate analysis of debt restructuring attempts at year 0
3. Correlation matrix of independent variables
4. Methodology of multivariate analysis
5. Results from Two-step (Durbin-Wu-Hausman) regressions
6. Methodology of cumulative abnormal return estimation

Table 4.10: Summary of hypotheses and testable predictions

Hypothesis	Theoretic framework	Explanation	Proxy variables	Expected impact on restructuring outcome	Expected impact on market reaction
H1: Firm Value	Jensen (1989)	Firms with higher going-concern value have more to gain from a private workout	Tobin's Q, Distress duration, Return on assets	Higher Tobin's Q, shorter distress duration, and higher return on assets increases the likelihood of a workout	Firms with higher firm value will experience more favorable market reactions
H2: Leverage	Jensen (1989), Harris and Raviv (1990)	Higher pre-default leverage serves as catalyst for value-preserving reorganization and thus fosters a private workout	Total leverage, Fraction of bank-debt	Higher pre-default leverage increases the likelihood of a successful workout	Firms with higher leverage will experience more favorable market reactions
H3: Information asymmetry	Giammarino (1989), Heinkel and Zechner (1993)	Creditors with informational disadvantage may prefer a court-supervised restructuring even if private renegotiation is less costly	Firm-age, Stock return volatility	Higher stock return volatility and lower firm-age increases the likelihood of bankruptcy	Firms with higher informational asymmetry will experience less favorable market reactions
H4: Creditor conflicts	Gertner and Scharfstein (1991), Bolton and Scharfstein (1996)	A heterogeneous debt structure fosters conflicts between creditor-groups and may thus prevent efficient private bargaining	Fraction of bank-debt, Fraction of secured debt, Fraction of public debt, Bank-pool	Bank-pools, higher fractions of bank-debt and lower fractions of public and secured debt increases the likelihood of a workout	Bank-pools, higher amounts of bank-debt and lower amounts of secured debt will experience more favorable market reactions

Table 4.11: Univariate analysis of distressed debt restructuring at year 0

Selected mean and median attributes for the sample of 57 successful and 59 unsuccessful distressed debt restructuring attempts between 1997 and 2004. Figures are based on the first year of coverage shortfall, i.e. year 0. Variable definitions are from Table 4.6. Test statistics between both sub-samples are based on a simple two-sided *t*-test of differences in means, and on a non-parametric Wilcoxon signed rank test, respectively.

	Successful restructurings			Unsuccessful restructurings			Difference	
	Mean	Median	Std. dev.	Mean	Median	Std. dev.	*t*-test	Wilcoxon
Assets in Mio. EUR	874.33	151.51	1903.71	380.70	58.56	1341.37	-1.61	-3.76***
Return on assets	-0.04	0.00	0.18	-0.08	-0.03	0.26	-1.20	-2.55**
Coverage	-20.54	-3.71	111.14	-38.00	-7.61	91.63	-1.14	-1.47
Tobin's Q	1.00	0.79	75.99	4.53	1.14	12.78	1.68	1.62
Leverage	0.54	0.61	0.29	0.38	0.23	0.34	-2.56**	-2.59***
Fraction of bank-debt	0.63	0.70	0.27	0.47	0.41	0.31	-2.91***	-2.72***

Table 4.12: Correlation matrix of independent variables

Correlation matrix of independent variables used in multivariate analysis. Figures are based on the last available business year predating the onset of restructuring. Variable definitions are from Table 4.6. Each column contains correlation coefficients and and their respective p-values in parentheses below.

		(1)	(2)	(3)	(4)	(5)	(6)	(7)	(8)	(9)	(10)	(11)	(12)
(1)	Log (Assets)	1.000											
(2)	Leverage	0.412	1.000										
		(0.000)											
(3)	Fraction of bank-debt	0.382	0.501	1.000									
		(0.000)	(0.000)										
(4)	Return on assets	0.335	0.237	0.145	1.000								
		(0.000)	(0.010)	(0.119)									
(5)	Distress Duration	-0.039	0.266	0.101	-0.031	1.000							
		(0.673)	(0.003)	(0.278)	(0.737)								
(6)	Fraction of secured debt	-0.018	0.136	0.291	-0.139	0.017	1.000						
		(0.846)	(0.142)	(0.001)	(0.135)	(0.848)							
(7)	Fraction of tangible collateral	0.024	0.195	0.301	-0.178	0.104	0.769	1.0000					
		(0.798)	(0.0352)	(0.001)	(0.055)	(0.265)	(0.000)						
(8)	Bank-pool	0.439	0.530	0.350	0.237	0.041	0.100	0.037	1.000				
		(0.000)	(0.000)	(0.000)	(0.010)	(0.655)	(0.285)	(0.693)					
(9)	Age	0.233	0.314	0.130	0.074	0.225	-0.071	0.162	0.180	1.000			
		(0.011)	(0.000)	(0.163)	(0.427)	(0.014)	(0.448)	(0.080)	(0.053)				
(10)	Volatility	-0.461	-0.307	-0.287	-0.273	0.006	0.040	-0.026	-0.427	-0.154	1.000		
		(0.000)	(0.000)	(0.001)	(0.003)	(0.941)	(0.668)	(0.778)	(0.000)	(0.100)			
(11)	Neuer Markt	-0.2538	-0.4532	-0.299	-0.116	-0.312	-0.043	-0.150	-0.359	-0.557	0.378	1.000	
		(0.0060)	(0.0000)	(0.001)	(0.212)	(0.000)	(0.641)	(0.107)	(0.000)	(0.000)	(0.000)		
(12)	Back-to-back	0.203	0.220	0.189	-0.007	0.338	0.238	0.253	0.109	0.066	-0.108	-0.101	1.000
		(0.028)	(0.017)	(0.041)	(0.939)	(0.000)	(0.009)	(0.006)	(0.241)	(0.477)	(0.250)	(0.278)	

Methodology of multivariate analysis

The following description of the methodology for my multivariate analysis as well as the augmented regression test is based on the general exposition in Pindyck and Rubinfeld (1998) and Davidson and MacKinnon (1993).

Mathematically, the structure of any binary response model assumes an unobserved and continuously distributed variable y^* that is related to the observed independent variables by the structural equation

$$y^* = X_i\beta + \varepsilon_i, \tag{A-1}$$

where i indicates the observation, X is the vector of independent variables, and ε is a random error. This equation is identical to those for the linear regression model with the crucial difference that the dependent variable is latent, i.e. unobserved. The link between the observed binary y and the latent y^* is made with a simple measurement equation:

$$y_i = \begin{cases} 1 & if \;\; y_i^* > 0 \\ 0 & if \;\; y_i^* \leq 0 \end{cases}. \tag{A-2}$$

Cases with positive values of y^* are observed as $y = 1$, while cases with negative or zero values of y^* are observed as $y = 0$. For a given vector X of the independent variables, the probability of $y = 1$ is given by

$$Prob(y = 1|X) = Prob(y^* > 0|X). \tag{A-3}$$

Substituting the structural model A-1 and rearranging terms, I get

$$Prob(y = 1|X) = Prob(\varepsilon > -[\alpha + \beta X]|X). \tag{A-4}$$

This equation shows that the probability depends on the distribution of the error ε, which can be modelled in several, non-linear ways causing the probability to be strictly between zero and one. In this chapter I assume ε to be normally distributed with $E(\varepsilon) = 0$ and $Var(\varepsilon) = 1$, which leads to the following binary probit model that is estimated by maximum-likelihood:

$$Prob(y = 1|X) = G(\beta_0 + X\beta). \tag{A-5}$$

In my context $Prob(y = 1|X)$ is the probability that a firms successfully restructures its debt in a workout while $Prob(y = 0|X)$ is the probability that the workout attempt fails and the firms files a formal bankruptcy petition.

$$G(z) = \frac{1}{\sqrt{2\pi}} \int_{-\infty}^{z} \exp\left(\frac{-t^2}{2}\right) dt \tag{A-6}$$

is the cumulative normal distribution function, β_0 is the intercept, and $X\beta$ is $\beta_1 x_1 + \ldots + \beta_k x_k$. Since due to the non-linear nature of $G(\cdot)$ the magnitudes of each β_i are not, by themselves, easily interpreted, I report the coefficients for the variables x_k as marginal effects on $p(X) = prob(y = 1|X)$:

$$\frac{\delta p(x)}{\delta x_j} = f(\beta_0 + X\beta)\beta_j, \tag{A-7}$$

where $f(z) \equiv \frac{dF}{dz}(z)$.

I call A-5 the original equation. Under the hypothesis H_0 that my regressors x_i in equation A-5 are uncorrelated with error term in the underlying latent variabel model A-1, ε_i, the regression of equation A-5 will yield consistent and efficient estimates of the bankruptcy likelihood. However, under the hypothesis H_1 that some or all of the x_i are endogenous, i.e. correlated with ε_i, all of the estimators will be biased and inconsistent. Therefore, if I want to know whether my approach produces correct results, I need to explicitly test for endogeneity.[46]

I consequently conduct an augmented regression test (Durbin-Wu-Hausman test), which is formed by including the residuals of each endogenous right-hand side variable z_i, as a function of all exogenous variables, in the regression of my original model A-5. Essentially, I calculate

$$Prob(y = 1|X) = G(\beta_0 + X\beta + Z_{res}\gamma), \tag{A-8}$$

where $X\beta$ is again $\beta_1 x_1 + \ldots + \beta_k x_k$ and Z_{res} is a vector of fitted values from regressing Z on a matrix of instruments. In this parlance, the Durbin-Wu-Hausman test is simply F-test for $\gamma = 0$. The results of this two-step procedure are contained in Tables 4.13 and 4.14.

[46] One alternative to deal with allegedly endogenous variables z_i is to apply Instrumental Variable (IV) estimation in which the respective variable is replaced by a suitable instrument, v, that fulfills the exogeneity assumption, i.e. $Cov(v, \varepsilon) = 0$, while being correlated with x, i.e. $Cov(v, x) \neq 0$. However, when I apply this alternative when in fact there is no endogeneity, the IV method yields estimator that are consistent but no longer efficient. See Davidson and MacKinnon (1993), p. 237.

Table 4.13: Two-step (Durbin-Wu-Hausman) regressions (Part I)

Models 1-4 contain Maximum-Likelihood and Ordinary Least Squares estimation of the reduced form equations for all allegedly endogenous variables applied in the original equation in Table 4.6 as a function of all exogenous variables. Regressions are based on a sample of 116 distressed debt restructurings by publicly listed corporations in Germany between 1997 and 2004. *No. of banks* is the total number of a firm's bank relationships. *Banks missing* is a dummy variable that equals one if the variable No. of banks is missing for a firm and zero otherwise. Bank owner is a dummy variable that equals one if a firm's bank is among its five largest shareholders and zero otherwise. *Liquidity* is cash and equivalents over total assets. All other variable definitions are from Table 4.6. The notation (Year 0) indicates that the respective values are from the first year of a firm's coverage shortfall. Each model contains the coefficient estimates as well as robust asymptotic standard errors reported in parentheses. *, **, and *** denote the parameters are statistically significant at the 10%, 5%, and 1% level, respectively. The Wald χ^2 and F-statistic test the hypothesis that all coefficients in the model are simultaneously equal to zero.

	Model 1		Model 2		Model 3		Model 4	
	Bank-pool		Collateral		Leverage		Fraction of bank-debt	
	dF/dx	se	$\widehat{\beta}$	se	$\widehat{\beta}$	se	$\widehat{\beta}$	se
Log (Assets) (Year 0)	0.167	0.041***	-0.060	0.338*	0.014	0.016	0.027	0.017
Leverage (Year 0)	0.277	0.203	0.556	0.176***	0.521	0.087***		
Fraction of bank-debt (Year 0)	-0.402	0.203**	0.213	0.186	0.054	0.084	0.575	0.097***
Return on assets (Year 0)	0.206	0.216	0.251	0.200				
No. of banks	0.006	0.005						
Banks missing	-0.377	0.124***						
Bank owner	-0.405	0.144***						
Liquidity (Year 0)			0.461	0.221*				
Volatility	-2.227	2.313	-0.649	1.698	0.017	0.863	-0.822	0.836
Age	-0.069	0.109	0.083	0.111	0.066	0.062	0.011	0.055
Neuer Markt	-0.223	0.159	0.194	0.113*	-0.021	0.063	0.005	0.057
N	96		100		102		104	
R^2	0.503		0.123		0.521		0.522	
χ^2-/ F-Statistic	60.410	***	2.380	**	18.920	***	26.780	***

Table 4.14: Two-step (Durbin-Wu-Hausman) regressions (Part II)

Models 5-7 contain Maximum-Likelihood and Ordinary Least Squares estimation of the reduced form equations for all allegedly endogenous variables applied in the original equation in Table 4.6 as a function of all exogenous variables. Model 8 contains the original equation of the restructuring outcome, i.e. model 1 in 4.6 plus the residuals of each endogenous right-hand side variable (notation (res)) as calculated from models 1-7 in Tables 4.13 and 4.14. Each model contains the coefficient estimates as well as robust asymptotic standard errors reported in parentheses. *, **, and *** denote the parameters are statistically significant at the 10%, 5%, and 1% level, respectively.

	Model 5		Model 6		Model 7		Model 8	
	Log (Assets)		Return on assets		Tobin's Q		Outcome	
	$\widehat{\beta}$	se	$\widehat{\beta}$	se	$\widehat{\beta}$	se	dF/dx	se
Log (Assets) (Year 0)	0.752	0.082***	0.041	0.019**	-0.186	0.099*		
Return on assets (Year 0)			0.126	0.248				
Tobin's Q (Year 0)					0.011	0.007*		
Volatility	-4.867	3.014	-3.147	1.571**	-1.689	3.937	-15.364	21.618
Age	0.359	0.229	0.022	0.096	-0.252	0.236	0.168	0.404
Neuer Markt	0.484	0.198	0.047	0.098	-0.075	0.205	-0.127	0.889
Log (Assets)							0.844	0.852
Leverage							-3.514	3.699
Fraction of bank-debt							1.658	1.195
Return on assets							-5.075	7.997
Distress duration							-0.177	0.065***
Tobin's Q							0.619	1.703
Collateral							1.959	3.627
Bank-pool							0.632	0.158***
Back-to-back restructuring							-0.445	0.149***
Log (Assets) (res)							-0.959	0.865
Leverage (res)							4.468	3.668
Fraction of bank-debt (res)							-0.099	1.089
Return on assets (res)							5.162	8.058
Tobin's Q (res)							-0.739	1.691
Bank-pool (res)							1.123	0.775
Collateral (res)							-2.856	3.582
N	115		114		109		95	
R^2	0.747		0.099		0.129		0.259	
χ^2-/ F-Statistic	41.510	***	4.440	***	3.460	***	52.500	***

Methodology of cumulative abnormal return and buy-and-hold abnormal return estimation

The following exposition of the event study methodology applied in section 4.3 essentially is based on the work of Brown and Warner (1985) and Scholes and Williams (1977). My description of the estimation of abnormal buy-and-hold returns below largely draws from Ritter (1991).

The daily abnormal return for the common stock of each firm i, AR_{it}, is calculated for each day of the event window ranging from -10 to +10 days around the event. AR_{it} are calculated as

$$AR_{it} = R_{it} - E(R_{it}), \tag{A-9}$$

where R_{it} presents the actual rate of return for firm i and $E(R_{it})$ stands for the expected rate of return for that firm's stock. Since $E(R_{it})$ is never known for certain it is approximated by the market model, which specifies a statistical relationship between security and market returns. The most widely used formulation was of the market model in the expected estimates relationship was adopted. It is presented by

$$E(R_{it}) = \alpha_i + \beta_i R_{Mt} + \epsilon_{it}, \tag{A-10}$$

where R_{Mt} is a proxy value that mimics the market return, in my case, the return of the German Composite DAX performance index. By standard, the market model parameters $\widehat{\alpha_i}$ and $\widehat{\beta_i}$ are calculated as simple ordinary squares parameters of contemporaneous security and market returns. However, in the absence of continuous trading equation A-10 cannot be observed at all times, which will result in errors in variables when measured returns are used as proxies for true but unobservable returns [Scholes and Williams (1977)]. With errors in variables in the observed market model ordinary least squares applied directly to equation A-10 generates estimators of the market model that are biased and inconsistent. This occurs because, as typical in models with errors in variables, the regressor R_{Mt} in A-10 covaries with residual ϵ_{it}.

Infrequent trading and thus the peril of inconsistent market model estimation is pronounced for bankrupt and financially distressed firms [e.g. Altman (1984)]. I thus calculate my abnormal returns in A-9 based on Scholes and Williams (1977) regression estimates of the market model parameters:

$$\widehat{\alpha_i} \equiv \frac{1}{T-2}\sum_{t=2}^{T-1} r_{it} - \widehat{\beta_i}\frac{1}{T-2}\sum_{t=2}^{T-1} r_{Mt} \tag{A-11}$$

and

$$\widehat{\beta_i} \equiv \frac{b_i^- + b_i + b_i^+}{1 + 2\widehat{\rho_M}}, \tag{A-12}$$

where

$$b_i^- \equiv \frac{\operatorname{cov}(R_{it}, R_{Mt-1})}{\operatorname{var}(R_{Mt-1})}, \tag{A-13}$$

$$b_i \equiv \frac{\operatorname{cov}(R_{it}, R_{Mt})}{\operatorname{var}(R_{Mt})}, \tag{A-14}$$

$$b_i^+ \equiv \frac{\operatorname{cov}(R_{it}, R_{Mt+1})}{\operatorname{var}(R_{Mt+1})}, \tag{A-15}$$

and

$$\rho_M \equiv \frac{\operatorname{cov}(R_{Mt}, R_{Mt-1})}{std(R_{Mt})std(R_{Mt-1})}. \tag{A-16}$$

Following Scholes and Williams (1977), this approach produces consistent estimates of $\widehat{\alpha_i}$ and $\widehat{\beta_i}$ without depending on detailed assumptions about the probability distribution generating the sequences of trading and non-trading times.[47]

I estimate the market model for each sample firm over the -230 to -31 day estimation window prior to the respective event. After calculating the AR_{it}, the average abnormal return for the entire sample on day t, AAR_t, is calculated as the cross-sectional arithmetic mean of the individual securities' abnormal return on their common dates relative to day 0:

$$AAR_t = \frac{1}{N}\sum_{i=1}^{N} AR_{it}, \tag{A-17}$$

where N is the number of securities in the sample with abnormal returns in day t. For example, the average abnormal return on day -5 is the arithmetic mean of the daily abnormal return on all securities five days prior to their respective event days.

Finally, cumulative abnormal returns are of interest for assessing the overall impact of abnormal returns over an extended time window. They are computed by summing average abnormal returns over a specified event window $[T_1; T_2]$ as

$$CAAR[T_1; T_2] = \sum_{t=T_1}^{T_2} AAR_t. \tag{A-18}$$

[47] Precisely, Scholes and Williams (1977) only demand that the true return generating process is uncorrelated through time.

The test statistic for any event window under the null hypothesis $CAAR[T_1;T_2] = 0$ is

$$t = \frac{CAAR[T_1;T_2]}{\sqrt{\left(\sum_{t=T_1}^{T_2} \widehat{\sigma^2}(CAAR[T_1;T_2])\right)}}, \tag{A-19}$$

where

$$\widehat{\sigma}(CAAR[T_1;T_2]) = \sqrt{\frac{1}{T_2 - T_1 - 1} \sum_{t=T_1}^{T_2} \left(CAAR_t - \overline{CAAR}\right)^2} \tag{A-20}$$

and

$$\overline{CAAR} = \frac{1}{T_2 - T_1} \sum_{t=T_2}^{T_2} CAAR_t. \tag{A-21}$$

Buy-and-hold returns are calculated as the geometrically compounded return on a stock i or a benchmark BM over a time window from day 1 to day T as follows:

$$BHR_T = \prod_{t=1}^{T} (1 + r_{i,t}) - 1 \tag{A-22}$$

and

$$BMBHR_T = \prod_{t=1}^{T} (1 + r_{BM,t}) - 1. \tag{A-23}$$

On basis of buy-and-hold returns the difference between BHR_T and $BMBHR_T$ is calculated to obtain the benchmark-adjusted or buy-and-hold abnormal return $BHAR_{i,T}$:

$$BHAR_{i,T} = \prod_{t=1}^{T} (1 + r_{i,t}) - \prod_{t=1}^{T} (1 + r_{BM,t}). \tag{A-24}$$

If $BHAR_{i,T} > 0$, stock i outperforms the benchmark. Finally, the aggregated buy-and-hold abnormal return $ABHAR_T$ is calculated as the equally-weighted average across the sample of N securities:

$$ABHAR_T = \frac{1}{N} \sum_{i=1}^{N} ABHR_{i,T}. \tag{A-25}$$

Chapter 5

Claimholder conflicts in distressed equity offerings: Evidence from German restructurings*

5.1 Introduction

When firms encounter financial distress, they typically pursue a going concern by restructuring their assets and liabilities. In recent years, several studies have tried to shed light on how firms respond to financial distress. Common operational responses are changes in organizational strategy [e.g. Wruck (1990)], asset divestitures [e.g. Brown, James, and Mooradian (1994)], or replacements of key-executives [e.g. Gilson (1989)]. Financial measures typically embrace bank-debt restructurings through workouts or public debt restructurings through exchange offers [e.g. Gilson, John, and Lang (1990), Mooradian and Harley (2005)]. Perhaps surprisingly, so far only little attention has been devoted to issues of fresh equity as a means to overcome financial distress. The ostensible rarity of distressed equity issues is based on a solid economic rationale. When a firm is financially distressed, it is likely that the liquidation value of its assets is below the face value of its liabilities. In such a setting, the firm's residual claims are essentially worthless and any infusion of equity solely reduces the riskiness of existing debt claims, thus implying wealth transfers to the firm's creditors [Myers (1977)]. This so called debt-overhang problem in-

* I would like to thank Ralf Elsas, Zacharias Sautner, Felix Treptow and Stefan Wagner for their detailed and thoughtful comments. An earlier version of this chapter was also a conference paper at the 1st International Conference on Accounting and Finance (ICAF), Thessaloniki 2006. Two anonymous referees provided helpful comments.

duces strong disincentives for shareholders to provide junior funding even in states where positive NPV investments could be financed.

There is more to the story, however. As Franks and Sanzhar (2003) point out, issues of distressed equity in workouts are much more frequent outside the U.S. domain. They argue that the important institutional difference lies in the Debtor-in-Possession (DIP) provision of the U.S. Chapter 11 Bankruptcy Code. DIP financing allows a bankrupt debtor to raise new debt funds with supra priority status even if doing so violates existing seniority covenants. This essentially nullifies wealth transfers and strongly encourages shareholders to pursue an in-court recapitalization rather than an unsolicited infusion of fresh equity.[1] Under the U.K. and German bankruptcy codes, by contrast, supra priority financing is not obtainable and formal proceedings are much aligned to creditors' interests. To sustain the firm as a going concern, therefore, distressed debtors much more often raise fresh funds through equity offerings.[2] The ability of a firm to successfully complete such a measure and the motivation of investors to subscribe the tendered shares under these circumstances is the subject of this chapter.

What factors promote the offering of distressed equity despite a potential debt--overhang? In this study I focus my attention on three non-mutually exclusive explanations that are of particular relevance for German firms. First, bankruptcy costs should matter. If bankruptcy cost are substantial (i.e. idiosyncratic growth opportunities are vast) and the gains from rescuing the firm through an infusion of equity exceed the wealth transfers to creditors, shareholders will find it in their self-interest to complete the issue. Especially in Germany where, until fairly recently, almost all bankruptcies resulted in a (piecemeal) liquidation of the debtor's estate, many of the observed offerings of distressed equity should be attributable to the bankruptcy cost argument. Alternatively, a firm's ownership structure, or changes therein, can affect the prospects of the transaction. For example, so-called strip financing in which creditors also hold equity claims (as is often the case in Germany), mitigates wealth transfers and helps solve information problems associated with outside finance [e.g. Wruck (1990)]. In a similar vein, workout specialists and strategic investors underwriting the issue can enhance the value of the restructuring making potential wealth transfers to creditors more endurable. Finally, managers may abuse equity offerings as entrenchment device to insulate themselves from hostile takeover bids. Because takeover threats increase as performance deteriorates, such managerial motives may well offset shareholder concerns about wealth transfers. In fact, in a recent

1 See Chatterjee, Dhillon, and Ramirez (2004) for a study on DIP financing. Of course, there are other factors that influence the decision between formal and private reorganization such as relative administrative costs and conflicts among creditors. See Gilson, John, and Lang (1990) and the analysis in chapter 4 of this thesis.

2 See Franks and Sanzhar (2003), p. 3.

survey of the legal literature, Prigge and Oellermann (2005) conclude that due to the great discretion granted to managers in defining the terms of a capital raise, equity issues, if designed properly, present one of the most powerful takeover defense tactics in the German domain.

Existing evidence on distressed equity is sparse. In their survey of the literature, Senbet and Seward (1995) conclude that they "are unaware of any empirical study of this issue, [and that] their impression is that new equity infusions are not frequently utilized to resolve distress."[3] The pioneering work on distressed equity is a recent paper by Franks and Sanzhar (2003) who exhaustively study the significance of the debt overhang problem for a choice-based sample of 111 destressed equity issues by U.K. firms between 1988 and 1998. They find that provisions of new equity induce considerable wealth transfers to lenders, offset in one third of the cases by lender concessions including debt forgiveness and swaps of debt for equity. Where lenders do not grant any concessions they find evidence of higher going concern value, smaller wealth transfers to lenders and higher bankruptcy costs. They also report significant losses to old shareholders upon the announcement of a distressed equity offering. In a smaller study, Kiefer (2003) documents 54 cases in which German firms were rescued through infusions of distressed equity and compares them to a sample of firms that filed a bankruptcy petition under the out-dated bankruptcy code between 1973 and 1998. He finds some evidence for debt forgiveness accompanying infusions of equity, however he is unable to document its size.

By taking a more comprehensive approach to distressed equity offerings, this study challenges and significantly extents these previous findings. For example, Franks and Sanzhar (2003) conclude that the debt-overhang problem may not be sufficient to explain why many distressed equity issues occur. They note that they "do not wish to exclude the possibility that shareholders lose as a result of the restructuring undertaken by management in pursuit of its own private benefits".[4] Yet, they do not examine this issue further. Moreover, as opposed to Kiefer (2003), I examine the ramifications of the new bankruptcy code and explicitly capture the valuation effects provoked by the restructuring.

My analysis is based on a sample of 267 German corporations that experienced sustained financial distress between 1996 and 2004. Of these firms 123 firms complete an infusion of fresh equity. This presents exogenous stratified sampling, which allows to analyze not only the terms of the issue but also the factors inducing a distress debtor to complete such a measure in the first place. In case both are interrelated my approach avoids problems of sample selection potentially incurred under choice-based sampling [e.g. Hausman and Wise (1983)].

3 Senbet and Seward (1995), p. 942.
4 Franks and Sanzhar (2003), p. 21.

I first analyze the managerial motives for the recapitalization using a Heckman two-stage selection model. I find that the propensity to complete such a measure as well as the amount raised through the issue are negatively related to the firms' indebtedness and positively related to future growth opportunities. Also, firms are more inclined to complete an issue if they are accommodated by creditors through debt concessions. Both results offer strong support for the prediction that wealth transfers to creditors constitute a major obstacle for a successful restructuring. Managerial discretion and firms' ownership distribution, by contrast, do not seem to substantially affect the issuance process. A subsequent analysis of stock price reactions confirms the wealth transfer hypothesis from a market perspective. Market reactions are significantly lower for highly levered firms. However, the market also seems to seriously contemplate motives for managerial entrenchment as well as ownership changes induced by the issue. Announcement returns are substantially lower for firms issuing equity while being subject to takeover threats and substantially higher for firms replacing top-management in the course of the issue. Market reactions are also significantly more favorable if the issued shares are subscribed by existing blockholders or incoming strategic investors. The results suggest that there exists some discrepancy between managerial motives for capital structure decisions and market perceptions thereof. I attribute this finding to the high uncertainty and informational opacity that typically burden distressed restructurings.

The remainder of this study is organized as follows. Section 2 briefly surveys the theoretic literature and derives testable hypotheses. Section 3 provides the descriptives for the sampled firms and equity issues. The applied methodology, the results and interpretations are presented in Section 4. Finally, Section 5 concludes.

5.2 Theory and hypotheses

5.2.1 Financial theory and distressed equity

5.2.1.1 Wealth transfers

In response to Myers' (1977) identification of the debt-overhang problem, which provides strong incentives for shareholders to forego valuable investment opportunities in the state of high indebtedness, Gertner and Scharfstein (1991) describe the circumstances under which distressed restructurings actually do succeed. They analyze a situation where a distressed debtor can renegotiate either with a bank-lender or with a dispersed group of public bondholders, or issue fresh equity to raise the funds required for the investment in the going concern. Any bilateral agreement will result in wealth transfers to the party not involved. For example, a renegotiation between shareholders and bank-lenders that involves some impairment of bank-debt causes a wealth transfer to the (unimpaired) public bondholders. Crucially, Gertner and Scharfstein (1991) show that the size of the wealth transfer increases when new funds come from more junior claimants. While bank-lenders only contemplate wealth transfers to bondholders, the infusion of fresh equity by shareholders will cause wealth transfers to banks and bondholders.

In this setting, shareholders will decide to provide new funds only if the NPV of the going concern exceeds the wealth transfers to bank-lenders and bondholders. Benefits from going concern may constitute profitable future growth opportunities or low liquidation value, both of which are equivalent to high bankruptcy costs. However, if wealth transfers are large, there are investments that are not undertaken despite their worthiness in absolute terms and shareholders will deliberately bankrupt the firm. The result is a costly underinvestment that linearly increases *ex ante* with higher fractions of secured and short-term debt.[5] In these cases, creditors have a self-interest to forgive or postpone part of their claims to reduce wealth transfers and thus reinstate the incentives of shareholders to complete the issue and keep the firm alive. However, because dispersed bondholders suffer from a coordination problem a restructuring of the public bond is much more expensive to implement.[6] The expected debt-concession is therefore more likely to be undertaken by the bank-lenders.[7]

In sum, following the Gertner and Scharfstein framework and related arguments set forth by Franks and Sanzhar (2003), I would expect firms to be more inclined to complete equity issues under two scenarios. First, when initial wealth transfers are comparably low and future growth opportunities are high, and second, when creditors accommodate shareholders with debt concessions. However, because banks have incentives to grant concessions, only when shareholders have no self-interest in completing the issue, I would expect debt concessions to coincide with equity infusions when wealth transfers are comparably high and growth opportunities are comparably low.

---

5 See Gertner and Scharfstein (1991), p. 1196.

6 Of course, public bonds have little empirical relevance in the financing of German corporations. Their position in the ranking order may well be taken by trade creditors, which are equally dispersed and due to their more heterogeneous nature even harder to renegotiate.

7 In the Gertner and Scharfstein model, the bank-debt restructuring not only dominates the public exchange offer for the bond but also the equity issue all together. In fact, Gertner and Scharfstein (1991), p. 1197 assert that "the firm never issues equity since an equity issue will transfer value to public debtholders not transferred by a debt issue."Clearly this statement is empirically incorrect as evidenced by Franks and Sanzhar (2003) and the sample in this chapter. However, the economic implications of the Gertner and Scharfstein model hold even if equity issues are observed.

5.2.1.2 Ownership structure

The trade-off outlined above may depend on the firm's ownership structure (or changes therein) in several ways. To begin with, overall ownership concentration might matter. Following Shleifer and Vishny (1986), concentrated ownership overcomes the free-rider problem in management monitoring, ensuring that an equity issue is completed to benefit the wealth of the shareholders. In a similar vein, concentrated ownership enhances the information collection required for any capital raise. Thus, it helps reducing the cost of adverse selection in the market and preserves the firm's going concern value. This should hold especially if blockholders themselves underwrite the shares tendered in the issue [Gebhardt, Heiden, and Daske (2001)]. If the blockholder is a family owner, however, the prospects of a successful capital raise may be reduced. Individuals and family investors are potentially cash constraint. Therefore, they have incentives to impede the infusion of fresh cash if they want to avoid ownership dilution due to private benefits of control but cannot afford to provide the money for a capital raise. Private benefits of control for blockholders are common in German firms that exhibit complex ownership structures such as cross-holdings and ownership-pyramids which cause departures from one-share one-vote [Grossman and Hart (1988)].

Blockholdings by creditors should also matter. If considerable fractions of a firm's credit and equity claims are held by the same party, it seems more likely that the external costs of leverage-induced underinvestment are internalized and thus a more efficient investment path is chosen. For example, Wruck (1990) argues that "strip financiers" have less incentives to jockey for advantage in the event of distress. Similarly, banks have more incentives to grant concessions if their equity claims benefit from their generosity. In consequence, I should observe firms with bank ownership to find it easier to tab the equity markets. However, bank ownership of distressed equity is limited by regulation, so I cannot expect banks to load significant amounts of stock in the issuance process.[8]

Finally, a firm's ability to provoke changes in the ownership structure in the course of the issue should make a difference. For example, workout specialists that combine financial might with ample restructuring experience can positively impact a firm's going concern value thus making the downsides of a distressed equity infusion more worthwhile. Consistent with this proposition, recent evidence by Hotchkiss and Mooradian (1997) suggest that the engagement of so-called "vulture investors" significantly affects firm value. They find positive abnormal returns for the target's common stock and bonds

[8] According to German legislation, banks who take equity in distressed firms deliberately subordinate their remaining debt claims in the firm and thus always fare worse than without the swap in case the restructuring attempt does ultimately fail. See Finsterer (1999), pp. 18-19 and Buth, Hermanns, and Janus (1998), pp. 238-239.

in the two days surrounding the announcement of a vulture purchase of public debt or equity.[9] In a similar vein, strategic investors that attach a high idiosyncratic value to the target's estate can afford to purchase even less marketable assets thus augmenting the firm's value over its piecemeal liquidation value [e.g. Williamson (1988)]. Crucially, to any new investor a capital raise provides an attractive vehicle to acquire a stake in the firm since it avoids paying premiums typically caused by a blocktrade of existing shares.[10] However, allowing incoming investors to pick up new shares at high discounts adds another layer of wealth transfers from old shareholders that needs to be overcome by the value they add as investors.

5.2.1.3 Managerial discretion

Most capital structure decisions are at least in part affected by managerial objectives. Thus, shareholder incentives for or against a distressed equity issue may be undermined if the transaction is fostered by management in pursuit of its own private benefits. Conflicts of interest between managers and their principals are pronounced in distress. For example, while shareholders and creditors dispute over the firm's waning resources, managers have strong incentives to ally with the side that is least likely to fire them. Accordingly, managers may use equity issues to pay out recalcitrant creditors even if doing so collides with the interest of their shareholders [Lang, Poulsen, and Stulz (1995)]. Managers of distressed firms might also use equity issues as entrenchment device to insulate themselves against hostile takeover threats. Scharfstein (1988) shows that disciplinary replacement of management following takeovers is more likely when firm performance is poor. Issues of equity, especially when completed at high discounts and placed in the hands of friendly investors, are among the most widespread takeover defense tactics that are widely covered by standard finance textbooks [e.g. Brealey, Myers, and Allen (2005)]. However, in Germany their importance is pronounced due to the great discretion granted to managers in defining the terms of a capital raise. For example, a large number of equity issues in Germany occur pursuant to an authorized capital as of § 202 AktG (*genehmigtes Kapital*). An authorized capital is granted to the management by the general assembly and allows the discretionary completion of an equity issue, notably at terms not reconfirmed by the assembly. Consistent with this view, Prigge and Oellermann (2005), in a recent survey of

---

9 "Vulture investors" that deliberately invest in distressed targets and actively engage in the firm's restructuring present a comparatively novel trend on the German capital market, which has garnered considerable attention in the financial press. See Becker (2003) and the analysis in chapter 3 of this thesis.

10 In fact, issues of distressed equity are frequently completed at considerable discounts to current share prices. See Franks and Sanzhar (2003) and my evidence presented below.

the legal literature, conclude that equity issues, if designed properly, present one of the most powerful takeover defense tactics in the German domain.

Existing evidence on the abuse of managerial discretion in distress is ambiguous. For example, Khanna and Poulsen (1995) analyze restructurings undertaken by a sample of financially distressed firms as well as a control sample of non-distressed counterparts and find no evidence that managerial self-serving behavior differs across samples. Brown, James, and Mooradian (1994), by contrast, do obtain evidence that managers' pursuit of job security and shareholders pursuit of wealth are more likely to collide in distress.[11] In this study I investigate managerial discretion by inspecting the coincidence of equity offerings and takeover threats under financial distress. Under the managerial entrenchment hypothesis, equity issues are more likely *ceteris paribus* when firms are subject to takeover speculation. Conversely, harmful issues of equity should be less likely when managers hold significant equity claims in their firm since stock-based compensation causes stronger interest alignment between managers and owners [Jensen and Meckling (1976)].

5.2.2 Hypotheses and variables

From the preceding analysis I summarize the following hypotheses on factors promoting or dejecting a firm's willingness and ability to raise fresh equity in the state of distress:

- H1: Companies are more inclined to raise distressed equity when wealth transfer are low, future growth opportunities are high, and creditors grant debt concessions.
- H2: Creditors are more inclined to grant concessions when wealth transfers are high and future growth opportunities are low.
- H3: Concentrated ownership, and shareholding by banks promote the issuance of distressed equity. Shareholding by insiders and family owners hamper it.
- H4: Concurring hostile takeover threats promote the issuance of distressed equity.

Hypotheses H1 and H2 follow directly from the model in Gertner and Scharfstein (1991). I approximate wealth transfers to creditors by the firm's ratio of *debt to assets* (Leverage), the *fraction of short-term debt*, and a dummy variable *default*. A default on privately held debt is unobservable and is therefore proxied by mandatory filings pursuant to § 92

[11] Brown, James, and Mooradian (1994) study asset sales under financial distress. They find that in some firms increased creditor pressure provokes sales proceeds to be used to redeem debt despite profitable growth prospects thus extinguishing future upside potential for equity claims. Managers in these firms, in turn, are less likely to be replaced suggesting that managers and creditors team up against shareholders.

I AktG according to which a firm must declare the loss of more than half of its equity book value. Thus, a default can be interpreted as a sudden and substantial increase in (market) leverage.

Following among others Gilson, John, and Lang (1990), I define a debt-*concession* as a transaction in which a firm obtains relief from its creditors either by a reduction or deferral of contractual payments, the swap of debt securities against securities with residual or mezzanine claim, or even a provision of fresh money. Future growth opportunities are measured by *Tobin's Q*, which presents the ratio of the market value of a firm's assets to their piecemeal liquidation value and is measured by total market value of equity plus book value of total debt divided by book value of total equity plus book value of total debt.

Hypothesis H3 captures the idea that different *ownership* structures should increase or decrease the attractiveness of distressed equity issues as means to counter financial distress. Measures for ownership type and concentration are the same as in Chapter 3 of this thesis.

Hypothesis H4 refers to the managerial entrenchment argument. To examine whether an equity issue is at least partly induced by hostile takeover threats, I gather information about sample firms that either received a competing bid or were subject to takeover speculation as reported in news accounts identified in the BÖRSENZEITUNG, LEXIS-NEXIS, and the DOWJONES&REUTERS news retrieval (i.e. firms that "heard footsteps") during the sampling interval. For example, during spring 2003 Winter AG, which initially entered the sample in 2002, received several takeover bids by Eurocoin AG, which were successfully opposed by Winter's management.[12] The definition of the *footsteps* variable is based on Lehn and Poulsen (1989) who investigate the relation between takeover speculation and going private activity between 1980 and 1987.

[12] See "Winter-Vorstand sieht feindliche Übernahme", in: *Frankfurter Allgemeine Zeitung*, 20 May 2003.

5.3 Data and descriptives

5.3.1 Sample description

The study in this chapter is based on the total sample of 267 financially troubled corporations in Germany over the period 1996 to 2004.[13] Similar to Franks and Sanzhar (2003), a firm is assigned to the sub-sample of distressed equity issuers, if it raises fresh funds through a cash deposit (*Bareinlage*) in the state of distress.[14] In order to get a more thorough understanding of the motives behind the issue and the severity of the firm's financial condition I further examine the commercial register filings and news accounts surrounding the offering. Thereby obtained anecdotal evidence clearly suggests that distressed equity offerings follow a different rationale than equity issues by financially sound companies. In fact, in most cases the filings explicitly state that the recapitalization is required to maintain the firm as a going concern. For illustration, consider the following excerpt from the commercial register's filing of CBB Holding AG, which is a typical, albeit particularly drastic, statement accompanying the equity issues in our sample:

> "The capital raise against cash deposit is part of a recapitalization program, which is essential to the continuity of the firm. [...] The holding of shares in the firms thus bears exceptional risks, which can cause the short-term loss of the entire exposure. The purchase of the offered shares should only be carried out under the deliberate consideration of theses risks." CBB Holding AG, 9 January 2004

Table 5.1 contains the time-series distribution of the sampled equity offerings over the sampling period. The German Companies Act (AktG) requires that the issuing company offers new shares to existing shareholders first (§ 186).[15] If shareholders make use of their subscription rights, the issue is completed as a rights issue to shareholders in proportion to the shares held prior to the issue (*Bezugsrechtsemission*). Subscription rights not exercised may be sold to outsiders in an open offer. § 186 III AktG specifies the conditions under which new shares may be issued under the exclusion of subscription rights and sold in a (private) placement. For example, placements require the approval by 75% of shareholders attending the general assembly unless the issue amounts less than 10% of the firm's outstanding common stock. Yet, according to commentaries, the exclusion is also justified if it offers scope for the engagement of specialized investors (*Sanierungshelfer*) that provide recapitalization services that existing owners cannot or will not offer.[16] In

[13] The sampling methodology as well as the relevant data sources are described in chapter 2 of this thesis.

[14] In-kind contributions (*Sacheinlagen*) are not considered because they are by definition inappropriate to overcome liquidity shortages. See Buth, Hermanns, and Janus (1998).

[15] For a more detailled description of the equity issuance process in Germany see Gebhardt et al. (2001).

[16] See Buth, Hermanns, and Janus (1998), § 14.

Table 5.1: Time series of distressed equity issues

Calender time distribution of a sample of 123 distressed equity offerings. Figures are based on a sample of 267 German corporations that suffered from financial distress between 1996 and 2004. Rights issues occur under obeyance of §186 AktG. Placings and open offers imply a prior exclusion of subscription rights according to §186 III AktG. Takeover offers (*footsteps*) indicate news announcements in the financial press on an existing or likely takeover offer to the distressed company. All figures are obtained from BÖRSENZEITUNG, LEXIS-NEXIS, and DOWJONES&REUTERS.

	Relative frequency of distressed equity issues				
Year	All issues	Rights issue	Placing and open offer	Firms with footsteps	Firms in sample
1996	1	0	1	3	37
1997	2	1	1	1	49
1998	2	2	0	3	71
1999	6	4	2	1	122
2000	17	7	10	13	196
2001	36	4	32	25	229
2002	18	5	13	7	235
2003	18	6	12	4	254
2004	23	13	10	0	247
Total	123	42	81	57	267

consequence, I observe an abnormally high number of placements among our sampled issues of which most embrace the subscription of new shares by financial investors and large incumbent blockholders.

Table 5.1 also provides information about the frequency and distribution of the *footsteps* events over the sampling interval, i.e. the number of firms that either received a competing bid or, according to the financial press, were subject to takeover speculation. From the figures in Table 5.1 it is obvious that footsteps, alike equity issue activity, are most common in the years 2000 and 2001, which coincides with the zenith of the technology bubble on the global stock market.

5.3.2 Summary statistics

Tables 5.2 and 5.3 present selected summary statistics of the companies in the equity issue sub-sample and the details of the equity issues. Due to the skewness in the distribution of some variables, I focus on medians rather than means. Panel A of Table 5.2 contains firm characteristics of all issuers partitioned by the type of issue and whether the issuing firm received bank-concessions in the course of the recapitalization. 20 firms received concessions accompanying their equity offering.[17] Such firms are considerably bigger and

[17] Bank-concessions are about evenly divided between rights-issues and placements with 11 bank-concessions accruing in the former and 9 accruing in the latter category.

higher leveraged than the majority of firms, which complete the equity issue as a stand alone operation. Median total assets and book-leverage in the concessions sample are roughly 150 Mio. EUR and 0.73 compared to the sample average of roughly 42 Mio. EUR and 0.47, respectively. In contrast, *Tobin's Q*, the proxy for future growth opportunities, is clearly lower at 0.63 compared to 0.95 for all issuers. The combination of higher leverage and lower growth opportunities in the concession-group is consistent with hypothesis H2 arguing that creditors have stronger incentives to grant concessions to firms in which wealth transfers are large and growth prospects are insufficient to provide shareholders a self-interest to contribute new funds.[18]

Concerning pre-issue ownership characteristics, only one substantial difference among the sub-groups can be identified. Managerial ownership appears to foster the exclusion of subscription rights for existing owners. In more than 80% of the firms in the placing and open offer category, managers hold blocks of voting stock exceeding 5% compared to only 46% in the rights issue category. A possible explanation is that managers who are also owners can more credibly convince shareholders of the necessity to exclude subscription rights in accordance with § 186 III AktG. Alternatively, this finding could result from managers using their additional power as shareholders to foster the placement of new shares in friendly hands thus promoting their entrenchment (hypothesis H3).

Panel B of Table 5.2 contains equity issue characteristics. As would be expected, the amount raised in rights issues exceeds the amount raised in placements and open offers. In rights issues, firms raise a median of 6.5 Mio. EUR, roughly 50% of the book value of total equity and 15% of total assets. Corresponding figures for placements and open offers are 2.4 Mio. EUR, 12%, and 6%. Most likely, the difference in magnitude mirrors the legal constraints that the exclusion of subscription rights depends on.

[18] In an ancillary analysis, I confirm this finding in a multivariate setting by running a simple probit regression with the bank concession dummy as dependent variable and *leverage*, *Tobin's Q* and several control variables as predictors. For the sake of brevity, the results of this analysis are not reported here, however, they can be obtained upon request.

Table 5.2: Summary statistics of distressed equity issues

Selected summary statistics for equity issues and equity issuing firms. Figures are based on a panel of 267 German corporations that suffered from financial distress between 1996 and 2004. Unless otherwise specified, all accounting measures are from the last business year preceding the equity offering. Panel A contains firm characteristics. *Leverage (Book)* is (lagged) book value of total debt over book value of total capital. *Leverage (Market)* is (lagged) book value of total debt over market value of common equity plus book value of total liabilities.*Short-term debt* represents the fraction of debt due within one year. *Tobin's Q* is total market value of equity plus book value of total debt divided by book value of total equity plus book value of total debt. *Herfindahl* is the Herfindahl index of total ownership concentration. *Family ownership* present average shareholdings by family investors or their descendants. *Management ownership* is a dummy variable indicating whether or not a member of the management team holds a block of voting stock exceeding 5%. *Bank ownership* is a dummy variable indicating whether or not one of the firm's lending banks holds a block of voting stock exceeding 5%. Panel B describes the equity issues. *Issue discount* presents the ratio of the offering price to the market price on the trading day preceding the offering announcement.

	All		Rights issues		Placings and open offers		Bank-concessions	
	Mean	Median	Mean	Median	Mean	Median	Mean	Median
Panel A: Firm characteristics								
Total Assets (in Mio. EUR)	231.159	42.097	351.695	57.993	179.403	40.377	743.449	149.770
Leverage (Book)	0.55	0.47	0.69	0.67	0.46	0.43	0.72	0.73
Leverage (Market)	0.41	0.42	0.46	0.45	0.38	0.40	0.70	0.71
Fraction of short-term debt	0.63	0.72	0.52	0.56	0.68	0.77	0.67	0.73
Tobin's Q	2.19	0.95	1.86	0.99	2.06	0.90	1.91	0.63
Herfindahl	0.20	0.15	0.25	0.16	0.18	0.15	0.25	0.21
Family ownership	0.04	0.00	0.05	0.00	0.09	0.00	0.10	0.00
Management ownership dummy	0.69	1.00	0.46	0.00	0.82	1.00	0.48	0.00
Bank ownership dummy	0.10	0.00	0.15	0.00	0.09	0.00	0.24	0.00
Panel B: Equity issue characteristics								
Amount raised (in TEUR)	17114	4363	26212	6500	11549	2416	11864	7775
Relative to book equity	2.47	0.21	1.72	0.48	2.96	0.12	0.64	0.36
Relative to total assets	0.47	0.08	0.35	0.15	0.57	0.06	0.11	0.07
Issue discount (in %)	0.11	0.00	0.17	0.08	0.07	0.00	0.20	0.02
Issue year in distress time	1.82	2.00	1.96	2.00	1.78	2.00	2.60	2.00
N	123		42		81		20	

However, it may also (in part) result from the fact that rights issues are less fraught with problems of informational asymmetry [e.g. Myers and Majluf (1984)]. The issue discount is also much bigger for rights issues with an average of 17% compared to the entire sample's average of 11%. This is consistent with evidence obtained by Franks and Sanzhar (2003) who argue that the discount in placements represents the value of free rights given to new investors, as in the case with open offers when existing owners do not take up their subscription rights. Finally, Panel B shows that infusions of equity are on average completed after two consecutive years in distress. In this respect, sub-groups are relatively similar.

Table 5.3 comprises summary statistics partitioned by the different types of investors subscribing the new shares. Following earlier studies, I focus my attention on management, existing blockholders, banks, strategic investors, and financial sponsors. The depicted categories are not mutually exclusive, i.e. offerings can be subscribed by two or more types of investors. However, due to inconsistencies across firms in the disclosure of the issue details, I only have subscription data on 106 of my sampled equity issues. Evidently, not all types are equally common. Similar to Franks and Sanzhar (2003), the bulk of issues is subscribed by financial sponsors and existing blockholders. Management and strategic investors play a subordinate role. Banks subscribe new shares in only three cases. Presented figures must therefore be interpreted with caution. Panel A comprises issue characteristics. Perhaps surprisingly, the amount raised through the issue is quite similar for all investors.[19] Solely blockholders subscribe slightly higher amounts of equity. Issue discounts, by contrast, are considerably higher when blockholders and management subscribe the issue. This may be the result of discretionary leeway for both investors concerning the determination of the issue terms. Thus, tacit collusion between blockholders and management at the expense of minority holders in this aspect appears not implausible.

Panel B contains pre-issue ownership characteristics of the issuing firm. As would be expected, firms that issue new shares to existing blockholders either through rights issue or open offers exhibit higher ownership concentration, which increases their incentives to take up the tendered shares. Moreover, prior managerial ownership is an important determinant for subscribing new shares. In the median, management holds at least one block of shares exceeding the 5% threshold in all categories other than that of bank-subscribers. Prior family ownership and bank ownership, by contrast, only plays a dismal role in determining the type of subscriber of fresh equity.

[19] We report both equity raised relative to book equity and total assets. However due to numerous cases in which the issuer has negative book equity, the quotient relating the issue amount to total assets may be the more accurate measure.

Table 5.3: Distressed equity issues by subscriber-type

Selected summary statistics for equity issues separated by different groups of buyers of the new shares. Figures are based on a panel of 267 German corporations that suffered from financial distress between 1996 and 2004. Unless otherwise specified, all measures are from the last business year preceding the equity offering. Panel A describes the equity issues. *Issue discount* presents the ratio of the offering price to the market price on the day preceding the announcement. Panel B contains pre-issue ownership characteristics. *Herfindahl* is the Herfindahl index of total ownership concentration. *Family ownership* present average shareholdings by family investors or their descendants. *Management ownership* is a dummy variable indicating whether or not a member of the management team holds a block of voting stock exceeding 5%. *Bank ownership* is a dummy variable indicating whether or not one of the firm's lending banks holds a block of voting stock exceeding 5%.

	Subscribers of distressed equity									
	Management		Financial		Strategic		Bank		Blockholder	
	Mean	Median	Mean	Median	Mean	Median	Mean	Median	Mean	Median
Panel A: Equity issue characteristics										
Amount raised (in TEUR)	33639	2160	8135	2700	13409	2000	24200	24200	22447	6000
Relative to book equity	1.84	0.07	0.25	0.13	0.66	0.06	0.71	0.36	5.06	0.41
Relative to total assets	0.83	0.06	0.11	0.06	0.31	0.05	0.04	0.06	0.87	0.13
Issue discount	0.14	0.07	0.11	0.01	0.00	0.00	0.02	0.02	0.13	0.05
Relative to onset of distress	2.42	2.00	1.68	2.00	1.66	1.00	4.00	4.00	1.72	2.00
Panel B: Pre-issue ownership structure										
Herfindahl	0.14	0.09	0.18	0.12	0.13	0.15	0.09	0.09	0.27	0.20
Management ownership dummy	0.86	1.00	0.77	1.00	0.89	1.00	0.00	0.00	0.69	1.00
Bank ownership dummy	0.00	0.00	0.11	0.00	0.11	0.00	1.00	1.00	0.07	0.00
Family ownership	0.00	0.00	0.05	0.00	0.03	0.00	0.00	0.00	0.06	0.00
N	9		39		9		3		46	

5.4 Methodology and empirical results

5.4.1 The firm perspective

5.4.1.1 Model specification

The aim of this section is to examine the determinants of a distressed equity infusion in a multivariate setting. I follow a two-step approach in which I analyze (1) the determinants of a firm's choice to complete a equity issue in the state of distress and (2) the determinants of the amount raised through the issue.[20] Crucially, both issues may be interrelated. Consider the following set of equations:

$$y_i = x_{1i}\beta_1 + \varepsilon_i \tag{5.1}$$

$$e_i^* = x_{2i}\beta_2 + \nu_i \tag{5.2}$$

For my purposes, equation (1) determines the amount raised by a firm involved in an equity issue, whereas (2) is a selection equation, describing a distressed firm's propensity to complete an equity issue, i.e. e_i^* is a latent variable. The vectors of observed explanatory variables in both equations are depicted by x_{1i} and x_{2i}. Finally, ε_i and ν_i are mean-zero stochastic errors representing the influence of unobserved variables affecting y_i and e_i^*. The parameter vectors of interest are β_1 and β_2. Because the latent variable e_i^* is unobserved, I define a dummy variable $e_i = 1$ if $e_i^* \geq 0$ and $e_i = 0$, otherwise. Equations (1) and (2) are interdependent if ε_i and ν_i exhibit non-zero correlation. For example, this is the case if firms with higher benefits from issuing equity, given x_{1i} and x_{2i}, are more likely to complete an issue. Failure to recognize this selectivity generally produces inconsistent estimates of the parameters in equation (1).

Heckman (1979) suggests a simple method to tackle this selection problem. Note that the conditional mean of ε_i can be written as:

$$E(\varepsilon_i | e_i^* \geq 0) = E(\varepsilon_i | \nu_i \geq -x_{2i}\beta_2), \tag{5.3}$$

and therefore

$$E(y_i | x_{1i}, e_i = 1) = x_{1i}\beta_1 + E(\varepsilon_i | \nu_i \geq -x_{2i}\beta_2). \tag{5.4}$$

Hence, the regression equation on the selected sample depends on both x_{1i} and x_{2i}. Omitting the conditional mean of ε_i biases the estimates of β_1 unless ε_i and ν_i are uncorrelated. The problem is to find an empirical representative of the conditional mean of ε_i and in-

[20] A more detailed description of the applied methodology is provided by Greene (2003), pp. 782-787.

clude this variable in the regression equation (1). Under the assumption that ε_i and ν_i are drawn from a bivariate normal distribution, I can derive the regression equation

$$E(y_i|x_{1i}, e_i = 1) = x_{1i}\beta_1 + \rho\sigma_1\lambda_i, \tag{5.5}$$

where ρ ist the correlation coefficient between ε_i and ν_i, σ_1 is the standard deviation of ε_i, and λ, the inverse Mill's ratio, is given by

$$\lambda_i = \frac{\phi(x_{2i}\beta_2/\sigma_2)}{\Phi(x_{2i}\beta_2/\sigma_2)}. \tag{5.6}$$

In (5.6) ϕ and Φ are the density and distribution functions of the standard normal distribution and σ_2 is the standard deviation of ν_i. Heckman (1979) shows how to estimate equation (5.6) in a two-stage procedure. A standard maximum-likelihood probit model first estimates equation (2) using the entire sample. These estimates are then used to compute λ_i for each observation. In the second step, (5.5) is estimated for the selected sample of issuing firms by ordinary least squares regression, treating $\rho\sigma_1$ as the regression coefficient for λ.

The advantage of the Heckman-approach to sample selectivity is that it allows different sets of variables and coefficients in equations (1) and (2). The Tobit model, by contrast, uses the same set of variables to determine both the probability of selection and the value of the dependent variable in the OLS regression and thus does not allow a theoretical distinction between these two. However, one concern when using the Heckman model is its sensitivity to alternative specifications. Thus, I report regression results for different subsets of predictors as well as for two different specifications of the dependent variable y.

I allocate the set of explanatory variables as follows: Because both Myers (1977) and Gertner and Scharfstein (1991) model a linear relationship between wealth transfers, future growth opportunities, and the incentives to restructure, the core interest in equation (1) is restricted to the debt overhang problem implied by these models. Precisely, I include variables on *leverage*, *Tobin's Q*, and *bank-concessions*. As control variable I include a measure for liquidity assuming that more liquid firms will raise lower amounts of external finance. Following Wooldridge (2003), these variables are also included in the selection equation (2). This is to assess whether the debt overhang problem not only affects the terms of the issue but also the censoring of the sample.[21] All remaining variables are also included in the selection model. In particular, I test the ownership and

[21] Wooldridge (2003), p. 589 recommends that x_1 be a subset of x_2 since excluding them incorrectly may cause inconsistencies.

managerial discretion hypotheses using variables for *ownership* type and concentration as well as the *footsteps* variable. Not including these variables in the linear equation (1) is an assumption: I assume that ownership and managerial discretion affects selection but has no partial effect on y. Likewise, I use *return on assets* and the *Neuer Markt* dummy variable as controls for the selection, the identifying assumptions being that more profitable firms are less inclined to tab equity markets while technology-prone firms are more inclined to do so.[22]

5.4.1.2 Estimation results

Results from the two-stage estimation procedure are presented in Table 5.4. The dependent variable in the regression model (equation (1) of the Heckman procedure) is the amount raised through the distressed equity offering. To inspect the sensitivity of the results, I complete the analysis for both the amount raised relative to book value of total assets and relative to book value of common equity. It shows that the results are largely equivalent, thus I focus my attention to the first measure (models 1 and 2). The dependent variable in the selection model (equation (2) of the Heckman procedure) is a dummy variable that equals one if a firm in the sample completes an equity issue in a given firm-year, and zero otherwise. To allow for some variation in the specification of the selection model, I report results for two different sets of independent variables.[23]

The OLS estimates in the regression model offer strong support for the hypothesis that the debt overhang problem inhibits infusions of distressed equity. Higher *leverage* ratios (in book values) and higher *fractions of short-term debt* provoke lower infusion levels. The coefficients of both variables have the predicted negative sign and are statistically significant at the 1% level of confidence.[24] In contrast, future growth opportunities significantly increase the amount raised in an issue. The estimated coefficient of the *Tobin's Q* variable is positive, as predicted, and significant at the 5% level. Thus, the argument set forth by Gertner and Scharfstein (1991) that equityholders will provide more funds the higher the future value potential of the firm and the lower present wealth transfers to debtholders is supported by my findings.

---

[22] Technology firms formerly listed on Neuer Markt, the growth segment of the German Stock Exchange produce less cash flow and face higher agency costs of debt, which makes equity finance more appealing.

[23] Table 5.8 in the Appendix of this chapter provides a correlation matrix across the number of different covariates to shed further light on the univariate relations in the data.

[24] In models 3 and 4, the coefficient of the *leverage* variable is positive but insignificant. While I have no reasonable intuition for this discrepancy, I attribute this results to the more noisy nature of the dependent variable in these models, which results from the fact that book value of equity is negative for some firms in the sample.

There is also some evidence that the debt-overhang problem influences the initial censoring of the sample. The coefficient of the *leverage* variable in the selection model is negative and significant at the 5% level. On the other hand, a prior default of the firm appears to foster an equity issue. The positive and significant coefficient of the *default* variable in the selection model is not in line with the wealth transfer hypothesis (H1). Yet, the positive effect of default on the propensity to issue equity may be a result of increased creditor bargaining power provoked by a default. Prior studies show that upon default, creditors gain significant influence on corporate decision making.[25] Put more drastically, upon default, shareholder incentives whether or not to tab equity markets may no longer matter. Consistent with this interpretation, the actual terms of the issue in the regression model are not affected by the default variable.

As predicted, bank-concession also significantly increase the likelihood of an equity issue. The estimated coefficient of the *concession* variable is positive and significant at the 1% level in all specifications. This also is consistent with Gertner and Scharfstein (1991) that concessions mitigate wealth transfers to lenders and thus reinstate shareholders' incentives to provide fresh funds (H1). Perhaps surprisingly, however, the actual amount of debt forgiven has no partial effect on the amount raised in an issue. The coefficient of the *debt forgiven* variable, although positive, is insignificant in all models.

The results for corporate ownership structures are more ambiguous. I would expect that firms with significant bank holdings are more inclined to pursue an equity issue since wealth transfers more or less affect the same party. However, the estimated coefficient of the *bank ownership* variable remains insignificant. Similarly, ownership concentration and holdings by family investors neither promote nor inhibit the likelihood of an issue. Managerial holdings, by contrast, strongly affect the selection. The estimated coefficient of the *management ownership* variable is positive and significant at the 1% level. This is consistent with the univariate finding above and supports the theoretic argument that blockholdings by corporate managers help overcoming the informational barriers to an equity issue.

---

[25] For example, Gilson (1990) shows that upon default creditors take more seats in the board of directors of the distressed debtor. Likewise, the previous chapter has shown that, upon default, creditors actively replace poorly performing managers.

Table 5.4: Multivariate analysis of distressed equity issues

Maximum-Likelihood estimation of the Heckman (1979) selection model. The dependent variable in the regression model is the amount of equity raised, the dependent variable in the selection model is a dummy variable indicating whether an equity issue is completed or not. Standard errors are reported in parentheses. *, **, and *** denote the parameters are statistically significant at the 10%, 5%, and 1% level, respectively.

	Issue amount relative to total assets				Issue amount relative to book equity			
	Model 1		Model 2		Model 3		Model 4	
	Coeff.	se	Coeff.	se	Coeff.	se	Coeff.	se
Regression Model (Eq. 1)								
Leverage (Book)	-0.849	(0.269)***	-0.914	(0.285)***	1.420	(1.126)	1.183	(1.130)
Fraction of short-term debt	-0.403	(0.139)***	-0.439	(0.141)***	-1.162	(0.558)**	-1.308	(0.563)**
Default	0.125	(0.180)	0.163	(0.181)	0.618	(0.736)	0.666	(0.735)
Tobin's Q	0.042	(0.017)**	0.039	(0.017)**	0.150	(0.077)**	0.142	(0.077)*
Liquidity	-1.341	(0.310)***	-1.379	(0.323)***	-2.296	(1.297)*	-2.569	(1.287)**
Debt forgiven	0.037	(0.045)	0.042	(0.043)	0.095	(0.216)	0.114	(0.215)
Constant	0.269	(0.332)	0.213	(0.431)	0.353	(0.337)		
Selection Model (Eq. 2)								
Leverage (Book)	-0.630	(0.269)**	-0.657	(0.284)**	-0.413	(0.229)*	-0.413	(0.227)*
Fraction of short-term debt	0.081	(0.171)	0.076	(0.183)	0.310	(0.144)**	0.321	(0.142)**
Default	0.571	(0.225)**	0.502	(0.223)**	0.604	(0.228)***	0.532	(0.227)**
Tobin's Q	-0.011	(0.012)	-0.017	(0.014)	-0.007	(0.009)	-0.011	(0.011)
Liquidity	-0.854	(0.322)***	-0.815	(0.340)**	-0.468	(0.275)*	-0.396	(0.268)**
Concession	0.666	(0.190)***	0.639	(0.201)***	0.836	(0.193)***	0.846	(0.192)***
Bank ownership	0.038	(0.163)	0.046	(0.157)	-0.060	(0.184)	-0.061	(0.179)
Majority owner	0.078	(0.104)			0.050	(0.122)		
Management ownership	0.448	(0.103)***			0.492	(0.113)***		
Family ownership	-0.434	(0.324)			-0.604	(0.377)		
Footsteps	0.110	(0.223)			0.090	(0.253)		
Return on assets	-0.355	(0.123)***	-0.402	(0.330)***	-0.409	(0.135)***	-0.473	(0.130)***
Neuer Markt	0.184	(0.106)*	0.330	(0.097)***	0.157	(0.121)	0.323	(0.113)***
Constant	-1.529	(0.212)***	-1.366	(0.227)***	-1.852	(0.157)***	-1.727	(0.145)***
Mills Ratio								
λ	0.536	(0.089)**	0.551	(0.096)**	0.666	(0.335)**	0.783	(0.333)**
ρ	0.796	(0.102)**	0.814	(0.107)**	0.281	(0.134)**	0.328	(0.129)**
N(obs.)	1024		1024		1024		1024	
N(firms)	267		267		267		267	
Wald-χ^2	30.42	***	30.41	***	12.05	*	12.95	**

On the other hand, the positive effect of managerial ownership is inconsistent with the managerial discretion hypothesis. If managers use their discretionary leeway to complete equity issues for their own benefit and despite costly wealth transfers for shareholders, I should observe managerial stockholdings to reduce the likelihood of an issue. Also inconsistent with the discretion hypothesis (H4), the dummy variable *footsteps* is positive but insignificant. A possible explanation for this finding is that managers have little incentive to insulate themselves even against unfriendly takeovers. If the alternative to a takeover is, eventually, a formal bankruptcy proceeding, managers are almost certain to lose their employment because court-appointed insolvency administrators usually assume all residual control rights.[26] This sharply contrasts to U.S. legislation under which managers have considerable scope for entrenchment in bankruptcy [e.g. Bradley and Rosenzweig (1992)].

As for the controls, the results are as predicted. Selection is negatively related to operating performance. The coefficient of the *return on assets* variable is negative and significant suggesting that, if profitability allows it, firms try to avoid external finance. The *Neuer Markt* dummy is positive, which supports the argument that technology firms rely more on outside equity, *ceteris paribus*.

Concerning the variables that adjust for sample selectivity, the results justify the application of the Heckman procedure. The estimated coefficient of the Mill's ratio is positive and significant at the 5% level. Since λ_i is a decreasing function of the possibility of sample selection and ρ is positive, it follows that the β-coefficients on variables that are likely to affect both participation and the amount raised, such as *leverage*, *concession*, and *Tobin's* Q, would be biased downwards (in absolute values) if the Heckman technique were not applied [Heckman (1979)].

Finally, the χ^2-statistic reported in all regressions ranges between 12.05 in the third model and 30.42 in the first model. The hypothesis that all parameters are simultaneously equal to zero is rejected at conventional levels of confidence for all models.

---

[26] The previous chapter offers a more detailed description of the German bankruptcy law and provides further references.

5.4.2 The market perspective

5.4.2.1 Valuation effects of offering announcements

The results presented above indicate that there are distinctive characteristics that influence the equity issuance process in a state of distress. The existence of such characteristics suggests that information is conveyed to the market when the terms of the restructuring are announced. To examine this hypothesis the following sections investigate the market valuation effects of firms' equity offering announcements.[27]

Abnormal common stock returns around the announcement of the scrutinized equity issues are reported in Table 5.5. Event window abnormal returns present simple market model residuals calculated over an estimation window from 230 trading days to 31 trading days before the respective event. Market model parameters are adjusted for non-synchronous trading following the Scholes and Williams (1977) approach. The used market model index is the Composite Dax (CDAX) performance index.[28] Unfortunately, I do not have accurate announcement dates for all sampled equity issues, so that the sample size is slightly reduced.

Figures in Panel A refer to the full sample. The results indicate that, on average, the market responds positively to the equity offerings in our sample. However, abnormal returns are less favorable for longer event windows. Mean one-day, two-day and three-day abnormal announcement returns are 4.9%, 4.2% and 3.7%, respectively. Also, corresponding median abnormal returns are considerably lower and indistinguishably different from zero at the three-day and 21-day event window. The results are consistent with earlier findings by Gebhardt et al. (2001) who report slightly positive and significant valuation effects to seasoned equity offerings by a cross-section of German corporations.[29]

Panel B distinguishes abnormal announcement returns by whether or not subscription rights for existing owners are excluded. It is obvious that the average positive effect is almost exclusively driven by the sub-sample of placings and open offers. Rights issues, by contrast, seem to trigger neutral valuation effects. This is clearly counterintuitive: Given the informational advantages typically inherent in rights issues, I should expect rights issues to be drivers of the overall positive valuation effect [e.g. Gebhardt et al. (2001)]. A plausible explanation for this discrepancy may lie in the restructuring value created

[27] The applied event study methodology is explained in detail in the Appendix of Chapter 4 of this thesis.

[28] The reported results are robust with respect to different indices or estimation windows.

[29] Yet, this strand of literature is not very much established so that existing evidence should not be interpreted as conventional wisdom.

Table 5.5: Stock price reactions around distressed equity offering announcements
Stock price announcement returns around distressed equity offerings. Abnormal returns are based on Scholes and Williams (1977) estimation of market model parameters over -230 to -30 day interval. Test statistics are based on a simple two-sided t-test for means and a non-parametric Wilcoxon signed rank test for medians. ** and *** denote the returns and their differences are statistically significant at the 5%, and 1% level, respectively.

Panel A: Abnormal announcement returns for all issues				
Event Window	Mean	Median	Fraction > 0	N
[0]	0.049***	0.010***	0.610	118
[-1;0]	0.042***	0.008**	0.551	118
[-1;+1]	0.037**	0.002	0.517	118
[-10;+10]	0.036	-0.013	0.449	118

Panel B: Abnormal announcement returns by type of issue						
	Rights issues $N = 40$			Placing and open offers $N = 78$		
Event window	Mean	Median	Fraction > 0	Mean	Median	Fraction > 0
[0]	0.044	0.007	0.625	0.060***	0.023***	0.577
[-1;0]	0.031	-0.006	0.475	0.056***	0.022***	0.564
[-1;+1]	0.024	-0.002	0.475	0.052**	0.015**	0.506
[-10;+10]	0.050	-0.062	0.350	0.028	0.003	0.448

by incoming investors, which may be appreciated more highly by the market despite the greater opacity in placings and open offers.

In sum, the observed non-negative announcement returns indicate that, despite the incurred wealth transfers, the market rewards equity issues as an effective means to sidestep bankruptcy.[30] This interpretation also corresponds to the above finding that a firm's ability to deal with the debt overhang problem is crucial to the sample selection (i.e. the results of the Heckman model). However, average abnormal returns only reflect a net-effect and may disguise the true complexity of the market perspective. In order to fully capture the market's assessment of distressed equity issues, a cross-sectional decomposition of the announcement returns is required. The subsequent sections will elaborate on this issue.

5.4.2.2 Cross-sectional hypotheses

As for the managerial motives of issuing equity in a state of distress, criteria for the market's assessment of the restructuring should be manifold. Thus, the hypotheses derived above should also hold for the market perspective. To begin with, valuation effects should be affected negatively by wealth transfers to creditors and and positively by future growth opportunities. Accordingly, I expect event window stock returns to be decreasing in *leverage* and increasing in *Tobin's Q*. Moreover, I expect less favorable announcement

[30] Notably, Franks and Sanzhar (2003) report vastly negative announcement returns to their sample of distressed equity offerings.

returns to firm's that *default*, i.e. firms that have registered a § 92 I AktG filing. However, to avoid contamination by the information effects associated with a § 92 I AktG filing, I only inspect defaults that precede the offering announcement.[31]

Furthermore, the market may consider managerial discretion. If managers use equity issues to insulate themselves from a disciplinary (and thus value enhancing) takeover, I would expect the market to respond negatively for that subset of firms. As before, this hypothesis is tested by employing the *footsteps* variable. Alternatively, equity issues may actually promote disciplinary turnover of key executives. Recent studies by Franks, Mayer, and Renneboog (2001) and Hillier, Linn, and McColgan (2005) show that firms, which tab equity markets to meet liquidity shortages, exhibit significantly higher turnover rates. I analyze this issue by including a dummy variable, *management turnover*, that equals one in cases in which the equity issuance process coincides or is shortly forestalled by an extraordinary replacement of a key executive. This event is defined as any turnover of an officer holding the position of CEO or CFO that is not due to retirement, health issues, death, or promotion.[32] According to the managerial discretion hypothesis, this variable should be positive and significant in the cross-section.[33]

If the value of the restructuring is dependent upon the type of investor subscribing the new shares, market reactions to offering announcement should vary between different types of investors. For example, provided that the state of distress requires more specialized monitoring, the market may appreciate if the shares are placed in the hands of a financial sponsor rather than sold to a dispersed group of retail investors. Similarly, when the buyer is an existing blockholder, a further engagement may convey favorable information about the firm's prospects and should thus also result in a more favorable valuation effect.

Finally, I include several control variables that may affect the cross-section of announcement returns but are not directly affiliated with the hypotheses in question. Standard controls are the natural *logarithm of total assets* representing firm size and the *Neuer Markt* dummy variable. Moreover, I include a dummy variable, *climate*, which captures the "hot-issue-period" on equity markets between 1999 and 2000. This latter variable aims

---

31 This restriction is to ensure that, by the time the equity announcement is made, the negative information affect about assets in place that is caused by a § 92 I AktG filing, is already reflected in the share price. Accordingly, the observed announcement return is likely to reflect the incremental effect of the wealth transfers incurred by the issue given that the firm has previously defaulted.

32 A display of the time-series distribution of the *management turnover* events in our sample is provided in Chapter 3 of this thesis.

33 Note, that endogeneity prevented me from considering the *management turnover* variable on the firm perspective: It is not plausible to assume that a management turnover is exogenous to the equity issue decision. Thus any evidence in favor of this proposition would be spurious.

at filtering out allegedly extreme stock return patterns observed during that time, which, if not controlled for, could potentially distort the estimates of the remaining regressors.[34]

5.4.2.3 Cross-sectional regression results

Least squares estimation results of cross-sectional regressions are contained in Table 5.6. I report results for both one-day and two-day announcement returns as dependent variable. The results are largely equivalent, however, the overall model appears to fit better for the two-day window. This most likely reflects the common wisdom that "it cannot be determined from published sources whether the initial post-announcement market transaction preceded or followed the close of trading on the trading day prior to the published announcement".[35] Thus, the longer event window is more likely to reflect the announcement's full valuation effect.

From the results in Table 5.6, I draw the following inference: First, the market responds negatively to wealth transfers. The *leverage* and *default* variables have the predicted negative signs and are statistically significant at the 10% and 5% level, respectively. Across the sample an increase in leverage of 0.01 reduces the abnormal announcement return by 0.14 percent. However, unlike in the firm-perspective, *Tobin's Q*, the proxy for future growth opportunities, remains insignificant in all specifications.

Second, the market explicitly considers managerial discretion issues. The estimated coefficient of the *management turnover* variable is positive, as expected, and significant at the 5% level. Thus, if equity issues provoke (or at least coincide with) disciplinary management replacements, the market views this as effective internal governance at working and appreciates the stock accordingly. The estimated coefficient of the *footsteps* variable is also significant at the 5% level. If the market suspects equity issues to be undertaken as a takeover defense tactic, abnormal announcement returns are significantly lower. This is a particularly stern result given that, on the firm level, hostile takeover threats were not found to affect the equity issue decision (Table 5.4). However, the results may be distorted by sample selection on the market perspective because announcement returns are conditioned upon the actual incidence of an equity issue, while on the firm-level results are adjusted for censoring. Thus, I inspect the robustness of the results by rerunning the OLS regressions using the inverse Mill's ratio from equation 5.2 in the Heckman model as additional regressor.

[34] Shiller (2000) analyzes abnormal investor behavior during recent market bubbles.
[35] Dann and Mikkelson (1984), p. 162.

Table 5.6: Cross-sectional analysis of stock price reactions

Ordinary least squares estimates of cross-sectional regressions of cumulative abnormal returns on a vector of explanatory firm-specific variables. Abnormal returns are based on Scholes and Williams (1977) regression estimates of the market model parameters. Models 1 and 2 are based on returns at the [-1,0] day event window around the initial offering announcement. Models 3 and 4 are based on the day 0 event window. All accounting and ownership measures are from the last available business year ending before the onset of the restructuring. All other variable definitions are from Tables 5.2 and 5.3. Robust asymptotic standard errors are reported in parentheses. *, **, and *** denote the parameters are statistically significant at the 10%, 5%, and 1% level, respectively. The F-statistic tests the hypothesis that all coefficients in the model are simultaneously equal to zero. The reported Mean *VIF* is the Chatterjee, Hadi, and Price (2000) measure for the model's average variance inflation factor calculated from regressions of each independent variable x on the the other x variables.

	Two-day announcement returns				One-day announcement returns			
	Model 1		Model 2		Model 3		Model 4	
	$\widehat{\beta}$	se	$\widehat{\beta}$	se	$\widehat{\beta}$	se	$\widehat{\beta}$	se
Log (Assets)	-0.003	(0.009)	-0.005	(0.010)	-0.008	(0.008)	-0.011	(0.009)
Leverage (Book)	-0.137	(0.069)**	-0.144	(0.083)*	-0.110	(0.072)	-0.125	(0.082)
Default	-0.122	(0.048)**	-0.140	(0.065)**	-0.078	(0.034)**	-0.097	(0.048)**
Tobin's Q	-0.002	(0.002)	-0.001	(0.002)	0.000	(0.002)	0.001	(0.003)
Management turnover	0.106	(0.051)**	0.116	(0.057)**	0.105	(0.054)**	0.117	(0.061)*
Footsteps	-0.110	(0.049)**	-0.098	(0.048)**	-0.084	(0.034)**	-0.073	(0.036)**
Buyer Management			0.065	(0.042)			0.069	(0.044)
Buyer Blockholder			0.087	(0.039)**			0.106	(0.040)***
Buyer Strategic			0.089	(0.052)*			0.089	(0.048)*
Buyer Financial			0.046	(0.035)			0.058	(0.035)*
Buyer Bank			0.120	(0.081)			0.147	(0.078)*
Climate	-0.079	(0.037)**	-0.051	(0.033)**	-0.084	(0.035)**	-0.079	(0.037)**
Neuer Markt	-0.049	(0.031)	-0.073	(0.038)	-0.044	(0.029)	-0.049	(0.031)
Constant	0.145	(0.112)	0.106	(0.126)	0.185	(0.103)*	0.145	(0.115)
N	114		114		114		114	
R^2	0.17		0.20		0.16		0.18	
F-Statistic	2.12	**	1.98	**	1.76	*	1.78	*
Mean *VIF*	1.29		1.59		1.29		1.59	

All results hold with the explicit consideration of sample selection.[36] Accordingly, the observed discrepancy in the results from the firm- and market perspective suggests that the pricing of distressed securities is very much afflicted by investors' sceptics and informational opacity about managerial motives and firm quality. In fact, this may also explain why the estimated coefficient of the *Tobin's Q* variable has a negative sign in all regression models.[37]

Third, changes in corporate ownership incurred by the equity issue have a significant valuation effect.[38] In cases where existing blockholders increase their stakes in the course of the restructuring or new strategic investors pick up the tendered shares, the market responds particularly favorable. This result also differs from the firm perspective, where the amount raised was not found to vary substantially across subscriber types (Table 5.3). The estimated coefficient of the *financial investor* variable, by contrast, is only significant in the one-day event window regression. Typically, strategic investors are better informed about asset quality than financial sponsors. Therefore, the difference in significance may be due to more valuable information effects associated with the subscription of fresh equity by a strategic rather than a financial buyer. Alternatively, in the sense of Shleifer and Vishny (1992), strategic buyers picking up distressed securities may transfer favorable information to the market concerning the overall financial health of the industry.

Of the control variables, solely the estimated coefficient of the *climate* variable is statistically significant. Not controlling for the oversensitive stock price behavior during the hot-issue period may thus potentially distorts the remaining regression estimates. Firm size and industry affiliation (*Neuer Markt*) do not explain any of the cross-sectional variation of the announcement returns.

The results in Table 5.6 hold with the alteration of the set of predictors. A *rights issue* dummy as well as the *issue discount* variable remain insignificant when added to the regression without undermining the explanatory power of the other right-hand side variables. Also, the incidence of debt forgiveness does not substantially affect the announcement return. This should not be surprising given adverse information effect associated with debt concessions (Table 5.2). Finally, the R^2 varies between 0.16 in model 3 and 0.2 in model 2. The hypothesis that all regression parameters are simultaneously equal to zero in rejected at conventional levels of confidence for all model specifications. Multicollinearity

[36] For the sake of brevity, I don't report the results in a table.

[37] If information asymmetry is high investors may find it more difficult to assess equity offerings by firms with high intangible assets and unobservable synergies (as measured by *Tobin's Q*) and thus put a discount on such firms.

[38] Note that the subscriber variables are not mutually exclusive so that I can include each of them as right-hand side variables.

inspected by the mean variance inflation factor does not distort the results [Chatterjee, Hadi, and Price (2000)].

5.5 Summary and conclusion

In this study I analyze equity offerings by a sample of financially distressed corporations in Germany between 1996 and 2004. I focus on three distinct economic determinants of distressed equity infusions, i.e. wealth transfers due to the debt-overhang problem, corporate ownership, and managerial entrenchment. I consecutively analyze the restructuring from the firm- as well the market perspective. My key findings can be summarized as follows:

1. From the firm perspective, the restructuring is dominated by the debt-overhang problem. Controlling for firm quality, I find that firms are more likely to complete an equity issue and raise higher amounts of funds the lower the wealth transfers to creditors incurred through the issue and the higher the firm's future value potential.

2. Firms are also more likely to raise new equity finance if wealth transfers are mitigated through bank-concessions. Bank-concessions, in turn, are more likely for firms with excessive leverage and limited future growth opportunities. These first two results provide strong support for the theoretic arguments set forth by Gertner and Scharfstein (1991).

3. Other than the debt overhang problem, the firm perspective seems not to be considerably affected by efforts of managerial entrenchment or distributions of corporate ownership.

4. From the market perspective, responses to distressed equity offerings are, on average, favorable. This result suggests that the market rewards firms that are able to issue equity despite a potential debt overhang. However, in the cross-section, abnormal announcement returns are lower for firms facing high wealth transfers to creditors.

5. Unlike the firm, the market does seem to contemplate managerial entrenchment and ownership changes. Announcement returns are substantially lower for firms issuing equity while being subject to takeover threats and substantially higher for firms replacing top-management in the course of the issue. Market reactions are also significantly more favorable if the issued shares are subscribed by existing blockholders or strategic investors.

The results suggest that there exists some discrepancy between managerial motives for capital structure decisions and market perceptions thereof. While it is yet to be confirmed that this finding is not specific to my sample, this picture may be a common side-effect of financial distress. Accordingly, one implication of the above results is that investor relations quality deteriorates under preserving distress. This would be consistent with the theoretic argument that the major (indirect) cost of financial distress results from the fact that managers in fear of existence are hampered from doing business as usual. I am unaware of any study comparing investor relations for sound and ailing firms. Therefore, whether or not better capital market communications can help firms mitigate the negative wealth effects of distress is yet open to debate.

Bibliography for Chapter 5

Becker, W. (2003): "Geier oder Notärzte? US-Investoren wittern in deutschen Turnaround-Kandidaten hohe Renditen," *Börsen-Zeitung*, (158 [08.19.03]), 13.

Bradley, M., and M. Rosenzweig (1992): "The Untenable Case for Chapter 11," *The Yale Law Journal*, 101, 1043–1095.

Brealey, R. A., S. C. Myers, and F. Allen (2005): *Principles of Corporate Finance.* McGraw Hill, Upper Saddle River, N.J.

Brown, D. T., C. M. James, and R. M. Mooradian (1994): "Asset Sales by Financially Distressed Firms," *Journal of Corporate Finance*, 1, 233–257.

Buth, A., M. Hermanns, and R. Janus (1998): "Finanzwirtschaftliche Aspekte der Fortführung von Krisenunternehmen," in *Restrukturierung, Sanierung, Insolvenz*, ed. by A. Buth, and M. Hermanns, pp. 224–245, München. Beck.

Chatterjee, S., U. S. Dhillon, and G. G. Ramirez (2004): "Debtor-in-Possession Financing," *Journal of Banking and Finance*, 28, 3097–3111.

Chatterjee, S., A. Hadi, and B. Price (2000): *Regression Analysis by Example.* John Wiley and Sons, New York, 3rd edn.

Dann, L. Y., and W. H. Mikkelson (1984): "Convertible Debt Issuance, Capital Structure and Financing-Related Information: Some New Evidence," *Journal of Financial Economics*, 13, 157–186.

Finsterer, H. (1999): *Unternehmenssanierung Durch Kreditinstitute: Eine Untersuchung unter Beachtung der Insolvenzordnung.* Gabler, Wiesbaden.

Franks, J. R., C. Mayer, and L. Renneboog (2001): "Who Disciplines Management in Poorly Performing Companies?," *Journal of Financial Intermediation*, 10, 209–248.

Franks, J. R., and S. V. Sanzhar (2003): "How Do Firms Overcome The Debt Overhang Problem?," Working Paper, London Business School.

GEBHARDT, G., S. HEIDEN, AND H. DASKE (2001): "Determinants of Capital Market Reactions to Seasoned Equity Offers by German Corporations," Goethe University Working Paper No. 85.

GERTNER, R., AND D. SCHARFSTEIN (1991): "A Theory of Workouts and the Effects of Reorganization Law," *The Journal of Finance*, 46, 1189–1222.

GILSON, S. C. (1989): "Management Turnover and Financial Distress," *Journal of Financial Economics*, 25, 241–262.

——— (1990): "Bankruptcy, Boards, Banks, and Blockholders," *Journal of Financial Economics*, 27, 355–387.

GILSON, S. C., K. JOHN, AND L. H. LANG (1990): "Troubled Debt Restructurings, An Empirical Study of Private Reorganization of Firms in Default," *Journal of Financial Economics*, 27, 315–353.

GREENE, W. H. (2003): *Econometric Analysis*. Prentice Hall, Upper Saddle River, 5th edn.

GROSSMAN, S. J., AND O. D. HART (1988): "One Share - One Vote and the Market for Corporate Control," *Journal of Financial Economics*, 20, 175–202.

HAUSMAN, J. A., AND D. A. WISE (1983): "Stratification on Endogenous Variables and Estimation: The Gary Income Maintenance Experiment," in *Structural Analysis of Discrete Data with Econometric Applications*, ed. by C. Manski, and D. McFadden, pp. 365–390, Boston, MA. MIT Press.

HECKMAN, J. J. (1979): "Sample Selection Bias as a Specification Error," *Econometrica*, 47, 153–161.

HILLIER, D., S. C. LINN, AND P. MCCOLGAN (2005): "Equity Issuance, CEO Turnover and Corporate Governance," *European Financial Management*, 11, 515–538.

HOTCHKISS, E. S., AND R. M. MOORADIAN (1997): "Vulture Investors and the Market for Corporate Control of Distressed Firms," *Journal of Financial Economics*, 43, 401–432.

JENSEN, M. C., AND W. MECKLING (1976): "Theory of the Firm: Managerial Behavior, Agency Costs, and Ownership Structure," *Journal of Financial Economics*, 3, 305–360.

KHANNA, N., AND A. B. POULSEN (1995): "Managers of Financially Distressed Firms: Villains or Scapegoats?," *The Journal of Finance*, 50, 919–940.

KIEFER, R. (2003): "Essays on Corporate Distress and the German Financial System," Ph.D. thesis, European University Institute Florence.

LANG, L., A. POULSEN, AND R. STULZ (1995): "Asset Sales, Firm Performance, and the Agency Costs of Managerial Discretion," *Journal of Financial Economics*, 37, 3–37.

LEHN, K., AND A. POULSEN (1989): "Free Cash Flow and Stockholder Gains in Going Private Transactions," *The Journal of Finance*, 44, 771–787.

MOORADIAN, R. M., AND R. E. HARLEY (2005): "Out-of-Court Restructurings and the Resolution of Financial Distress: Section 3(a)(9) Compared to Investment-Bank-Managed Exchange Offers," *Journal of Business*, 78, 1593–1624.

MYERS, S. C. (1977): "Determinants of Corporate Borrowing," *Journal of Financial Economics*, 5, 147–175.

MYERS, S. C., AND N. S. MAJLUF (1984): "Corporate Financing and Investment Decisions When Firms Have Information That Investors Do Not Have," *Journal of Financial Economics*, 13, 187–221.

PRIGGE, S., AND R. OELLERMANN (2005): "Potenzielle Präventivmaßnahmen gegen Übernahmen: Verbreitung und Stärke des Übernahmemotives," *Finanzbetrieb*, 7, 581–592.

SCHARFSTEIN, D. S. (1988): "The Disciplinary Role of Takeovers," *Review of Economic Studies*, 55, 185–200.

SCHOLES, M., AND J. WILLIAMS (1977): "Estimating Betas from Nonsynchronous Data," *Journal of Financial Economics*, 5, 309–327.

SENBET, L. W., AND J. K. SEWARD (1995): "Financial Distress, Bankruptcy and Reorganization," in *Finance*, ed. by R. A. Jarrow, V. Maksimovic, and W. T. Ziemba, pp. 921–957, Amsterdam, N.H. Elsevier.

SHILLER, R. J. (2000): "Measuring Bubble Expectations and Investor Confidence," *The Journal of Psychology and Financial Markets*, 1, 49–60.

SHLEIFER, A., AND R. W. VISHNY (1986): "Large Shareholders and Corporate Control," *Journal of Political Economy*, 94, 461–488.

——— (1992): "Liquidation Values and Debt Capacity: A Market Equilibrium Approach," *The Journal of Finance*, 47, 1343–1366.

WILLIAMSON, O. E. (1988): "Corporate Finance and Corporate Governance," *The Journal of Finance*, 43, 567–592.

WOOLDRIDGE, J. M. (2003): *Introductory Econometrics*. Thomson South-Western, Mason, Ohio.

WRUCK, K. H. (1990): "Financial Distress, Reorganization, and Organizational Efficiency," *Journal of Financial Economics*, 27, 419–444.

Appendices

1. Summary of variable definitions and data sources
2. Correlation matrix of independent variables in Heckman estimation
3. Correlation matrix of independent variables in cross-sectional abnormal return estimation

Table 5.7: Summary of variable definitions and data sources

Variable	Definition	Data source
Panel A: Ownership data		
Herfindahl	Herfindahl index across all blocks of common voting stock defined as $HI = \sum_{i=1}^{N} s_i^2$, where $s_i (i = 1, ..., N)$ is the fraction of common stock owned by the party i.	Hoppenstedt Financial Information Stock Guide
Majority owner	Single shareholder comprising absolute majority of voting rights ($\geq 50\%$)	Hoppenstedt Financial Information Stock Guide
Management ownership	Share of common stock held by members of the board of executives (Vorstand)	Hoppenstedt Financial Information Stock Guide
Family ownership	Share of common stock held by families or individual investors (shares held by different family members were aggregated)	Hoppenstedt Financial Information Stock Guide
Bank ownership	Share of common voting stock held by corporate and investment banks	Hoppenstedt Financial Information Stock Guide
Panel B: Restructuring data		
Bank-concession	Out-of-court reduction or deferral of contractual payments, provision of fresh money, or swap of claims	LexisNexis and Dow Jones&Reuters news retrieval
Default	Mandatory filing in accordance with § 92 I of the German Companies Act (AktG)	LexisNexis and Dow Jones&Reuters news retrieval
Footsteps	Dummy variable indicating firms that received a competing bid or were subject to takeover speculation as reported in news accounts	LexisNexis and Dow Jones&Reuters news retrieval
Buyer variables	Subscribers of new shares tendered in the issue categorized by management, (existing) blockholders, strategic invenstors (non-financial corporates), financial investors (investement funds, private equity funds, and insurance companies) , banks	LexisNexis and Dow Jones&Reuters news retrieval
Management turnover	Extraordinary replacement of firm's CEO or CFO position not due to retirement, health issues, death, or promotion	LexisNexis and Dow Jones&Reuters news retrieval

Table 5.8: Correlation matrix of independent variables in Heckman estimation

Correlation matrix of independent variables used in Table 5.4. All variable definitions are from Tables 5.2 and 5.3. Each column contains correlation coefficients and and their respective p-values in parentheses below.

		(1)	(2)	(3)	(4)	(5)	(6)	(7)	(8)	(9)	(10)	(11)	(12)	(13)
(1)	Leverage (Book)	1.000												
(2)	Fraction of short-term debt	0.064	1.000											
		(0.009)												
(3)	Default	0.061	0.034	1.000										
		(0.013)	(0.145)											
(4)	Tobin's Q	-0.014	-0.050	-0.033	1.000									
		(0.585)	(0.047)	(0.184)										
(5)	Liquidity	-0.181	-0.208	-0.048	0.085	1.000								
		(0.000)	(0.000)	(0.038)	(0.001)									
(6)	Concession	0.072	0.075	0.245	-0.022	-0.087	1.000							
		(0.003)	(0.001)	(0.000)	(0.385)	(0.000)								
(7)	Bank ownership	0.048	0.068	0.054	-0.046	-0.064	0.084	1.000						
		(0.046)	(0.003)	(0.008)	(0.067)	(0.005)	(0.000)							
(8)	Management ownership	-0.081	0.040	0.009	-0.030	0.203	0.068	0.058	1.000					
		(0.001)	(0.079)	(0.648)	(0.229)	(0.000)	(0.001)	(0.002)						
(9)	Majority owner	-0.004	0.066	0.063	-0.072	-0.098	0.062	0.065	0.154	1.000				
		(0.880)	(0.004)	(0.002)	(0.004)	(0.000)	(0.002)	(0.000)	(0.000)					
(10)	Family ownership	0.038	0.043	-0.006	-0.035	-0.036	0.040	0.068	0.135	0.261	1.000			
		(0.113)	(0.065)	(0.782)	(0.161)	(0.114)	(0.048)	(0.000)	(0.000)	(0.000)				
(11)	Footsteps	-0.012	0.059	0.031	-0.001	0.047	0.057	0.089	0.115	0.043	0.021	1.000		
		(0.608)	(0.011)	(0.120)	(0.957)	(0.040)	(0.005)	(0.000)	(0.000)	(0.018)	(0.258)			
(12)	Return on assets	-0.048	-0.005	-0.043	0.000	-0.100	0.002	-0.010	-0.155	-0.022	0.008	-0.021	1.000	
		(0.049)	(0.821)	(0.064)	(0.996)	(0.000)	(0.939)	(0.656)	(0.000)	(0.314)	(0.727)	(0.342)		
(13)	Neuer Markt	-0.112	-0.070	-0.074	0.138	0.318	-0.052	-0.065	0.253	-0.097	-0.077	0.016	-0.081	1.000
		(0.000)	(0.002)	(0.000)	(0.000)	(0.000)	(0.011)	(0.000)	(0.000)	(0.000)	(0.000)	(0.373)	(0.000)	

Table 5.9: Correlation matrix of independent variables in cross-sectional abnormal return estimation

Correlation matrix of independent variables used in Table 5.6. All variable definitions are from Tables 5.2, 5.3 and 5.6. Each column contains correlation coefficients and and their respective p-values in parentheses below.

		(1)	(2)	(3)	(4)	(5)	(6)	(7)	(8)	(9)	(10)	(11)	(12)	(13)
(1)	Log (Assets)	1.000												
(2)	Leverage (Book)	0.046	1.000											
		(0.056)												
(3)	Tobin's Q	-0.209	-0.014	1.000										
		(0.000)	(0.585)											
(4)	Neuer Markt	-0.353	-0.112	0.138	1.000									
		(0.000)	(0.000)	(0.000)										
(5)	Management turnover	0.168	-0.004	-0.053	0.047	1.000								
		(0.000)	(0.873)	(0.033)	(0.011)									
(6)	Default	0.021	0.061	-0.033	-0.074	0.140	1.000							
		(0.386)	(0.013)	(0.184)	(0.000)	(0.000)								
(7)	Footsteps	0.107	-0.012	-0.001	0.016	0.190	0.031	1.000						
		(0.000)	(0.608)	(0.957)	(0.373)	(0.000)	(0.120)							
(8)	Climate	-0.129	0.034	0.217	0.097	0.008	-0.055	0.023	1.000					
		(0.000)	(0.159)	(0.000)	(0.000)	(0.673)	(0.007)	(0.214)						
(9)	Buyer Management	-0.020	-0.017	-0.014	0.022	0.009	0.082	-0.008	-0.026	1.000				
		(0.396)	(0.489)	(0.580)	(0.232)	(0.641)	(0.000)	(0.675)	(0.156)					
(10)	Buyer Blockholder	0.012	-0.002	-0.017	0.041	0.061	0.060	0.002	0.011	-0.007	1.000			
		(0.627)	(0.921)	(0.509)	(0.026)	(0.001)	(0.003)	(0.896)	(0.538)	(0.707)				
(11)	Buyer Strategic	-0.014	-0.019	-0.006	0.022	0.032	0.036	-0.008	-0.010	-0.003	-0.007	1.000		
		(0.565)	(0.425)	(0.819)	(0.232)	(0.078)	(0.072)	(0.675)	(0.579)	(0.869)	(0.707)			
(12)	Buyer Financial	0.002	-0.021	-0.014	0.076	0.129	0.003	0.092	-0.016	-0.006	-0.014	-0.006	1.000	
		(0.944)	(0.376)	(0.566)	(0.000)	(0.000)	(0.894)	(0.000)	(0.377)	(0.730)	(0.431)	(0.730)		
(13)	Buyer Bank	0.070	0.033	-0.009	-0.030	0.074	0.231	-0.004	0.012	-0.002	-0.004	-0.002	-0.004	1.000
		(0.003)	(0.167)	(0.724)	(0.104)	(0.000)	(0.000)	(0.809)	(0.499)	(0.924)	(0.828)	(0.924)	(0.842)	

Chapter 6

A study of firm exit and survival in financial distress*

6.1 Introduction

The impact of financial distress on a firm's operations traditionally presents one of the cornerstones in the literature on corporate finance and investment. For example, one of the liveliest and most persistent debates is concerned with the relevance of financial distress costs and whether they have a significant economic impact or not [e.g Kraus and Litzenberger (1973), Haugen and Senbet (1978)]. A related field of study highlights the benefits of financial distress in triggering value preserving operational change [e.g. Jensen (1989), Wruck (1990)]. Furthermore, in the empirical strand of the literature, studies have recently focused on how firms respond to distress and why they may prefer a private workout over a formal reorganization [e.g. Ofek (1993), Denis and Rodgers (2006)]. One intuitive assumption implicitly endorsed by most of these studies is that sustained distress poses a threat to a firm's very existence. Failure to respond timely and effectively, it is commonly understood, will ultimately result in the liquidation of a firm's estate or a wholesale transfer of control to a new owner. Yet, perhaps surprisingly, the more fundamental question of what actually determines the ultimate outcome of financial distress for a given firm has remained largely unexplored.

In the following chapter I address this issue by analyzing the determinants of firm exit and survival in financial distress. I follow a sample of firms through their restructuring

* I would like to thank Oren Sussman, Karin Thorburn and Stefan Wagner for their detailed and thoughtful comments. The study in this chapter also benefitted doctoral seminar presentations at the Financial Management Association European Meeting, Stockholm 2006, and the University of Oxford (2006).

interval and document factors that influence the ultimate outcome of distress (i.e. the type of exit) as well as the time elapsed until that outcome occurs. I distinguish between the two common types of firm exit, acquisition and bankruptcy, and contrast them against the sample's survivors.[1] Studying firm exit and survival for a sample conditioned on financial distress is of particular relevance since both the time spent in distress as well as the type of exit chosen are major determinants of a firm's total direct and indirect distress costs. In this respect, financial theory argues, both forms of exit have merits and shortcomings. For example, formal bankruptcy proceedings offer institutional features that mitigate information asymmetries and bargaining deadlocks between the debtor and different types of creditors [e.g. Jackson (1982), Brown (1989)]. On the other hand, it involves high administrative expenses and, especially in Germany, often fosters premature liquidation [e.g. Gilson, John, and Lang (1990) and Chapter 4 of this thesis]. Acquisitions, by contrast, allow the going concern of the firm's operations and the exploitation of its intangible assets. However, insufficient purchasing power by strategic bidders and high valuation uncertainties for industry outsiders often reduce the price feasible in a sale [e.g. Shleifer and Vishny (1992)].

The existing body of evidence on firm exit has so far largely focused on its evolutionary implications, questioning whether firm failure is the result of an efficient Darwinian selection in which firms with inferior product market combination are forced to exit. The common insight gained by these studies is that acquisition and bankruptcy are closely related forms of exit that tend to be *influenced by common economic factors.*[2] For example, poor operating performance [e.g.Altman (1968), Maksimovic and Phillips (2001)], macroeconomic pressure [e.g. Buehler, Kaiser, and Jaeger (2006)], young age and small firm size [e.g. Harhoff, Stahl, and Woywode (1998), Bethel, Liebeskind, and Opler (1998), are commonly identified as factors that make failure as well as control transfers more likely. Overall, the results are consistent with a controversial argument set forth by Dewey (1961) that "most mergers are merely a civilized alternative to bankruptcy."[3]

In this study I take a different approach. Starting off by analyzing the *economic consequences* of acquisition and bankruptcy as alternative ways to resolute financial distress, I find that both differ substantially in their impact on a firm's market value. While bankruptcy filings provoke announcement returns of below -40% around a 20 day event window, corresponding returns for takeover agreements between a bidder and a distressed

[1] I do not discuss voluntary liquidations as a third possible form of exit typically discussed in the literature. Voluntary liquidation rarely occurs at large public corporations and thus has little relevance for my study. An exception is IG Farben AG whose voluntary liquidation was initially decided in 1952. More than 50 years later, the completion of the liquidation was forestalled by the groups bankruptcy filing in 2003. Voluntary liquidations are analyzed in detail by Harhoff, Stahl, and Woywode (1998).
[2] A more detailed account of these factors is provided by Köke (2002), pp. 75-76.
[3] Dewey (1961), p. 257.

target are significantly positive ranging between 12% and 17%. This suggests that, contrary to the established view, both forms of exit may present two distinct economic phenomena and that specific features may exist that help identifying the potential candidates of either form of exit beforehand.

Using simple multinomial logit and Cox proportional hazard rate models, I find these differences across firms' financial structure and ownership distribution as well as in the success of their restructuring efforts and the financial condition of their industry. Crucially, these characteristics not only affect the likelihood of the ultimate outcome but also the time spent in distress until that outcome occurs: Acquired firms exit distress earlier than their bankrupt counterparts and, and the onset of distress, are characterized by low leverage, high ownership concentration, and high industry liquidity. By contrast, bankruptcies are largely driven by high leverage, low liquidity, low ownership concentration, and low industry growth opportunities. Bankruptcies are also accelerated in cases where managers hold significant blocks of voting stock. Finally, firms seem to be able to retard their exit by issuing fresh equity and divesting considerable amounts of assets.

Most likely, the novelty of my findings is attributable to my unique data set, which is drawn from a largely unexplored population, a panel of German public corporations, and focuses solely on distressed firms. In this more homogeneous population the most significant determinants of a firm's exit choice are more subtle than in a general cross-section since highly dominant economic factors such as poor performance and financial pressure are already controlled for. However, because the perils of exit and failure are much more pronounced for distressed firms, the insight gained in this study may be of high relevance for researchers and investors particularly interested in this specific asset class.

The investigation in this chapter proceeds as follows: In Section 2 I review the theoretical background as well as the related empirical evidence and condense my predictions into six testable propositions. In Section 3 I provide extensive descriptive statistics for the relevant sub-samples and briefly discuss the methodology for my multivariate analyses. The estimation results and their interpretations are contained in Section 4. Section 5 concludes the chapter with implications on capital structure and financial distress costs. In the Appendix I provide supplementary statistics as well as an overview of the variable definitions and their data sources.

6.2 Theory and propositions

6.2.1 Theoretical background

Distressed firms that fail to maintain their status as independent legal entities are typically forced to "exit" via acquisition or bankruptcy. By contrast, firms that avoid either outcome are typically declared as survivors, though actual survival may only be transient as it cannot be accurately captured due to right-censoring in the data. Figure 6.1 provides an illustration of a firm's potential path to exit from financial distress.

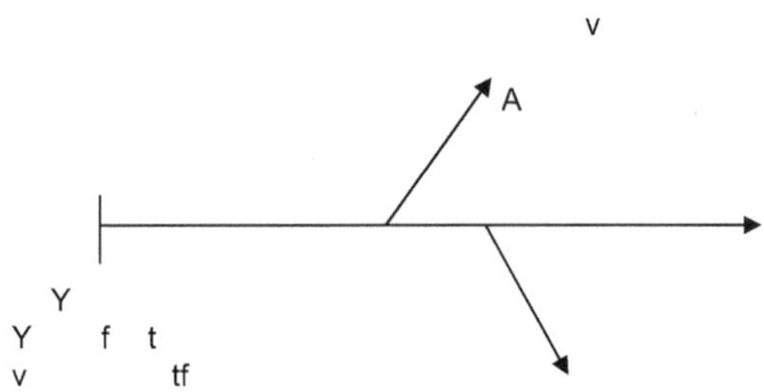

Figure 6.1: Firm exit and survival in distress

In this study I am interested in detecting the economic drivers of firm exit versus survival as competing outcomes of financial distress. Moreover, I am interested in how firms "chose" between acquisition and bankruptcy as alternative forms of exit. Presumably, such a knowledge is useful for policy makers interested in how financial distress affects the allocation of corporate resources across firms and industries. Moreover, a model of firm exit likelihood could provide a useful guidepost for a more thorough understanding of the intricate risk-return characteristics typically observed in the trading of distressed securities. In this section I briefly review the theoretical literature as well as related empirical evidence that provide the foundation for the formulation of testable hypotheses in the subsequent section.

6.2.1.1 Firm size, firm age, and performance

There is a large body of theoretical and empirical studies, especially in the Industrial Organization and Organizational Ecology literature, explaining business turnover and firm survival on real-economic terms, in analogy to Darwinian selection. A good overview on this literature in provided by Hannan and Freeman (1989). In this study, however, I only rely on the most conventional firm characteristics, i.e. firm size, age, and operating performance, which mostly serve as controls for the financial covariates motivated below. Firm size, to begin with, should be a significant determinant of failure rates. For example, Schultz (1993), Hensler, Rutherford, and Springer (1997) and Harhoff, Stahl, and Woywode (1998) report that smaller firms who are more likely to operate below the minimum efficient scale exhibit higher failure rates and thus a higher hazard of bankruptcy. Large firms, by contrast, have better access to capital markets and are thus better equipped to withstand rough market conditions or unfavorable outcomes of investment choices [e.g. Botman and Van der Goot (2004)]. Large firms may also face lower risk of performance induced exit as disciplinary takeover markets are illiquid for large conglomerates and the external costs of large bankruptcies make public intervention more likely.[4] Similarly, I expect firm age to be inversely related to failure probability. Audretsch (1995) argues that firm age is a proxy for the knowledge of technology and the competitive environment, which a firm accumulates over its life-cycle. A greater stock of cumulated information should lead to higher survival chances. Finally, operating performance should affect the risk of exit. Firms with strong operating performance generate enough cash, which reduces financing costs and gives the firm more leeway to overcome economic turmoil and excessive leverage. Also, sound operating performance reduces the threat of involuntary takeovers [e.g. Manne (1965)]. Empirical evidence for the inverse relation between operating performance and failure and acquisition is provided by, among others, Altman (1968), Powell (1997), and Köke (2002).

6.2.1.2 Capital structure

The predictions of capital structure theory on firm exit are more ambiguous and differ with respect to bankruptcy and acquisition. The established view is that, *ex ante*, high leverage increases the hazard of bankruptcy because relatively small declines in operating performance might lead to insufficient interest coverage and hence default, which in turn leaves the firm at the mercy of creditors. Put more bluntly, firms with no debt cannot default and thus face no risk of bankruptcy. The predicted impact of financial pressure on firm-failure is confirmed by several studies not conditioned on distress [e.g. Köke (2002), Altman (1968)]. *Ex post* however, high leverage may be value preserving. For example,

[4] Bethel, Liebeskind, and Opler (1998), and Mulherin and Boone (2000) find that large firms are less vulnerable to takeover threats. Köke (2002) describes the case of Philipp Holzmann AG in Germany (a firm in this sample) that—under the lead of German chancellor Schröder—received considerable creditor concessions. However, though ultimately, it went bankrupt in 2002.

the study in Chapter 4 of this thesis found that upon default, firms with higher leverage and higher fractions of debt owed to bank-lenders are more likely to restructure privately. This is consistent with Jensen (1989) who argues that high leverage has benefits because it will hasten a firm's attempts to restructure its operating business as well its financial claims, thereby preserving higher fractions of its firm value. Thus, distressed firms that end up in bankruptcy may not necessarily be less economically viable than firms that lack the disciplinary effect of leverage and thus face lower risk of bankruptcy.

As for acquisitions, I expect the effect of leverage to be the opposite. For one, acquisitions of poorly performing firms in many ways serve the same purpose as leverage. Similar to the contractual obligations induced by high debt levels the takeover market disciplines management to respond to operating deficiencies in a timely and orderly manner. If both mechanisms are substitutive it is reasonable to argue that they should coincide less often. In the special case of distressed firms, acquisitions are further inhibited by wealth transfers. In a takeover, the buyer almost always assumes the debt of the target and therefore reduces the riskiness of the outstanding claims. A potential acquirer would like to avoid such a transfer to debt-holders and could, for example, make the acquisition contingent on a successful restructuring of the firm's debt. Incumbent shareholders may also be opposed to agreeing to a takeover in which mostly the creditors benefit. When the firm is heavily distressed, it is likely that the liquidation value of its assets is below the face value of its liabilities. In such a setting, the firm's residual claims are essentially worthless and thus shareholder receive little of the payment in a merger. Instead, the transaction would reduce much of their equity's option value and thus eliminate the scope for risk shifting [e.g. Jensen and Meckling (1976)]. These arguments suggests that highly levered firms are less likely to be acquired in a merger.[5] Prior research on this hypothesis is sparse. For example, for a sample of junk-bond issuers that became distressed Asquith, Gertner, and Scharfstein (1994) find that the most highly leveraged firms are less likely to be acquired. Furthermore, Clark and Ofek (1994) find that acquisitions of distressed targets are more likely to succeed after debt restructurings. The significance of shareholder-creditor wealth transfers in inhibiting distressed restructurings is also demonstrated by Franks and Sanzhar (2003) as well as the findings in the previous chapter of this thesis, which hold that infusions of distressed equity are less likely to go through when the firm is highly indebted.

[5] Crucially, such wealth transfers occur regardless of wether the takeover is friendly or hostile.

6.2.1.3 Corporate ownership

If firm performance is poor or the firm's financial condition is strained there is an increased need for effective monitoring in which corporate ownership takes a pivotal role [e.g. Demsetz and Lehn (1985), Fama and Jensen (1983)]. Therefore, a firm's ownership distribution, and especially the concentration of ownership, should influence the hazard of exit. Yet again theory prescribes that a distinction between acquisition and bankruptcy as competing types of exit is made. Grossman and Hart (1980) suggest that effective takeovers of poorly performing firms require concentrated ownership of the target. Under dispersed ownership individual shareholders have incentives to hold on to their shares and thus free-ride on the improvement of the firm value undertaken by the acquirer. Similarly, Burkart, Gromb, and Panunzi (2000) show that the existing and bidding blockholders prefer to complete a transfer of control over-the-counter rather than through the market because they anticipate the harmful effect of free-riding at their expense. Hence, a higher concentration of ownership at the beginning of distress should make firm exit through acquisition more likely, *ceteris paribus*. Holmström and Tirole (1993), on the other hand, claim that takeovers require low ownership concentration because only then is the company's stock sufficiently liquid for the market to determine whether a takeover would be value enhancing or not. Concentrated ownership, it is argued, reduces the benefits of market monitoring by reducing market liquidity. This dispute, it follows, needs to be resolved empirically. Perhaps surprisingly, not much related evidence has been gathered. Köke (2002) suggests that takeovers should be less likely for firms with very low and very high ownership concentration. He finds some support for this trade-off hypothesis, however, the positive effect of ownership concentration appears to be stronger, giving more support for Grossman and Hart (1980) argument.

Concerning firm exit via bankruptcy, the influence of ownership concentration is more easy to predict. Higher share ownership concentration reduces the scope for agency conflicts and shareholders can alleviate the downside of managerial discretion through more effective monitoring. As firms slide deeper into trouble and managers become ever more distracted from running the business, this monitoring will be of increasing value [Shleifer and Vishny (1986)]. Accordingly, I expect the hazard of bankruptcy to be inversely related to ownership concentration.

For similar reasons, managerial shareholdings may affect a firm's hazard of exit. For one, managers that hold significant amounts of voting stocks are more able to insulate themselves against unwelcome takeovers. Scharfstein (1988) shows that disciplinary replacement of management following takeovers is more likely when firm performance is poor. Consistent with this view, the findings in Chapter 3 of this thesis show that management turnover in distress increases after takeovers. Thus, managers may have an incentive to sidestep takeover attempts even if they would be economically favorable to the firm's shareholders. As for bankruptcies, the impact of managerial ownership is unclear theoretically. On the one hand, managers with stock ownership may work harder thus reducing the likelihood of failure. This would be consistent with, among others, Baker, Jensen, and Murphy (1988) who show that the incentive related virtues of compensating managers with firm's stock are greatest when the firm is in feeble health. If, however, managers have private information about hidden flaws or simply believe the firm is doomed, they have strong incentives to actually speed up the processing of the firm.

6.2.1.4 Market valuations

It is a common wisdom that firms whose market values are low compared to their book values are likely takeover targets [e.g. Powell (1997)]. As Hasbrouck (1985) points out, firms that wish to expand would *de facto* compare the costs of a setting up a new business with the costs of acquiring assets in place through a takeover. The appropriate measure for this comparison is the ratio of the market value of a firm to the replacement costs of its assets, i.e. the firm's Tobin's Q or, in a simplified version, the market-to-book value. In this parlance, the lower a firm's market-to-book valuation is, the higher the hazard of a potential acquirer preferring to take over the firm rather than start afresh. Furthermore, acquirers are commonly said to prefer targets with lower price-earnings multiplies for the transaction to have an accretive effect on the reported earnings per share ratio. This in turn is appreciated by the market, which, other things being equal, makes firms with comparably low market valuations "cheap bargains".[6]

Not surprisingly, high market valuations should also lower the risk of bankruptcy. As Jensen (1989) and Wruck (1990) suggest, firms that encounter financial distress despite the market's believe of valuable future growth opportunities face high costs of liquidation that give all claimants strong incentive to pursue an out-of-court solution of distress. Consistent with this argument, previous evidence by Gilson, John, and Lang (1990) suggests that in distressed debt restructurings firms with comparable high market-to-book valuations are less likely to end up in bankruptcy. Only if this valuation advantage is absorbed by continued distress, bankruptcy becomes a more likely scenario.

---

6 For a more detailed description of this so-called bootstrap effect on earnings, see Brealey, Myers, and Allen (2005), pp. 878-879.

6.2.1.5 Industry condition

Firm exit and survival in distress may not solely depend on firm-specific attributes but also on the condition of the industry as a whole. For example, Shleifer and Vishny (1992) argue that most corporate assets are not easily redeployable. The highest value users of a firm's assets and operations therefore usually come from the same industry. If, however, distress is widespread across the industry, competitors, also, may be cash constraint and have problems meeting their own debt obligations. In this case a firm that seeks to sell assets or even its entire operations would have to turn to industry outsiders as potential acquirers. Such investors are likely to have more troubles managing these resources, face additional agency conflicts when hiring specialists to run these resources on their behalf, and, moreover, fear overpaying because they cannot value these resources properly. Because information asymmetries and debt-overhang are pronounced in a downturn these drawbacks reduce the price feasible in a sale, and thus make a sale less attractive. Consistent with this view, the analysis in Chapter 3 of this thesis found that only a small number of distressed acquisitions in this sample actually involved financial bidders. Similarly, Asquith, Gertner, and Scharfstein (1994) in their study of distressed high-yield bond issuers find that asset divestitures are aggravated by industry distress. As a result, I expect acquisitions of a distressed debtor to be less likely when there is a lack of purchasing power among its industry peers.

Again, there is a related intuition for bankruptcies as alternative outcome of distress. When industry liquidity is high and acquisitions more likely, bankruptcies should be observed less often. However, the bankruptcy hazard should also be affected by real-economic industry prospects. If a firm's industry outlook is dismal, for example because it is technologically outdated, investors will be increasingly reluctant to provide fresh funds or invest in a turnaround even if liquidity is abundant. Consistent with this view, Maksimovic and Phillips (1998) provide evidence that the outlook for the industry is an important determinant of the fate of individual plants of distressed firms. Similarly, Denis and Rodgers (2006) find that a more favorable industry climate increases the survival chances for firms in a Chapter 11 reorganization. A higher ratio of bankruptcies in less prosperous industries is also economically more favorable as it suggests that resources are reallocated to presumably higher value uses. Thus, industry factors fostering firm-failure are indicative of the bankruptcy process as an effective screening device [e.g. Mooradian (1994) and Kahl (2001)].[7]

[7] The predicted influence on industry growth prospects on the hazard of acquisition is unclear. On the one hand, firms in highly valued industries present promising investments in future company growth. This effect in undermined by the threat of overpaying by purchasing firms in industries with high current market valuations.

6.2.1.6 Corporate restructuring

Finally, I expect corporate restructuring to negatively affect the hazard of exit. When firms are in financial distress they typically respond by restructuring their assets and liabilities. Existing empirical evidence indicates that the market generally responds favorably to restructuring announcements by distressed firms. For example, Brown, James, and Mooradian (1994) report a 2% increase in market value for distressed firms that successfully divest assets to raise funds for future investments. Similarly, the evidence in the previous chapter of this thesis found that firms that manage to raise new funds in an equity offering are rewarded by the market with an average stock price appreciation of roughly 4%. Provided that financial distress is most often caused by firm-specific malfunction, the positive announcement effects should at least in part reflect the value of the increase in operating efficiency associated with the restructuring. Alternatively, they may also contain an information effect about the efficiency of the assets already in place. Higher operating efficiency should come along with a lower hazard of exit as it increases a firm's prospects of maintaining the status of an independent entity. Therefore, the observed announcement effects may also be indicative of higher survival likelihoods for firms that restructure. Some related evidence in favor of this hypothesis has been generated. For example, anecdotal evidence by Asquith et al. (1994) suggests that high-yield bond issuers that divest significant fractions of their assets have better prospects to avoid bankruptcy. Similarly, of those firms that do ultimately end up in Chapter 11 bankruptcy, Denis and Rodgers (2006) find that significant reductions of assets and indebtedness increase the likelihood that a firm emerges as an independent firm. In this study, I also restrict my attention to asset divestitures and equity infusions. These measures are two most common forms of operational and financial restructuring observed in my sample and thus have the highest empirical relevance.

6.2.2 Propositions and variables

In this section I translate the findings from the previous analysis into six testable propositions and briefly describe the variables used to operationalize the relevant independent variables. I distinguish between the economic determinants of the hazards of firm exit in general, and the hazards of acquisition and bankruptcy in particular.

Proposition 1. *Firm exit and survival is affected by real-economics factors. In particular, higher firm size, age, operating profitability, and liquidity reduce the hazard of exit.*

Proposition 2. *Firm exit and survival is affected by a firm's capital and liability structure. In particular, higher leverage increases the hazard of bankruptcy and reduces the hazard of acquisition.*

Proposition 3. *Firm exit and survival is affected by a firm's distribution of ownership. In particular, higher ownership concentration reduces the hazard of bankruptcy and increases the hazard of acquisition. Management ownership reduces the hazard of acquisition.*

Proposition 4. *Firm exit and survival is affected by a firm's growth opportunities and market valuations. In particular, higher values of Tobin's Q reduce the hazard of exit.*

Proposition 5. *Firm exit and survival is affected by industry conditions. In particular, higher industry liquidity increases the hazard of acquisition and reduces the hazard of bankruptcy. Lower industry growth potential increases the hazard of bankruptcy.*

Proposition 6. *Firm exit and survival is affected by corporate restructuring. In particular, asset divestitures and issues of fresh equity reduce the hazard of exit.*

Propositions 1 and 2 essentially capture the effect of firm size, performance, and indebtedness on exit and survival. *Firm size* is measured as the natural logarithm of total assets. *Age* is the number of years elapsed between firm foundation and the onset of financial distress. Operating performance is measured as the *return on assets*, i.e. a firm's earnings before interest, taxes, depreciation, and amortization (Ebitda) deflated by total assets. *Liquidity* is the sum of a firm's 'cash and equivalents' positions deflated by total assets. A firm's leverage is defined as the ratio of total debt to capital as used by, among others, Köke (2002).

The measures ownership type and ownership distribution referred to in proposition 3 are the same as applied in Chapters 3 and 5 of this thesis. Ownership concentration is measured by a *Herfindahl* index, which is calculated as the sum of the squares of the individual blockholding positions in the ownership structure of each firm. Management ownership is a dummy variable that equals one if members of the management board own share-blocks exceeding 5% of the firm's voting stock. A firm's relative market valuation and growth opportunities are captured, as before, by *Tobin's* Q, which is calculated as the sum of total market value of common equity and book value of total debt divided by the book value of total capital.

Measures for industry prospects and liquidity referred to in proposition 5 are based on the median values of the universe of firms in WORLDSCOPE with the same two-digit FTSE Global Classification industry code. This is comparable to the industry variable definitions used by Denis and Rodgers (2006). *Industry liquidity* is measured as industry median of cash and equivalents to total assets multiplied by the number of firms in the two-digit industry segment. This is to capture the fact that industry purchasing power is positively related to the absolute amount of cash available as well as the number of potential buyer firms. *Industry Tobin's Q* is the median *Tobin's Q* of all firms in the same FTSE industry segment.

The effect of corporate restructuring activities summarized in proposition 6 is measured by dummy variables. Divestiture is a dummy variable indicating whether a firm divests parts of its production facilities, subsidiary units or abroad business activities during the distress interval. The measure relates to the asset sale definitions in Ofek (1993) and Brown, James, and Mooradian (1994). Similarly, equity issue is a dummy variable indicating whether or not a firm completes a capital raise through cash infusion (Barkapitaleinlage) during the distress interval. The measure is the same as investigated in Chapter 5 of this thesis.

In the subsequent analyzes I distinguish between time-variant and time-invariant independent variables. For firm size as well as measures relating to propositions 2, 3, 4, and 6 I employ time-invariant values that capture pre-distress (year 0) firm characteristics. This is to avoid problems of endogeneity potentially caused by look-ahead biases in a firm's capital and ownership structure as well as its market valuation: Under continuing distress, these variables are likely to reflect market participants expectations about the outcome of financial distress, which would distort the obtained regression estimates. However, in a hazard model, a firm's risk for exit changes through time, and its survival likelihood is a function of its latest economic health condition.[8] Thus, to exploit each firm's time-series data I include annual observations of measures relating to proposition 2 and 5 (*return on assets*, *liquidity*, *industry liquidity*, and *industry Tobin's Q*) as time-varying covariates. Notably, this is based on the assumption that a firm's economic health and industry surrounding is less likely to be endogenously determined than its ownership and financial structures as well as its market valuation.

Table 6.6 in the Appendix contains a summary of the variable definitions, the data sources and the corresponding propositions.

---

[8] The merits of hazard models in exploiting cross-sectional time-series data are discussed by e.g. Shumway (2001).

6.3 Data and methodology

6.3.1 Data structure and descriptive analysis

6.3.1.1 Data structure

The data used for this study contains information on the full sample of 267 German corporations that experienced repeated interest coverage shortfalls between 1996 and 2004. The sampling methodology as well as the relevant data sources are described in Chapter 2 of this thesis. Table 6.1 displays the data structure as well as the time-series distribution of firm exits. I observe a total of 121 firm-failures of which 50 are due to acquisition and 71 are due to bankruptcy.[9] Of the acquired firms 5 ultimately go bankrupt under new ownership, the mean (median) time-span between both events being 2.25 (2.0) years. However, for consistency purposes, coverage of these firms only embraces the first failure event.[10] The total number of censored observations, i.e. time-series of firm data that do not end with an explicit failure event, is 146. Table 6.1 also contains the observed hazard rates relating to the pooled failure event. It represents the instantaneous rate of failure, i.e. the probability that the denoted failure event occurs in a given interval, provided that the firm has survived to the beginning of that interval.[11] As can be inferred from Table 6.1, the hazard of exit for the firms in the sample is greatest in periods 5, 6, and 7 in distress time, with hazard rates amounting to 17.4%, 14.9%, and 25%, respectively. The resulting survivor function is the Kaplan and Meier (1958) estimate and reports the probability of surviving beyond time t. It is a monotone non-increasing function of time and presents the reverse cumulative distribution function of T, i.e. the time to a failure event.

Selected Kaplan and Meier (1958) product-limit estimates of the survivor functions are depicted in Figure 6.2. The top graph presents survivor functions for the competing risks of acquisition and bankruptcy. The censored observations are plotted along the upper horizontal line. The survivor curves indicate that acquired firms drop out strictly earlier than their bankrupt equivalents. At any point in time, the curve depicting survival of acquisitions is strictly below that of bankruptcies. A Peto and Prentice test for equality of survivor functions reveals that this difference is statistically significant at the

9 In total, 54 acquisitions are contained in the sample. 4 firms are acquired twice over the sampling period. For consistency, coverage of these firms is discontinued after the first control transfer.

10 Similarly, several firms are acquired under bankruptcy protection. Yet, in- and out-of-court acquisitions of firms are two economically distinct issues, so that for these firms the bankruptcy filing marks the relevant failure event.

11 Unless not all intervals have the same width, the hazard rate is divided by the width of a specific interval. In the methodology section the hazard rate is explained more formally.

Table 6.1: Data structure and frequency of exit

Time series distribution of failure and censoring events for a sample of financially distressed German corporations between 1996 and 2004. Time denotes the number of years spent in distress. Time 1 is equivalent to year 0 in distress time, i.e. the year of the initial coverage shortfall. The nonparametric estimate of the survivor function is the Kaplan and Meier (1958) estimate and denotes the probability of survival (all failures) past time t.

	Beg.	Number of failures			Number	Hazard	Survivor
Time	Total	Total failures	Takeover	Bankruptcy	Censored	Rate	Function
1	267	4	3	1	0	0.015	0.985
2	263	18	11	7	0	0.068	0.918
3	245	27	10	17	18	0.110	0.816
4	200	25	9	16	31	0.125	0.714
5	144	25	10	15	45	0.174	0.590
6	74	11	6	5	31	0.149	0.503
7	32	8	0	8	9	0.250	0.377
8	15	3	1	2	4	0.200	0.302
9	8	0	0	0	8	0.000	0.302

10% level [Prentice (1978)]. The evidence is consistent with earlier findings by, among others, Cockburn and Wagner (2005) and indicates a selection process in which buyers of distressed assets quickly identify potentially attractive bargains and leave the processing of alleged non-viable debtors to the courts.

Note furthermore that the survivor curves for both groups do not intersect. This can be interpreted as a first indication that the proportionality assumption underlying the Cox Proportional Hazard models applied later holds with regard to the different classification of the firms in my sample.

For illustration, the lower two graphs in Figure 6.2 depict survivor curves for firms partitioned by a binary variable indicating whether or not a certain restructuring measure is undertaken. The lower left graph considers equity issues the lower right graph considers asset divestitures. Both graphs indicate that corporate restructuring reduces the hazard of premature exit, however, the effect is more pronounced in the case of equity issues. Of course, the estimated effect may not solely represent the value of the restructuring *per se*. It may also reflect an unobserved correlation between restructuring and the underlying prospects and intangible assets of a firm. However, it does suggest a significant role of restructurings in the survival dynamics of firms in distress and thus present a potentially valuable guidepost to investors. Further below, the effect of restructuring on firm exit will be analyzed more extensively in a multivariate setting. Moreover, it will be analyzed whether corporate restructuring affects the hazards of acquisition and bankruptcy differently.

Figure 6.2: Kaplan-Meier survivor estimates for competing risks

Figures are based on a sample of 267 German corporations between 1996 and 2004. The non-parametric estimate of the survivor function is the Kaplan and Meier (1958) estimate. Displayed numbers on the top graph denote the number of censored observations at each interval in time.

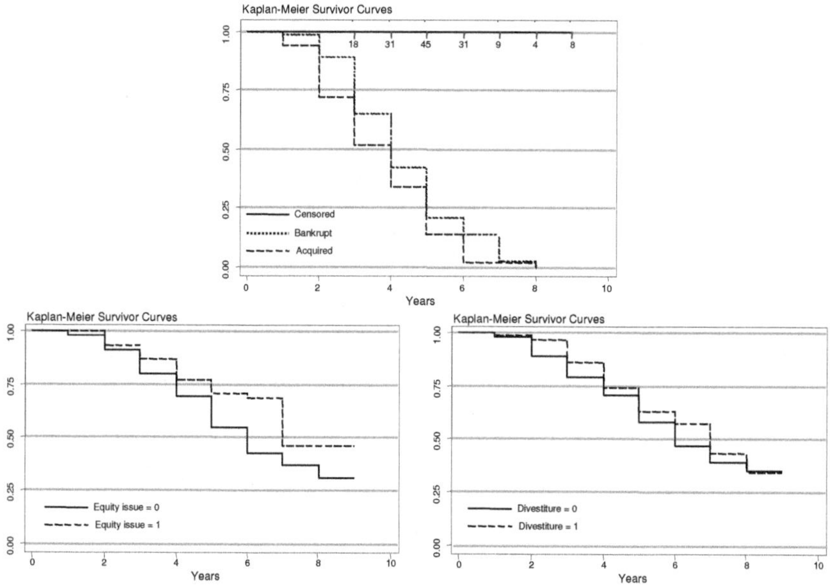

6.3.1.2 Descriptive analysis

Part of the motivation for this study stems from the argument that the economic effects of financial distress significantly depend on the type of exit a firm takes from distress. Different types of exit are presumably associated with different valuation effects, thus making them more or less favorable from shareholders' point of view. To inspect the economic impact associated with a particular type of exit I calculate their impact on firms' market valuations [Brown and Warner (1985)].[12] Abnormal common stock returns around the announcement of either a takeover agreement or a bankruptcy filing are contained in Table 6.2. Event window abnormal returns represent simple market model residuals calculated over an estimation window from 230 trading days to 31 trading days before the respective event. Returns are based on Scholes and Williams (1977) estimates of the market model parameters to accommodate for infrequent trading that typically bur-

[12] The applied event study methodology is explained in detail in the Appendix of Chapter 4 of this thesis.

Table 6.2: Economic effects of firm exit type

Stock price announcement returns around designated outcomes of financial distress. Abnormal returns are based on Scholes and Williams (1977) estimation of market model parameters over -230 to -30 day interval. The used market model index is the Composite Dax (CDAX) performance index. Test statistics are based on a simple two-sided t-test for means and a non-parametric Wilcoxon signed rank test for medians.

Event window	Mean	Median	Std. dev.	Fraction> 0	t-stat	Wilcoxon	N
Panel A: Abnormal announcement returns for acquisitions							
[0]	0.028	0.013	0.119	0.67	1.682	2.137	50
[-1;0]	0.066	0.285	0.191	0.68	2.465	3.356	50
[-1;+1]	0.103	0.057	0.259	0.71	2.828	3.628	50
[-10;+10]	0.173	0.123	0.421	0.67	2.938	3.037	50
Panel B: Abnormal announcement returns for bankruptcies							
Event window	Mean	Median	Std. dev.	Fraction> 0	t-stat	Wilcoxon	N
[0]	-0.259	-0.276	0.249	0.19	-7.949	-5.515	59
[-1;0]	0.299	-0.407	0.301	0.17	-7.561	-5.338	59
[-1;+1]	-0.402	-0.449	0.331	0.08	-9.265	-5.772	59
[-10;+10]	-0.515	-0.478	0.526	0.13	-7.456	-5.578	59

dens distressed securities. The used benchmark market model index is the Composite Dax (CDAX) performance index.[13] The results reveal an enormous difference between outcomes in their impact of firm value. Bankruptcies results in significantly negative announcement returns amounting to a median loss in firm value of roughly 48% over the 20 day window surrounding the announcement day. Acquisitions, by contrast, increase shareholder value by approximately 12% over the same interval. Most likely, this difference mirrors the more beneficial implications of the acquisition outcome for the value of a firm's intangible assets, its ability to reap future growth opportunities, and the avoidance of bankruptcy costs. In consequence, the evidence indicates that acquisitions and bankruptcy present economically distinct forms of exit that should be treated and valued accordingly and that the assertion that "mergers [...] are merely a civilized alternative to bankruptcy" [Dewey (1961), p. 257], at least in this sample, is without empirical merit.

The observed disparities between acquisitions and bankruptcies in the survivor functions as well as their economic consequences suggest that there may be fundamentally different determinants underlying both forms of firm exit. In this case there should be considerable variation in firm- and industry characteristics across exits. Table 6.3 contains selected summary statistics for the firms in the sample partitioned by their particular type of exit from financial distress. To increase the ease of inspection, all variable definitions and their underlying propositions are summarized in Table 6.6 in the Appendix. Due to

[13] Due to missing data on the exact dates of all bankruptcy filings the sample size is slightly reduced in that sub-sample.

the skewed distribution of some variables, I focus on medians rather than means. Figures relate to year 1 in survival time, i.e. the year of the initial coverage shortfall and thus only offer a static assessment. Nevertheless, univariate comparisons do reveal a number of interesting differences. For example, acquired firms exhibit lower levels of leverage than both ultimately bankrupt and surviving firms. Median *leverage*, measured as book value of total debt to book value of total capital, is 0.487 for firms that will be acquired, 0.640 for firms that end up bankrupt, and 0.542 for surviving firms. Ownership concentration, by contrast, is higher in the acquisition category. The *Herfindahl* index is 0.280 for acquisitions compared to 0.162 for bankruptcies, and 0.202 for survivors. Survivors enter financial distress with considerably higher liquidity positions. Median *liquidity*, measured as the ratio of total cash and equivalents to total assets, is 0.238 for surviving firms, compared to 0.068 for acquisition targets, and 0.118 for bankruptcies. Corporate restructuring activity also differs across sub-samples. Among the sample's survivors roughly 41% complete an *equity issue* while 43% announce at least one substantial asset *divestiture*. The corresponding figures for *equity issues* in the acquisition and bankruptcy category are substantially lower at 13%, and 32%, respectively. Other variables, such as *firm size*, measured by the logarithm of total assets, *return on assets*, measured as Ebitda to total assets, or *age* do not indicate considerable cross-sectional variation. Displayed figures in column 4 of Table 6.3 contain information about statistical significance in the observed differences across categories based on a Wilcoxon signed rank test of differences in medians.[14]

The results from pairwise comparison in Table 6.3 broadly correspond with the proposition formulated above. One problem with this type of analysis, however, is that is difficult to interpret the marginal contribution of the different determinants of the distress outcome. Moreover, observed differences could result from spurious correlation that could disguise actual causalities. This suggests that investigating the outcome and duration of financial distress requires a more complex procedure that involves the simultaneous consideration of the choices available. The following section discusses the applied methodology for the multivariate analysis.

[14] In the multivariate analysis that follows I transform *age* into a dummy variable *relage* that simply captures whether a given firm is older the total sample's median age or not. The underlying assumption is that firm age is more important in relative rather than in absolute term. However, the reported results are robust to alternative specifications of the firm-age variable.

Table 6.3: Selected sub-sample descriptives

Selected summary statistics on firm- and industry characteristics of firms in the survival, acquisition, and bankruptcy sub-samples. All measures refer to the onset of financial distress (year 1 in survival time), i.e. the year of the initial coverage shortfall. Test statistics between both sub-samples and the survivor reference group are based on a simple non-parametric Wilcoxon signed rank test of differences in medians. All variable definitions are from Table 6.6. Figures are obtained from WORLDSCOPE, LEXIS-NEXIS, and HOPPENSTEDT.

	(1) Survival (n=146)			(2) Acquisition (n=50)			(3) Bankruptcy (71)			(4) Difference		
	Mean	Median	Std.	Mean	Median	Std.	Mean	Median	Std.	(1)-(2)	(1)-(3)	(2)-(3)
Firm size	11.057	10.797	1.424	11.273	11.130	1.292	10.967	10.905	1.494	-1.158	0.359	1.237
Return on assets	-0.103	-0.048	0.185	-0.109	-0.028	0.217	-0.063	-0.028	0.190	-0.265	-1.471	-1.140
Leverage	0.663	0.542	1.090	0.467	0.487	0.270	0.660	0.640	0.326	1.271	-2.235	-2.196
Herfindahl	0.229	0.202	0.198	0.325	0.280	0.277	0.212	0.162	0.193	-1.721	0.827	1.950
Tobin's Q	4.181	0.986	8.824	2.111	1.002	2.857	4.528	1.449	12.109	1.097	-0.815	-1.650
Industry liquidity	8.322	2.746	11.344	9.260	2.475	12.839	8.171	1.718	11.688	-0.113	0.952	-1.187
Liquidity	0.318	0.238	0.285	0.241	0.068	0.292	0.223	0.118	0.236	1.945	2.124	1.949
Industry Tobin's Q	1.592	1.082	1.322	1.237	0.951	0.849	1.861	1.083	1.608	0.870	-0.708	0.818
Divestiture	0.432	0.000	0.496	0.414	0.000	0.494	0.429	0.000	0.496	0.194	-0.308	-0.408
Equity issue	0.414	0.000	0.493	0.127	0.000	0.334	0.325	0.000	0.469	2.958	0.562	-2.268
Age	29.092	11.000	45.790	30.267	13.000	37.598	39.958	12.000	53.050	-1.150	-1.631	-0.380

6.3.2 Methodology

To assess the determinants of firm exit and survival in financial distress I apply a two-stage estimation approach that takes into account the unordered categorical property of the exit variable as well as the data set's longitudinal structure. At first, I analyze the determinants of alternative exits of financial distress using a simple multinomial logit model (MNLM). The MNLM solely focuses on the determinants of the outcome of distress without explicitly considering the underlying time dimension. Thus, I consecutively conduct a duration analysis for competing risks of acquisition and bankruptcy. In doing so I inspect whether the economic factors that foster a certain outcome of distress also affect the speed at which this outcome is likely to occur.

The MNLM analyzes the determinants of alternative outcome of distress as a discrete choice problem.[15] Formally, the MNLM can be written as

$$\ln \Omega_{m|b}(X) = \ln \frac{\Pr(y = m|X)}{\Pr(y = b|X)} = X\beta_{m|b} \tag{6.1}$$

for $m = 1$ to J, where J is number of categorical outcomes and b is the designated base category, which is also referred to as the comparison group, and X is a vector of covariates. I consider three outcomes, *survival*, *acquisition*, and *bankruptcy*, i.e. $J = 3$. The three equations can be solved to compute the predicted probabilities where the model uses one outcome, in this case the most frequent outcome *survival*, as the reference. That is, any parameter estimate presents the *ceteris paribus* effect of the particular covariate on the outcome *acquisition* or *bankruptcy* relative to the outcome *survival*. Thus, the probability equations write:

$$\Pr(y = m|X) = \frac{\exp(X\beta_{m|1})}{\sum_{j=1}^{J} \exp(X\beta_{j|1})} \tag{6.2}$$

and I obtain estimates $\widehat{\beta}_{acquisition|survival}$ and $\widehat{\beta}_{bankruptcy|survival}$, where $\widehat{\beta}_{survival|survival} = 0$. The analysis uses a relatively simple multinomial logit approach in which I control for the fact that the number of observations is not the same for all firms.[16] Moreover, I estimate models using robust Huber/White sandwich standard errors to control for potential violations of the model's assumptions [e.g. White (1982)].

The second stage of the investigation proceeds with a survival analysis. Survival time in this context is measured as a nonnegative random time-variable T that depicts the

[15] A more detailed description of the model can be found in Greene (2003), chapter 21.

[16] Using a very similar study design and data sources Heiss and Köke (2001) show that using a mixed MNLM, which takes into account unobserved firm heterogeneity and allows for more involved correlation structure between the outcomes, leads to qualitatively similar results.

time elapsed until a particular form of exit occurs.[17] A basic concept for the analysis of survival times is the hazard function $\lambda(t)$, which is defined as the limit

$$\lambda(t) = \lim_{\Delta t \to 0} \frac{P(t \leq T + \Delta t | T \geq t)}{\Delta t} \tag{6.3}$$

and measures the instantaneous failure rate at time t given that the individual survives until t. The reference model for multivariate survival analysis is the Cox (1972) proportional hazard model (PHM) in which the firm's hazard of exit is modelled as a multiplicative function of a common baseline hazard and a firm-specific vector of covariates $X = (x_1, ...x_p)$:

$$\lambda(t|x_j) = \lambda_0(t) \exp(x_1\beta_1 + ... + x_J\beta_J) = \lambda_0(t) \exp(x_j\beta). \tag{6.4}$$

Because in the Cox model the baseline hazard remains unspecified and is estimated non-parametrically while the latter component is modelled as a parameterised function of firm characteristics, this approach is frequently referred to as a semi-parametric estimation technique.[18] I use a specification, which includes both time-variant regressors, x_{it}, such as the firm's operating performance and liquidity along with time-invariant regressors, x_j, such as firm ownership and capital structure characteristics at the onset of financial distress. Accordingly, my specification to be estimated augments to

$$\lambda(t|x_j) = \lambda_0(t) \exp(x_j\beta_j + x_{it}\beta_i).^{19} \tag{6.5}$$

In analogy to the MNLM I specify the PHM so as to distinguish between alternative forms of exit. I thus report separate estimation results for firms exiting through acquisition and bankruptcy, each adjusted for censoring of the survival-type exits, i.e. I estimate competing risks models. However, for comparison I also estimate MNLM and PHM using a pooled dependent variable that only distinguish between survival and exit and but not between different types of exit. To verify the appropriateness of the competing risk specification I estimate a test statistic proposed by Narendranathan and Stewart (1991), which tests the proportionality of the individual risks' hazard functions. The result clearly rejects the hypothesis that exits via acquisition and bankruptcy are not behaviorally distinct (see Appendix for details).

---

[17] Time 1 is the first year of the interest coverage shortfall. Time is measured in years however, exit in a particular year is measured in days using the OFFSET methodology in STATA.

[18] See also Harhoff, Stahl, and Woywode (1998), pp. 469-470.

[19] Table 6.7 in the Appendix of this chapter provides a correlation matrix across the different covariates to shed further light on the univariate relations in the data.

6.4 Estimation results

6.4.1 Outcomes of financial distress

Table 6.4 contains estimation results from multinomial logit regressions of firm exit in financial distress. Estimates are reported for two different sets of covariates. Models 1 and 2 contain only variables on firm and industry performance as well as several controls on firm size, age, and industry segment. In models 3 and 4 also variables on corporate ownership and restructuring are introduced. In models 1 and 3 I estimate a binary logit in which the dependent variable equals one if a firm exits the sample due to either acquisition or bankruptcy, and zero otherwise. In models 2 and 4 I distinguish between both forms of exit.

For the pooled outcome regressions large and negatively significant effects are estimated for firm *liquidity*, *return on assets* as well as *industry Tobin's Q*. Unsurprisingly, firms with higher liquidity, better operating performance and more industry growth prospects are more likely to survive distress as stand-alone entities. As expected, firms are also more likely to prevail if they manage to complete significant restructurings. The estimated coefficients of the *equity issue* and *divestiture* dummy variables have the expected negative sign, however, only the *equity issue* dummy is statistically significant. These findings are consistent with propositions 1, 5, and 6, which hold that firm exit of any kind is fostered by feeble economic health, poor industry prospects, and failed restructuring efforts. The effect of firm *Tobin's Q* is also negative, as predicted by proposition 4, however the coefficient is not significant. Perhaps surprisingly, controls on firm size and age have no effect on firm exit in distress. This conflicts with earlier findings by e.g. Harhoff, Stahl, and Woywode (1998) and Geroski (1995) who find firm size in particular to significantly affect the hazard of exit. A possible explanation for this discrepancy is that stratified sampling based on distress criteria is somewhat more tilted towards smaller and younger firms than random, cross-sectional sampling. While it is not clear *ex ante* whether and how this affects the results of this study, this finding is a potential caveat that should be kept in mind throughout the analysis.

However, the results from pooled model estimation also conceal some interesting differences across different forms of exit. Most importantly, the effects of corporate capital and ownership structure remained insignificant. Yet, the results of the competing outcome specifications clearly show that this preliminary finding is due to two offsetting effects between acquired and bankrupt firms. High indebtedness at the onset of distress strongly and significantly reduces the likelihood of acquisition while strongly and significantly increasing the likelihood of bankruptcy. Both coefficients of the *leverage* variable are about equal in magnitude and statistically significant at the 1% level of confidence. This evidence offers strong support for proposition 2 stating that leverage serves as catalyst for efficient operational change but also hampers takeover attempts due to the induced wealth transfers to lenders. Consistent with the efficiency argument, bankrupt firms are more profitable than the sample's survivors.[20] A similar effect holds for ownership concentration and managerial shareholdings. Consistent with arguments by Shleifer and Vishny (1986) and the prediction outlaid in proposition 3, the estimated coefficient of the *herfindahl* variable is positive and significant for firms that exit through acquisition. Clearly, high ownership concentration facilitates control transfers and thus makes acquisition a more likely form of exit for distressed firms. Low ownership concentration, on the other hand, strongly fosters bankruptcy as opposed to survival. The estimated coefficient of the *herfindahl* variable is negative and significant for the bankruptcy outcome suggesting that corporate failure is (at least in part) attributable to deficient monitoring by owners. Again, both estimates are similar in absolute terms and significant at the 1% level of confidence.

Also consistent with proposition 3, managerial ownership strongly affects the outcome of distress. Compared to the sample's survivors, acquired firms exhibit significantly less managerial ownership. The estimated coefficient of the *mgmt owner* variable in the acquisition category is negative and significant (at the 10% level) suggesting that manager-owners are better able to insulate themselves against takeover attempts. Even more intriguingly, also bankruptcy is strongly affected by managerial holdings. However, the effect is the exact opposite. Managers that hold voting stock exceeding 5% are significantly (at the 1% level) more likely to bankrupt their firm. An ostensible explanation of this finding would be that managers hold stock in poor firms or that managers who hold stock are themselves poorer performers. However, perhaps a plausible interpretation is that managers are likely to have private information about the prospects of their firms and, when equipped with share ownership, have stronger incentives to ensure a timely processing of the debtor's estate if doing so increases the chances that some of the firm's value may be preserved for shareholders.[21] The subsequent section will provide further evidence in favor of this argument.

---

[20] The coefficient of the return on assets variable is positive and significant at the 10% level suggesting that many of the surviving firms actually prevail as living dead and simply forego operational change due to low levels of leverage and thus low financial disciplining.

[21] Typically, of course, managers have strong incentives to keep the firm alive and thus protract their employment as long as possible. The argument is that share ownership will at least in part offset this incentive.

Table 6.4: Results from multinomial logit regressions

Maximum-likelihood estimates of multinomial logit models relating different outcomes of distress to a vector of explanatory variables. Models 1 and 3 are ordinary logit models where the outcomes of acquisition and bankruptcy enter as pooled dependent variable that equals one if, over the sampling interval, the firm is either acquired or bankrupt and zero if it stays alive. In Models 2 and 4 acquisition and bankruptcy enter separately whereas surviving firms constitute the comparison group. Time-constant (year 0) variables are from year 0 in distress, i.e. the year of the initial coverage shortfall. *Liquidity*, return on assets, *industry liquidity*, and *industry Tobin's Q* are time-inconstant variables taken from the respective lagged business year. All variable definitions are from Table 6.6. Robust asymptotic standard errors are reported in parentheses. *, **, and *** denote the parameters are statistically significant at the 10%, 5%, and 1% level, respectively. The χ^2-statistic tests the hypothesis that all coefficients in the model are simultaneously equal to zero.

	Model 1		Model 2				Model 3		Model 4			
	Pooled outcomes		Competing outcomes				Pooled outcomes		Competing outcomes			
	Survival		Acquired		Bankrupt		Survival		Acquired		Bankrupt	
	Coeff.	se	Coeff.	se	Coeff.	se	Coeff.	se	Coeff.	se	Coeff.	se
Assets (year 0)	-0.016	(0.090)	0.096	(0.063)	-0.008	(0.073)	0.024	(0.094)	0.090	(0.071)	0.009	(0.076)
Leverage (year 0)	-0.542	(0.814)	-1.621	(0.596)***	1.371	(0.480)***	-0.419	(0.820)	-1.514	(0.578)***	1.349	(0.492)***
Return on assets	-0.678	(0.321)**	0.212	(0.129)*	0.249	(0.138)*	-0.786	(0.327)**	0.166	(0.102)	0.206	(0.113)*
Liquidity	-2.637	(0.955)***	-1.428	(0.505)***	-1.809	(0.509)***	-2.802	(0.923)***	-1.517	(0.496)***	-2.101	(0.524)***
Tobin's Q (year 0)	-0.007	(0.021)	-0.061	(0.020)***	-0.001	(0.010)	-0.002	(0.019)	-0.050	(0.019)***	0.002	(0.009)
Relage (year 0)	-0.215	(0.284)	-0.250	(0.211)	0.216	(0.216)	-0.224	(0.299)	-0.439	(0.242)*	0.390	(0.217)*
Industry liquidity	0.030	(0.012)**	0.026	(0.009)***	0.016	(0.010)	0.032	(0.013)**	0.033	(0.010)***	0.008	(0.011)
Insdustry Tobin's Q	-1.450	(0.825)*	-0.188	(0.146)	-0.344	(0.091)***	-1.470	(0.845)*	-0.154	(0.147)	-0.373	(0.094)***
Herfindahl (year 0)							-0.117	(0.708)	1.279	(0.444)***	-1.417	(0.473)***
Mmgt owner (year 0)							-0.115	(0.309)	-0.437	(0.234)*	0.670	(0.218)***
Divestiture							-0.386	(0.274)	-0.030	(0.229)	-0.146	(0.180)
Equity issue							-0.578	(0.300)*	-1.342	(0.276)***	-0.390	(0.192)*
Neuer Markt	0.059	(0.301)	-0.699	(0.221)***	-0.455	(0.235)*	0.151	(0.321)	-0.288	(0.286)	-0.750	(0.241)
Constant	-0.762	(1.202)	-1.044	(0.778)	-1.220	(0.857)	-0.860	(1.268)	-0.976	(0.853)	-1.185	(0.911)
N (obs)	899		899				899		899			
N(firms)	267		267				267		267			
Pseudo R^2	0.085		0.078				0.098		0.128			
Wald-χ^2	24.37	***	108.60			***	39.40	***	197.25			***

Another striking result of the estimation is the effect of the industry condition on the form of exit. As argued in proposition 5, higher purchasing power of a firm's industry peers should considerable increase the likelihood of a takeover. As predicted, the estimated coefficient of the *industry liquidity* variable is positive and highly significant for the acquisition outcome. Thus, the theoretical postulate derived from Shleifer and Vishny (1992) that industry distress hampers merger activity is supported by my findings. Conversely, dismal future industry growth prospects strongly promote bankruptcy. The estimated coefficient of the *industry Tobin's Q* variable is negative and significant for the bankruptcy outcome, which suggests that firm bankruptcy is, to some extent, industry-determined. Growth opportunities on the firm-level, by contrast, are only relevant for the acquisition outcome. The estimated coefficient of the *Tobin's Q* variable is negative and significant at the 1% level for that sub-sample. This clearly supports proposition 4, which argues that buyers of distressed assets prefer cheap bargains and are reluctant against earnings dilutions. On bankruptcies, firm-level *Tobin's Q* does not seem to have a noticeable impact.

Turning to the control variables, firm-age and size do not differ significantly across outcomes. Yet, perhaps surprisingly, it does seem that firms formerly listed on the Neuer Markt are less likely to exit through either acquisition or bankruptcy. The coefficient of the *Neuer Markt* dummy is negative and significant for both outcomes. However, Neuer Markt firms are typically low leveraged and fraught with high technologically uncertainty, attributes that typically hamper bankruptcy and takeovers, respectively. Thus, this result may appear more plausible. Also, this result suggests that a bulk of the firms in the survival category may actually present "living deads" rather than successful turnarounds. This stresses the need for paying tribute to the censoring of the exit variable. Finally, the hypothesis that all coefficients are simultaneously equal to zero is rejected at conventional levels of confidence for all specifications. However, the reported R^2 and χ^2-statistics clearly suggest that the competing outcome specification is much more precise in predicting the outcome of financial distress. Thus, my analysis supports the claim that bankruptcy and acquisition should be treated as economically distinct forms of firm exit.

6.4.2 Duration of financial distress

The results of previous section suggest that there exist distinct economic characteristics that are likely to determine a firm's outcome of financial distress. In this section I am interested in whether these or similar characteristics also determine the time-span elapsed until a particular outcome of distress is realized. Crucially, the time spent financially distressed is a major component of a firm's overall distress costs [e.g. Jensen (1989)]. To analyze the determinants of the distress duration I analyze several Cox proportional hazard models using the same set of covariates previously employed in the MNLM estimation. Regression results are reported in Table 6.5. Note that I report the estimated hazard rates rather than the coefficients. As before, I analyze both pooled as well as competing risk specifications. The dependent variable in each specification is the time elapsed until a particular type of exit occurs. This estimation technique controls for right-censoring in the exit variable.

Similar to the above estimation, pooled outcomes are largely driven by firm and industry liquidity as well as industry growth prospects. For example, a 10% increase in liquidity (measured by total cash to assets) reduces the hazard of exit by roughly 9.4% in the pooled risks model. Also, firms seem to be able to significantly protract exit by divesting assets and raising fresh equity. In any given period, firms that complete an equity infusion decrease the hazard of exit by more than 40%. However, the estimated coefficient of the *equity issue* dummy variable is significant only at the 10% level.

Again, introducing the distinction between acquisition and bankruptcy reveals that pooling exit types is a major source of misspecification. Columns 2 and 4 contain the competing risks results. The patterns revealed by the coefficients broadly correspond with my propositions as well as the results obtained in the MNLM estimation. As before, leverage acts in opposite directions for acquired and bankrupt firms. For acquisitions the effect of the *leverage* variable is decreasing and significant, as predicted. Thus, firms that enter distress at comparably high leverage levels are not only less likely to be acquired at all. The time until an acquisition actually occurs also lasts longer. A 10% increase in pre-distress leverage reduces the hazard of exit through acquisition by more than 8%. This finding clearly supports proposition 2. Bankruptcy, in contrast, is more likely for highly levered firms. The estimated coefficient is positive (the hazard rate is larger than one), as would be expected. However, perhaps surprisingly, the impact is not statistically significant. In fact, *liquidity* appears to have a much stronger effect on the time-to-bankruptcy than *leverage*. A 10% increase in liquidity reduces the hazard of bankruptcy by almost the same amount, the effect being significant at the 1% level of confidence. This result is consistent with my finding in chapter 4 of this thesis that bankruptcy due to over-indebtedness is usually forestalled by cash flow based insolvency, which *per se* triggers a mandatory bankruptcy filing.

Table 6.5: Results from semi-parametric Cox proportional hazards regressions

Maximum-likelihood estimates of Cox proportional hazards models relating different outcomes of distress to a vector of explanatory variables. Models 1 and 3 are pooled pooled risks models where the outcomes of acquisition and bankruptcy enter as pooled dependent variable that equals one if the firm is either acquired or bankrupt and zero if it is still alive in a given firm year. In Models 2 and 4 acquisition and bankruptcy enter separately whereas surviving firms constitute the comparison group. Time-constant (year 0) variables are from year 0 in distress, i.e. the year of the initial coverage shortfall. *Liquidity, return on assets, industry liquidity* and *industry Tobin's Q* are time-inconstant variables taken from the respective lagged business year. All variable definitions are from Table 6.6. Standard errors are reported in parentheses. *, **, and *** denote the parameters are statistically significant at the 10%, 5%, and 1% level, respectively. The χ^2-statistic tests the hypothesis that all coefficients in the model are simultaneously equal to zero.

	Model 1		Model 2				Model 3		Model 4			
	Pooled Risks		Competing Risks				Pooled Risks		Competing Risks			
	Survival		Acquired		Bankrupt		Survival		Acquired		Bankrupt	
	Haz.	se	Haz.	se	Haz.	se	Haz.	se	Haz.	se	Haz.	se
Assets (year 0)	0.946	(0.093)	0.938	(0.127)	0.956	(0.133)	0.984	(0.103)	0.954	(0.139)	1.046	(0.155)
Leverage (year 0)	0.481	(0.359)	0.086	(0.107)**	1.573	(1.560)	0.494	(0.369)	0.132	(0.149)*	1.847	(1.965)
Return on assets	0.643	(0.201)	0.834	(0.403)	0.531	(0.212)	0.591	(0.192)	0.693	(0.393)	0.486	(0.208)*
Liquidity	0.063	(0.049)***	0.446	(0.390)	0.001	(0.002)***	0.055	(0.044)***	0.480	(0.439)	0.001	(0.002)***
Tobin's Q (year 0)	0.984	(0.016)	0.851	(0.080)*	1.005	(0.015)	0.989	(0.017)	0.852	(0.084)*	1.008	(0.015)
Relage (year 0)	0.772	(0.225)	0.975	(0.413)	0.566	(0.234)	0.752	(0.226)	0.860	(0.401)	0.649	(0.272)
Industry liquidity	1.030	(0.012)***	1.014	(0.018)	1.049	(0.017)***	1.031	(0.013)**	1.022	(0.020)	1.044	(0.018)**
Industry Tobin's Q	0.421	(0.207)*	0.733	(0.340)	0.153	(0.154)*	0.418	(0.211)*	0.784	(0.394)	0.159	(0.162)**
Neuer Markt	1.278	(0.436)	0.779	(0.362)	2.451	(1.305)	1.329	(0.500)	1.153	(0.655)	1.919	(1.042)
Herfindahl (year 0)							1.128	(0.697)	3.719	(2.894)*	0.079	(0.099)**
Mmgt owner (year 0)							1.059	(0.330)	0.693	(0.323)	2.149	(1.010)*
Divestiture							0.686	(0.192)	0.488	(0.213)*	0.773	(0.304)
Equity issue							0.566	(0.170)*	0.346	(0.195)*	0.843	(0.314)
N (firms)	267		267		267		267		267		267	
Time at risk	899		899		899		899		899		899	
χ^2	32.56	***	14.86	*	47.80	***	39.64	***	30.38	***	55.38	***

Turning to the impact of corporate ownership structure, the results very much resemble the evidence obtained above. High ownership concentration strongly increases the hazard of acquisition while low ownership concentration strongly increases the hazard of bankruptcy. The estimated hazard rates of the *herfindahl* variable are significant at the 10% and 5% level, respectively.[22] The effect of managerial ownership, also, is as predicted. The estimated hazard rates of the *mgmt owner* variable suggest that managerial ownership reduces the hazard of acquisition and increases the hazard of bankruptcy. However, the result is only significant for bankruptcies. Thus, of the firms that chose bankruptcy as their type of exit, those that exhibit significant managerial shareholdings fulfill their fate almost twice as fast as their less entrepreneurial equivalents. This confirms the argumentation above. Managers that are in charge of a distressed debtor's processing have an incentive to do so faster (and thus more efficiently) if they have an own financial interest in the firm.

In my industry-specific estimates, the results are somewhat surprising. The effect of the *industry Tobin's Q* variable on the bankruptcy hazard is negative and significant and thus confirms the earlier finding that corporate bankruptcies occur more frequently in less prosperous industries. However, while I would expect a higher hazard of acquisition due to high industry liquidity, I only find, quite surprisingly, a slightly positive but significant effect for the hazard rate of bankruptcy. The effect of the *industry liquidity* variable on the hazard of acquisition is positive but insignificant. Thus, the results with respect to proposition 5 and the regression analysis above are mixed.

As to the effect of *Tobin's Q* and corporate restructuring, the obtained evidence is again in line with the predictions. The estimated effect of the *Tobin's Q* variable on the hazard of acquisition is negative and significant indicating that high market valuations prevent firms from being bought up rapidly after falling into distress. Similarly, corporate restructuring retards exit *via* acquisition. The effects of the *divestiture* and *equity issue* dummy variables are strong and significant (albeit only at the 10% level) suggesting that broadening the equity base and selling off significant parts of assets may present promising takeover defense mechanisms.

The influence of the controls for firm size, age, and Neuer Markt affiliation does not seem to differ across competing risks. The estimated coefficients of the control variables remain insignificant in all specifications. Thus, the above finding of the negative influence of the *Neuer Markt* dummy on involuntary firm exit is not supported by the hazard estimates. My suggestion is that this discrepancy is most likely due to the explicit consideration of the right-censoring of the exit variable by the PHM procedure. Finally, the

[22] The interpretation of the Herfindahl index variable is traditionally difficult as it presents a synthetic and quadratic measure for ownership concentration.

hypothesis that all the estimated effect of all covariates equals zero at the same time is again rejected at conventional levels in all models.

6.5 Summary and conclusions

In this chapter I analyze the determinants of survival, acquisition, and failure for a sample of firms suffering from a sustained bout of financial distress. Using simple multinomial logit and Cox proportional hazard rate models, I find considerable differences across alternative exits in the economic factors determining the type of exit as well as the time elapsed until that particular exit occurs. Moreover, I find substantial differences in the economic impact of alternative types of exit. The evidence presented is consistent with a wide body of capital structure theory and offers valid support for the assertion that acquisition and failure present economically distinct forms of firm exit that should be investigated in combination. Thus, my results imply that studies analyzing either form of exit without considering the other potentially suffer from sample-selection that could lead to distortions of the estimation results.[23]

My results have several implications for the discussion of financial distress costs, which is currently enjoying a revival in the literature [e.g. Almeida and Philippon (2006)]. For example, my evidence suggests that high ownership concentration reduces distress costs in that it fosters acquisition as the more preferable outcome of distress for a firm's shareholders and significantly shortens a firm's distress duration. The effect of leverage, by contrast, is mixed. High leverage increases the speed at which bankrupt firms are wound up but it hampers and decelerates the acquisition of an otherwise viable debtor. To my knowledge this approach to estimating or at least explaining costs of distress is novel and compliments earlier studies that have, so far, mostly focused on estimating the actual amount, rather than the determinants, of financial distress costs.[24]

Moreover, the empirical methodology used in this chapter presents an important innovation. I use multinomial choice models to estimate the determinants of a firm's exit from distress as well hazard rate analysis to estimate a firm's distress duration. In combination, both methodologies provide a better understanding of the dynamics driving the final phase in a firm's life-cycle and allow an assessment of the effectiveness of financial distress as a selection mechanism. Survival methodology, in particular, only slowly diffuses into

[23] This argument is discussed in detail by Köke (2002), and Köke and Börsch-Supan (2002).

[24] Almeida and Philippon (2006) provides a summary of the literature on distress costs. A synopsis of the amount of direct and indirect distress costs found by several studies is also contained in Chapter 4 of this thesis. Existing studies that have also tried to shed a first light on the cross-sectional determinants of distress costs include Andrade and Kaplan (1998) and Pindado and Rodrigues (2005).

firm-level data analysis and especially empirical corporate finance. Hence, by the time, complimentary studies should emerge to test and potentially challenge the results of this chapter.

Bibliography for Chapter 6

ALMEIDA, H., AND T. PHILIPPON (2006): "The Risk-Adjusted Cost of Financial Distress," NBER Working Paper No. 11685.

ALTMAN, E. E. (1968): "Financial Ratios, Discriminant Analysis, and the Prediction of Corporate Bankruptcy," *The Journal of Finance*, 23, 589–609.

ANDRADE, G., AND S. N. KAPLAN (1998): "How Costly is Financial (Not Economic) Distress? Evidence from Highly Leveraged Transactions That Became Distressed," *The Journal of Finance*, 53, 1443–1493.

ASQUITH, P., R. GERTNER, AND D. SCHARFSTEIN (1994): "Anatomy of Financial Distress: An Examination of Junk-Bond Issuers," *The Quarterly Journal of Economics*, 109, 625–658.

AUDRETSCH, D. B. (1995): *Innovation and Industry Evolution.* MIT Press, Cambridge, MA.

BAKER, G. P., M. C. JENSEN, AND K. J. MURPHY (1988): "Compensation and Incentives: Practice Vs. Theory," *The Journal of Finance*, 43, 593–616.

BETHEL, J. E., J. P. LIEBESKIND, AND T. OPLER (1998): "Block Share Purchases and Corporate Performance," *The Journal of Finance*, 53, 605–634.

BOTMAN, M., AND T. VAN DER GOOT (2004): "What Determines the Survival of Internet IPOs?," University of Amsterdam Discussion Paper 2004/09.

BREALEY, R. A., S. C. MYERS, AND F. ALLEN (2005): *Principles of Corporate Finance.* McGraw Hill, Upper Saddle River, N.J.

BROWN, D. T. (1989): "Claimholder Incentive Conflicts in Reorganization: The Role of Bankruptcy Law," *The Review of Financial Studies*, 2, 109–123.

BROWN, D. T., C. M. JAMES, AND R. M. MOORADIAN (1994): "Asset Sales by Financially Distressed Firms," *Journal of Corporate Finance*, 1, 233–257.

BROWN, S., AND J. WARNER (1985): "Using Daily Stock Returns in Event Studies," *Journal of Financial Economics*, 14, 3–31.

BUEHLER, S., C. KAISER, AND F. JAEGER (2006): "Merge or Fail? The Determinants of Mergers and Bankruptcies in Switzerland, 1995-2000," *Economics Letters*, 90, 88–95.

BURKART, M., D. GROMB, AND F. PANUNZI (2000): "Agency Conflicts in Public and Negotiated Transfers of Corporate Control," *The Journal of Finance*, 55, 647–677.

CLARK, K., AND E. OFEK (1994): "Mergers as a Means of Restructuring Distressed Firm: An Empirical Investigation," *Journal of Financial and Quantitative Analysis*, 29, 541–565.

COCKBURN, I. M., AND S. WAGNER (2005): "Business Method Patents: What are They Good for? Patenting and the Survival of Internet-Related IPOs," Mimeo, Boston University and University of Munich.

COX, D. R. (1972): "Regression Models and Life-Tables," *Journal of the Royal Statistical Society*, Series B34, 187–220.

DEMSETZ, H., AND K. LEHN (1985): "The Structure of Corporate Ownership: Causes and Consequences," *Journal of Political Economy*, 93, 1155–1177.

DENIS, D. K., AND K. J. RODGERS (2006): "Chapter 11: Duration, Outcome, and Post-Reorganization Performance," *Journal of Financial and Quantitative Analysis (forthcoming)*, 41.

DEWEY, D. (1961): "Mergers and Cartels: Some Reservations About Policy," *American Economic Review*, 52, 255–262.

FAMA, E. F., AND M. C. JENSEN (1983): "Separation of Ownership and Control," *Journal of Law and Economics*, 26, 301–325.

FRANKS, J. R., AND S. V. SANZHAR (2003): "How Do Firms Overcome The Debt Overhang Problem?," Working Paper, London Business School.

GEROSKI, P. A. (1995): "What Do We Know About Entry?," *International Journal of Industrial Organization*, 14, 421–440.

GILSON, S. C., K. JOHN, AND L. H. LANG (1990): "Troubled Debt Restructurings, An Empirical Study of Private Reorganization of Firms in Default," *Journal of Financial Economics*, 27, 315–353.

GREENE, W. H. (2003): *Econometric Analysis*. Prentice Hall, Upper Saddle River, 5th edn.

GROSSMAN, S. J., AND O. D. HART (1980): "Takeover Bids, the Freerider Problem, and the Theory of the Corporation," *The Bell Journal of Economics*, 11, 42–64.

HANNAN, M. T., AND J. H. FREEMAN (1989): *Organizational Ecology*. Harvard University Press, Cambridge, MA.

HARHOFF, D., K. STAHL, AND M. WOYWODE (1998): "Legal Forms, Growth and Exit of West German Firms—Empirical Results for Manufactoring, Construction, Trade and Service Industries," *The Journal of Industrial Economics*, 46, 453–488.

HASBROUCK, J. (1985): "The Characteristics of Takeover Targets: Q and Other Measures," *Journal of Banking and Finance*, 9, 351–362.

HAUGEN, R., AND L. SENBET (1978): "The Insignificance of Bankruptcy Costs to the Theory of Optimal Capital Structure," *The Journal of Finance*, 33, 383–393.

HEISS, F., AND J. KÖKE (2001): "Dynamics in Ownership and Firm Survival: Evidence from Corporate Germany," ZEW Discussion Paper No. 01-63, Centre for Economic Research, Mannheim.

HENSLER, D. A., R. C. RUTHERFORD, AND T. M. SPRINGER (1997): "The Survival of Initial Public Offerings in the Aftermarket," *Journal of Financial Research*, 20, 93–110.

HOLMSTRÖM, B., AND J. TIROLE (1993): "Market Liquidity and Performance Monitoring," *The Journal of Political Economy*, 101, 678–709.

JACKSON, T. (1982): "Bankruptcy, Non-Bankruptcy Entitlements, and the Creditors Bargain," *Yale Law Journal*, 91, 857–907.

JENSEN, M. C. (1989): "Active Investors, LBO's and Privatization of Bankruptcy," *Journal of Applied Corporate Finance*, 2, 35–44.

JENSEN, M. C., AND W. MECKLING (1976): "Theory of the Firm: Managerial Behavior, Agency Costs, and Ownership Structure," *Journal of Financial Economics*, 3, 305–360.

KAHL, M. (2001): "Financial Distress as a Selection Mechanism: Evidence from the United States," University of California, Los Angeles Working Paper 16/01.

KAPLAN, E., AND P. MEIER (1958): "Nonparametric Estimation from Incomplete Observations," *Journal of the American Statistical Association*, 53, 457–481.

KÖKE, J. (2002): *Corporate Governance in Germany: An Empirical Investigation*. Physica, Heidelberg.

KÖKE, J., AND A. BÖRSCH-SUPAN (2002): "An Applied Econometrician's View of Empirical Corporate Governance Studies," *German Economic Review*, 3, 295–326.

KRAUS, A., AND R. H. LITZENBERGER (1973): "A State-Preference Model of Optimal Financial Leverage," *The Journal of Finance*, 28, 911–922.

MAKSIMOVIC, V., AND G. M. PHILLIPS (1998): "Asset Efficiency and Reallocation Decisions of Bankrupt Firms," *The Journal of Finance*, 53, 1495–1532.

——— (2001): "The Market for Corporate Assets: Who Engages in Mergers and Asset Sales and are their Efficiency Gains?," *The Journal of Finance*, 56, 2019–2065.

MANNE, H. G. (1965): "Mergers and the Market for Corporate Control," *The Journal of Political Economy*, 73, 110–120.

MOORADIAN, R. M. (1994): "The Effect of Bankruptcy Pretection on Investment: Chapter 11 as a Screening Device," *The Journal of Finance*, 49, 1403–1430.

MULHERIN, H. J., AND A. L. BOONE (2000): "Comparing Acquisitions and Divestitures," *Journal of Corporate Finance*, 6, 117–139.

NARENDRANATHAN, W., AND M. B. STEWART (1991): "Testing the Proportionality of Cause-Specific Hazards in Competing Risk Models," *Oxford Bulletin of Economics and Statistics*, 53, 331–340.

OFEK, E. (1993): "Capital Structure and Firm Response to Poor Performance," *Journal of Financial Economics*, 34, 3–30.

PINDADO, J., AND L. RODRIGUES (2005): "Determinants of Financial Distress Costs," *Financial Markets and Portfolio Management*, 19, 343–359.

POWELL, R. G. (1997): "Modelling Takeover Likelihood," *Journal of Business Finance and Accounting*, 24, 1009–1030.

Prentice, R. L. (1978): "Linear Rank Tests with Right-Censored Data," *Biometrika*, 65, 167–179.

Scharfstein, D. S. (1988): "The Disciplinary Role of Takeovers," *Review of Economic Studies*, 55, 185–200.

Scholes, M., and J. Williams (1977): "Estimating Betas from Nonsynchronous Data," *Journal of Financial Economics*, 5, 309–327.

Schultz, P. (1993): "Unit Initial Public Offerings: A Form of Staged Financing," *Journal of Financial Economics*, 59, 199–229.

Shleifer, A., and R. W. Vishny (1986): "Large Shareholders and Corporate Control," *Journal of Political Economy*, 94, 461–488.

——— (1992): "Liquidation Values and Debt Capacity: A Market Equilibrium Approach," *The Journal of Finance*, 47, 1343–1366.

Shumway, T. (2001): "Forecasting Bankruptcy More Accurately: A Simple Hazard Model," *The Journal of Business*, 74, 101–124.

White, H. (1982): "Maximum Likelihood Estimation of Misspecified Models," *Econometrica*, 50, 1–24.

Wruck, K. H. (1990): "Financial Distress, Reorganization, and Organizational Efficiency," *Journal of Financial Economics*, 27, 419–444.

Appendices

1. Summary of variable definitions and data sources
2. Correlation matrix of independent variables
3. Test of proportionality of competing risk specification

Table 6.6: Summary of variable definitions

Variable	Proposition	Definition	Time-varying
Firm size	1	Logarithm of total assets	No
Return on assets	1	Ebitda to total assets	Yes
Liquidity	1	Cash and equivalents to total assets	Yes
Leverage	2	Total debt to total capital ratio	No
Herfindahl	3	Herfindahl index of total ownership concentration	No
Mgmt owner	3	dummy variable indicating whether or not a member of the management team holds a block of voting stock exceeding 5%.	No
Tobin's Q	4	Total market value of common equity plus book value of total debt divided by book value of total equity plus book value of total debt.	No
Industry liquidity	5	Industry median of cash and equivalents to total assets multiplied by number of competitors based on universe of firms in the same two-digit FTSE industry code.	Yes
Industry Tobin's Q	5	Median *Tobin's Q* based on universe of firms in the same two-digit FTSE industry code.	Yes
Divestiture	6	Dummy variable indicating whether or not firm divests assets during disterss interval	No
Equity issue	6	Dummy variable indicating whether or not firm completes a capital raise through cash infusion (Barkapitaleinlage) during disterss interval	No
Relage	Control	Dummy variable indicating whether at onset of distress firm is older or younger than the sample median age	No
Neuer Markt	Control	Dummy variable indicating whether or not firm was formerly listed on the growth segment of the German stock exchange	No

Table 6.7: Correlation matrix of independent variables in MNLM and PHM estimation

Correlation matrix of independent variables used in Tables 6.4 and 6.5. Variable definitions are from Table 6.6. Each column contains correlation coefficients and and their respective p-values in parentheses below.

		(1)	(2)	(3)	(4)	(5)	(6)	(7)	(8)	(9)	(10)	(11)	(12)	(13)
(1)	Assets (year 0)	1.000												
(2)	Leverage (year 0)	0.247	1.000											
		(0.000)												
(3)	Return on assets	0.096	0.097	1.000										
		(0.003)	(0.003)											
(4)	Liquidity	-0.294	-0.429	-0.047	1.000									
		(0.000)	(0.000)	(0.148)										
(5)	Tobin's Q (year 0)	-0.273	-0.099	-0.063	0.088	1.000								
		(0.000)	(0.002)	(0.056)	(0.008)									
(6)	Relage (year 0)	0.163	0.274	0.122	-0.304	-0.201	1.000							
		(0.000)	(0.000)	(0.000)	(0.000)	(0.000)								
(7)	Neuer Markt	-0.214	-0.472	-0.054	0.349	0.164	-0.428	1.000						
		(0.000)	(0.000)	(0.096)	(0.000)	(0.000)	(0.000)							
(8)	Industry liquidity	-0.274	-0.242	-0.044	0.219	0.047	0.012	0.349	1.000					
		(0.000)	(0.000)	(0.179)	(0.000)	(0.156)	(0.710)	(0.000)						
(9)	Industry Tobin's Q	-0.175	-0.142	0.027	0.081	0.143	-0.067	0.136	0.173	1.000				
		(0.000)	(0.000)	(0.409)	(0.013)	(0.000)	(0.038)	(0.000)	(0.000)					
(10)	Herfindahl (year 0)	0.240	0.185	0.050	-0.265	-0.102	0.272	-0.315	-0.211	-0.021	1.000			
		(0.000)	(0.000)	(0.121)	(0.000)	(0.002)	(0.000)	(0.000)	(0.000)	(0.506)				
(11)	Mmgt owner (year 0)	-0.143	-0.203	-0.034	0.179	0.056	-0.194	0.424	0.281	0.082	-0.160	1.000		
		(0.000)	(0.000)	(0.299)	(0.000)	(0.088)	(0.000)	(0.000)	(0.000)	(0.011)	(0.000)			
(12)	Divestiture	0.332	0.137	0.020	-0.158	-0.048	0.090	-0.121	0.054	-0.028	0.028	-0.036	1.000	
		(0.000)	(0.000)	(0.543)	(0.000)	(0.143)	(0.005)	(0.000)	(0.095)	(0.376)	(0.386)	(0.254)		
(13)	Equity issue	-0.020	-0.101	-0.057	-0.009	0.131	-0.063	0.128	0.002	0.079	-0.170	0.134	0.088	1.000
		(0.533)	(0.002)	(0.079)	(0.773)	(0.000)	(0.048)	(0.000)	(0.961)	(0.013)	(0.000)	(0.000)	(0.006)	

Test of proportionality of competing risk specification

Narendranathan and Stewart (1991) provide a test of whether exits to different states are behaviorally distinct (rather than simply incidental) for continuous time proportional hazards models. This is a test of the hypothesis that the cause-specific hazards are all proportional to one another (i.e. that all parameters except the intercepts are equal across the hazards). The test statistic TS proposed by Narendranathan and Stewart (1991) is given by

$$TS = 2[ln(L_{CR}) - ln(L_{SR}) - \sum_{j} n_j ln(p_j)], \tag{A-1}$$

where $ln(L_{CR})$ is the maximized log-likelihood from the competing risk model (the sum of those from the component risk models), $ln(L_{SR})$ is the maximized log-likelihood from the single-risk model, n_j is the number of exits to state j and $p_j = n_j / \sum_j n_j$, where there are $j = 1, ..., J$ destination states. The test-statistic is χ^2-distributed with degrees of freedom equal to the number of restrictions. For the full model I can reject the null hypothesis of risk proportionality at 2.5% of significance ($TS = 24.227$), i.e., I reject that the two different forms of exit are behaviorally equal.

Beiträge zur betriebswirtschaftlichen Forschung

Herausgegeben von:

Prof. Dr. Dr. h.c. Sönke Albers, Kiel
Prof. Dr. Bernhard Pellens, Bochum
Prof. Dr. Dieter Sadowski, Trier
Prof. Dr. Martin Weber, Mannheim

Auswahl der erschienenen Bände:

Band 7 H. Albach
Wirtschaftlichkeitsrechnung bei unsicheren Erwartungen

Band 10 H. Hax
Vertikale Preisbindung in der Markenartikelindustrie

Band 14 D. Schneider
Die wirtschaftliche Nutzungsdauer von Anlagegütern

Band 40 B. Rudolph
Die Kreditwährungsentscheidung der Banken

Band 43 A. Luhmer
Maschinelle Produktionsprozesse

Band 46 H. Simon
Preisstrategien für neue Produkte

Band 59 T. Hartmann-Wendels
Dividendenpolitik bei asymmetrischer Informationsverteilung

Band 61 R. Ewert
Rechnungslegung, Gläubigerschutz und Agencyprobleme

Band 65 W. Neus
Ökonomische Agency-Theorie und Kapitalgleichgewicht

Band 66 U. Backes-Gellner
Ökonomie der Hochschulforschung

Band 71 M. Steven
Produktion und Umweltschutz

Band 72 E. Terberger
Neo-institutionalistische Ansätze

Beiträge zur betriebswirtschaftlichen Forschung

Herausgegeben von:

Prof. Dr. Dr. h.c. Sönke Albers, Kiel
Prof. Dr. Bernhard Pellens, Bochum
Prof. Dr. Dieter Sadowski, Trier
Prof. Dr. Martin Weber, Mannheim

Neuerscheinungen:

Band 100 C. Watrin
Internationale Rechnungslegung und Regulierungstheorie

Band 101 S. Valcárcel
Theorie der Unternehmung und Corporate Governance

Band 102 D. Simons
Kosten und Nutzen von Aktienoptionsprogrammen

Band 103 A. Mohren
Performancemessung und die Steuerung von Investitionsentscheidungen

Band 104 M. Spann
Virtuelle Börsen als Instrument zur Marktforschung

Band 105 P. Grundke
Modellierung und Bewertung von Kreditrisiken

Band 106 A. Walter
Technologietransfer zwischen Wissenschaft und Wirtschaft

Band 107 S. Gensler
Heterogenität in der Präferenzanalyse

Band 108 T. Pfeiffer
Corporate-Governance-Strukturen interner Märkte

Band 109 T. Mellewigt
Management von Strategischen Kooperationen

Band 110 C. Koziol
Valuation of Convertible Bonds when Investors Act Strategically

Band 111 A. Lambrecht
Tarifwahl bei Internetzugang

Band 112 S. Ruenzi
Optimale Gestaltung von Fondsfamilien

Band 113 T. Weber
Anreizsysteme für die betriebliche Foschung und Entwicklung

Band 114 M. Rummer
Going Public in Deutschland

Band 115 J. T. Martini
Verrechungspreise zur Koordination und Erfolgsermittlung

Band 116 P. Jostarndt
Financial Distress, Corporate Restructuring and Firm Survival

FSC
www.fsc.org
MIX
Papier | Fördert gute Waldnutzung
FSC® C083411

Kolibri 360 GmbH
Ferdinand-Jühlke-Straße 7
99095 Erfurt, Deutschland
produktsicherheit@kolibri360.de